A FIELD GUIDE TO

BIRDS

OF THE DESERT SOUTHWEST

GULF'S FIELDGUIDE SERIES

A FIELD GUIDE TO

BIRDS

OF THE DESERT SOUTHWEST

BARBARA L. DAVIS

Gulf Publishing Company
Houston, Texas

Gulf Publishing Company
Book Division
P.O. Box 2608 □ Houston, Texas 77252-2608

10 9 8 7 6 5 4 3 2 1

Library of Congress Cataloging-in-Publication Data

Davis, Barbara (Barbara L.)
    A field guide to the birds of the desert Southwest / by Barbara L. Davis.
        p.   cm.–(Gulf's field guide series)
    Includes bibliographical references (p.   ) and index.
    ISBN 0-88415-278-2
    1. Birds–Southwest, New–Identification.   2. Desert animals–Southwest, New.   3. Bird watching–Southwest, New.   I. Title. II. Series.
QL683.S75D38   1997
598′.0979–dc21   96-48172
                                                                              CIP

CONTENTS

ACKNOWLEDGMENTS

I am extremely grateful to my editor, **Claire Blondeau:** Thank you, Claire, for the opportunity to publish this book. Your smooth editing skills finely honed my finished product. It has been a genuine pleasure working with you.

My deepest gratitude goes to my friend, fellow bird photographer, and mentor, **Greg Homel:** I will always be indebted to your generous sharing, and thanks for your precise review of this book.

Much appreciation goes to **Richard Cachor Taylor:** Thank you for finding time to review my slides.

I would like to express my thanks to **Orville TeBockhorst:** Thank you for your computer skills.

With love and joy, I thank **Carol Bryniarski:** I'll never forget our first birding trip together. Who would have ever thought to take *me* to McNeal? I always look forward to our Mexico trips.

With appreciation, I thank **Dr. Beverly Allen:** Thank you for allowing a small piece of Mother Nature to renew herself, and thanks for the help in bird identifications.

I express thanks and admiration to my special equestrian friends, **Carol Jacques** and **Janie Benglis:** Thanks for spotting the Red-tailed Hawk's nest and the Great Horned Owls!

I extend much love and admiration to **Bernice Roberts:** How lucky I am to have you in my life!

I give love and thanks to **Pauline Davis:** Thanks, Mom, for an upbringing filled with nature. Thanks also for always encouraging my creativity!

I give unconditional love and thanks to **Lady MacIntosh:** You were there through it all—the traveling, the photographing, the writing, the re-writing, the sorting, and the finalizing. What a pal!

And ultimately . . . with total love and appreciation, I thank my life-mate, **Celia McMurry:** My most precious moments are those we share!

About the Author

Barbara L. Davis is a native Arizonan who grew up in the midst of nature—lots of it! She was raised on a large cattle ranch in southeastern Arizona where nature, animals, time, and space offered her the opportunity to develop an intimacy with life that continues to express itself in all her work.

Her firsthand knowledge of birds, and their habits and habitats comes as a result of her years of horseback riding, backpacking, camping, hiking, and photographing in the mountains, meadows, streams, and deserts of the Southwest. Her previous book is entitled *Birds of the Southwest,* and she has additionally photographed birds in Mexico, Central America, South America, and the Caribbean.

Barbara's formal education includes a Bachelor's degree in Spanish and French and a Master's degree in counseling. She has been a professional counselor in Tucson for twenty-seven years. She also pursues formal art instruction and spends many hours observing and photographing birds.

A Desert Awakening

THE cold, crisp, morning air made me shiver while I quickly loaded my remaining camera gear into the van. I had made most preparations the night before, but expensive lenses are always a last-minute addition. The heater was on in my van and I was ready to jump inside to get warm. The early spring desert temperatures would climb from the crisp, mid 30s to nearly 80 degrees Fahrenheit, and I was anticipating a great photo morning. The sky was clear overhead with brilliant stars twinkling among the many constellations. Only a few clouds hung low over the horizon, hopefully enough to reflect the beauty of the rising sun, but not so many as to interfere with my photo aspirations.

I couldn't wait to get to the Red-tailed Hawks' nest I had been watching from a distance for nearly two months. I had waited for the eggs to hatch before setting up my blind and attempting to photograph because I didn't want my intrusion to stress the adults, thus causing them to abandon the eggs. Now, two fuzzy white nestlings would be awakening to a new dawn and patiently waiting for the first feast of the day.

Still in darkness so the adults could not see my arrival, I carefully made my way over the brushy, rocky terrain and slipped inside my blind with fifty pounds of camera gear and my one-cup thermos of hot coffee. (It's a good thing hawks have no sense of smell!) Finally, with camera in place, I could relax while I waited for the perfect light and some fun action. In the meantime, I sat in awe, becoming a part of one of the most beautiful experiences nature has to offer: The awakening desert.

Crepuscular light allowed me to see some movement in the nest while behind me the eastern sky was beginning to come alive with ever-increasing intensity. Crimson hues intermingled with golden rays as the sunlight filtered through the cloud bank hovering over the mountainous horizon. Desert smells, especially those of dew-covered creosotes, mingled with my aromatic coffee while dawning light seemed to orchestrate the symphonic medley of the awakening, diurnal avian world. A Curve-billed Thrasher loudly greeted the day with its two-whistled call and was soon joined by Gambel's Quail, Mourning Doves, Gila Woodpeckers, Gilded Flickers, and Cactus Wrens. Breeding season had found these exquisite songsters energetic and with perfect vocal conditioning. To my left I could hear a Verdin's distinctive, incessant call as it twitted among the branches of a creosote bush while gleaning insects for its breakfast. Somewhere in the distance, I could hear the low, harsh whisper of the Black-tailed Gnatcatcher.

The cloud bank was rising with the sun and I would have to wait a bit longer for the appropriate light to capture the nest with my lens. The large, bulky structure made of sticks was securely resting in the arms of a giant saguaro growing on the edge of a dry wash. Ecotones, areas where one type of habitat cuts through another, such as this create ideal birding habitats. Dense mesquite, palo verde, catclaw, and creosote bushes along with saguaro and cholla cacti offer nesting sites and protection, while seeds, insects, rodents, reptiles, and nectar fulfill food needs.

I kept my focus on the birds' home. Two years ago a pair of Great Horned Owls raised two owlets in this same nest. Now I could clearly see the two Red-tailed nestlings anxiously watching the sky. Neither adult was visible, and I could only hope that the sun would break above the cloud bank before one of them came flying home with breakfast. Several times in the past two weeks they had brought food to the young in the pre-dawn light while I watched with total fascination. I needed full sunlight for photographing, however. Maybe I would luck out this morning.

Finally the sun emerged from behind me, and shortly thereafter I realized the young were reacting to something. Through small peepholes in my blind I scanned the sky and detected motion. One of the adults was flying low over the terrain and quickly dropped out of sight to approach from a wash. Swooping up from behind the saguaro, the magnificent raptor gracefully landed with a squirming snake in its talons. Suddenly the nest was full of activity! The youngsters watched with mouths agape and tiny wings upheld while the female skillfully gained control of the reptile.

When the young first hatched, the female had been brooding the nestlings while the male hunted and brought food to the nest, but this morning it was the larger female who triumphantly flew home with breakfast. Withholding my own excitement, I clicked away as she finally conquered the snake then began tearing away tiny pieces of flesh with her sharp beak while holding the rest of it down with her talons. Even though my camera made whirring sounds each time it advanced a frame, she paid little attention. She had accepted the presence of my blind, and because there was no apparent motion, she felt no threat.

I watched and photographed for some time while she fed the young and herself as well. After breakfast, she stayed with the now-subdued nestlings awhile, then disappeared into the sky, perhaps to join the male on another hunting foray. With full tummies, the young pair snuggled down for a morning nap. I searched the tops of bushes and saguaros, finally satisfying myself that the adults were away, then gathered my gear and left the sleeping nestlings in peace. What a way to wake up in the morning!

The photographing light had passed its peak, so I returned home to write during the less-productive birding hours. But before I sat down to my computer, I would relax, sit quietly, and revel in the morning's adventure. The joy I experience while photographing birds is spiritual, simple, and fulfilling. I never cease to be amazed by the colors, shapes, and designs displayed by every species, not to mention the special niche each plays in the order of life. Feeling at one with nature, I become part of the experience before me. We need scientific knowledge, but we also desperately need the intuitive knowledge that comes by: experiencing the purity of nature, and knowing we are part of it; seeing beauty, and realizing we cannot live without it; and respecting all life, because therein lies the key to our own existence. My thoughts carried me to a statement made by Sylvia Eral in speaking of her beloved sea, "Nature is vital to our well-being–to our own existence. We are putting ourselves in jeopardy. When it is gone, we are gone."

My purpose in this book is twofold: to provide the birder with descriptive and behavioral information about bird species found in the deserts and grasslands of the southwest; and to enhance and encourage the joy of living in harmony with nature. I have seen well-intentioned birders, including myself, unknowingly contribute to the demise of some bird species. A little knowledge adds to the joy and assures the protection of our beloved feathered friends. Knowledge and beauty go hand in hand. It is my hope that this book will assist you in your own "Desert Awakening."

Red-tailed Hawk Nestlings

HOT SOUTHWESTERN DESERTS

THE deserts of the world come in two types: Hot and cold. Hot deserts receive the majority of their precipitation in the form of rain, while snow is the main source of moisture in the cold deserts. Regardless of temperature, the single factor that defines a desert is dryness. This book is devoted to the hot deserts of southern California, southern Arizona, and southern New Mexico, specifically the regions of the Mojave, Sonoran, and Chihuahuan deserts as determined by Davis E. Brown and Charles H. Lowe in *Biotic Communities of the Southwest.* It also includes the grasslands that adjoin these areas or that are interspersed among them. Deserts separate mountains from and blend into grasslands. Because of the geographical proximity of these varied biomes, and because of the diversity created by the convergence of two or more ecotones, birding opportunities abound in the southwestern lowlands.

The lowest elevation, not only of the U.S. deserts but on the entire continent, is in the Death Valley National Monument in the **Mojave Desert.** At 282 feet below sea level, the habitat generally consists of sparse, low-growing vegetation. In the higher elevations within the same desert, the unique joshua tree with its spiny arms may reach 50 feet in height. The Mojave Desert borders a "cold desert"—the Great Basin Desert—to the north, the Sierra Nevada and Tehachapi Mountains to the west, and the San Bernardino Mountains to the south. The hot Sonoran Desert to the east transitions into a varied blend of vegetation. This desert-scrub biome is the smallest of the four North American deserts.

Less than one-third of the **Sonoran Desert** lies in Arizona and California; the remaining two-thirds extends southward into Baja California and Sonora, Mexico. Still, the Sonoran covers more area in the United States than either the Mojave or the Chihuahuan desert. Considered a subtropical desert, the Sonoran Desert's vast biome contains an amazing diversity of plant species, enough to even appear lush in some areas. As a result, higher numbers of birds abound here.

Seven subdivisions comprise the Sonoran Desert, only two of which are in the United States. The largest subdivision is the Lower Colorado River Valley encompassing the area between the Colorado River—the desert's eastern boundary, and the San Bernardino Mountains and Mojave Desert, which join it on the northern and western extremities. In this portion of the desert, riparian habitat and agricultural areas are surrounded largely by creosote bushes and white bur sage. The Salton Sea, Imperial Valley, and the Colorado River provide winter habitat for many bird species. As the elevation rises to the Arizona Upland Division, palos verdes, ocotillos, chollas, and ironwoods prevail. This portion receives more annual precipitation and is the least "desert-like." In fact, it is termed an arboreal desert, sometimes called the Arizona Desert, Paloverde-cacti Desert. The saguaro cactus is a specialty along with organ pipe cactus and a large diversity of other cacti. The Arizona portion of this profuse subdivision extends from the Mexican border and ends just north of Phoenix, and from the Colorado River eastward to the Buckskin Mountains. "Sky island"—mountains that rise abruptly from the desert floor—and grassy steppes provide additional habitats for a diverse array of bird species.

The **Chihuahuan Desert** reaches its lowest elevation at 1,000 feet above sea level along the Rio Grande River, which is the main drainage system for this area. It is the highest of the three deserts discussed in this book. Nearby, grasslands and desert-scrub may turn into rugged mountains reaching 5,000 feet above sea level. Four fingers of this vast desert extend between mountain ranges in the vicinity of the Mexican border, as far north and west as Socorro, New Mexico, and Benson, Arizona. Creosote and tarbush dominate this region.

The Mojave Desert receives most of its precipitation during winter while the Chihuahuan Desert benefits largely from summer monsoons. Located between them, the sub-tropical Sonoran Desert is bimodal, receiving both summer and winter moisture. In all three deserts, the precipitation averages less than ten inches per year, and rapid evaporation exacerbates dry conditions. Freezing temperatures occur in all three hot deserts, and summer temperatures often exceed 100 degrees Fahrenheit.

The diversity of the Southwestern deserts intrigues the visitor. Angles, shapes, patterns, contrasts, and colors begin to take form in one's perception, and are quickly followed by a realm of emotional responses and a variety of questions: "What grotesque shapes! How beautiful! How does life survive? How hot does the desert get? Why are some parts of the desert so different from others? How barren! What rugged mountains! How could this lush vegetation be called desert?" And, yes of course in some areas, "Look at those sand dunes!" Whatever the line of questioning or the degree of exclamation, one is usually left in a state of awe.

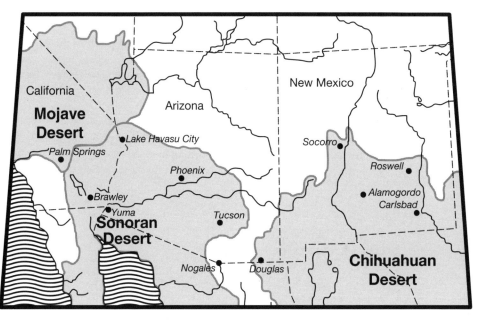

Map 1. *Hot Southwestern Deserts.*

Desert Birding

Birding the southwestern deserts and grasslands is an exciting adventure. Resident birds share their arena with multitudes of visiting and migrating species, while some tropical specialties sporadically appear north of the Mexican border to thrill the observant birder. Where water exists, bird populations are greatest, especially migratory and transitory species that may not be adapted to desert life and must drink water and bathe daily. Most resident birds are equipped to obtain moisture from the food they eat, but water sources are a precious commodity to them as well.

In the desert and grassland areas, the composite total of bird species ranging in abundance from common to occasional reaches a staggering 440. Eight bird charts from diversified locations in the Mojave, Sonoran, and Chihuahuan deserts are included, along with a section listing twenty prime desert birding locations. Descriptions, behavioral information, and photographs will assist the birder in identifying 200 common, uncommon, and rare birds who frequent desert habitats as residents, migrants, or winter residents.

Birding populations vary greatly according to season. Abundance is indicated within each chapter as well as on the charts in the appendix using the following codes:

C—Common to Abundant: Easily found in suitable habitat.

U—Uncommon to Fairly Common: Found where looked for in suitable habitat, but can be missed.

R—Rare to Very Uncommon: More often missed than seen, even when looked for in suitable habitat.

O—Occasional: Normally less than five individuals per season during any given year, but to be looked for.

X—Accidental: Less than ten records for the entire area, and not to be expected.

I believe that the majority of birders are hooked on birding for the pure and simple joy of it. There is nothing more freeing than hearing a medley of birdsongs announce the arrival of a new day, and quietly feeling as much a part of nature as the vocalists themselves. There is nothing more touching than watching a covey of newly hatched quail scamper after their parents. And there is nothing more inspiring than witnessing the sights and sounds of thousands of Sandhill Cranes as they fly into an intense desert sunset. It is my hope that this book will enhance your own special connection with nature.

Map 2. *Desert Birding Hotspots. Addresses listed in Appendix 2.*

Section 1

WATER/WETLAND BIRDS

WATER in the southwestern deserts and grasslands is a precious commodity to say the least. Where there is water, however, one can usually be assured that there are birds. Lakes, ponds, rivers, and streams attract many species, especially migratory and wintering birds. Included in this section are seabirds, waterfowl, wading birds, and shorebirds.

Pied-billed Grebe*
Eared Grebe*
Western Grebe*
American White Pelican
Brown Pelican*
Double-crested
    Cormorant*
American Bittern
Least Bittern
Great Blue Heron*
Great Egret*
Snowy Egret*
Cattle Egret*
Green Heron*
Black-crowned
    Night-heron*
White-faced Ibis*
Greater White-fronted
    Goose
Lesser Snow Goose*
Ross' Goose

Canada Goose*
Green-winged Teal*
Mallard*
Northern Pintail*
Blue-winged Teal
Cinnamon Teal*
Northern Shoveler*
Gadwall
American Wigeon*
Canvasback
Redhead
Ring-necked Duck*
Common Merganser
Red-breasted Merganser
Ruddy Duck*
Sora
Common Moorhen
American Coot*
Greater Sandhill Crane*
Killdeer*
Black-necked Stilt*

American Avocet*
Greater Yellowlegs*
Solitary Sandpiper*
Willet*
Spotted Sandpiper
Whimbrel
Long-billed Curlew*
Marbled Godwit
Western Sandpiper
Least Sandpiper*
Long-billed Dowitcher
Common Snipe
Wilson's Phalarope
Red-necked Phalarope
Heermann's Gull*
Ring-billed Gull*
California Gull
Caspian Tern
Forster's Tern

* See color section.

PIED-BILLED GREBE[*]
Podilymbus podiceps

Description: Small, gray-brown body; white undertail coverts;
breeding—buff-colored bill with dark ring, black chin;
non-breeding—plain bill; white chin

The Pied-billed Grebe measures twelve to fifteen inches long and is unique among grebes because it is the only one *without* a white wing patch or pointed bill. It does have the typical thin neck characteristic of other grebes, but the bill is rather thick, resembling that of a chicken.

Its upperparts are gray-brown while the underparts are whitish. Breeding plumage includes a black throat patch, white beneath the tail, and a ring around its buff-colored bill. In the fall, the Pied-billed Grebe loses its throat patch as well as the black ring. The bill then appears more yellowish.

The Pied-billed Grebe is perhaps the most aquatic of all birds, using lobed feet to expertly propel through the water. Seldom does this species appear on land, but when it does, this little grebe is extremely awkward, and can therefore be quite comical.

The Pied-billed Grebe is most noted for a continual *cow-cow-cow-cow-cow-cow-hu* sound during nesting season, but it also has a very low yelping call. This boisterous water bird sings all day and can even be heard at night, beginning slowly at first, then getting faster and faster.

Its stubby little body may be seen "running" across the surface of the water as it gains speed and momentum for takeoff. Once in the air, it is a strong flier. In the water it floats with its rear above the surface, making the white tail covert very conspicuous.

Nesting and Mating Behaviors

The Pied-billed Grebe is one of the season's first nesting water birds in the Southwest, and may be seen constructing its floating nest as early as February. This rather wary grebe is very secretive, and often only one pair is seen on a pond. It does mix with other waterfowl, however, which makes it even more inconspicuous. When other grebes are on the same water source, it claims an area of thirty yards or more from other nests.

This seclusive grebe can sink out of sight in a split second with only a trace of a ripple to indicate its existence. Often, only the head emerges like a periscope as it scans the area before completely showing itself.

* Plate 1

The nest is constructed by both sexes in shallow water where aquatic vegetation thrives. It approximates one foot in diameter and is made of decaying plant parts attached to an underwater foundation, which allows it to float above the water but secures it from sliding away.

The three to ten eggs are incubated by both parents, and are covered with pliable nesting materials to camouflage and regulate temperature if both adults leave the nest at the same time. The eggs are pale blue at first, then turn to a buff coloration during incubation. They are oval in shape with a smooth or sometimes chalky finish.

Both sexes also aid in the rearing of the young and, characteristic only of Grebes, carry the young on their backs while diving underwater. At night the family stays in the vicinity of the nest. It is thought that because of these close bonding behaviors, it is difficult for the fledglings to break the ties with their parents. Once the young can fend for themselves, the parents may actually drive the fledglings away by pecking at them. Occasionally the adult will even peck the youngster to death if it continually resists leaving.

Habitat and Diet

The Pied-billed Grebe may be seen year round in the Southwestern lowlands on freshwater ponds, marshes, and lakes, as well as salt bays in winter. It prefers open water with aquatic vegetation.

Its diet consists of fish, frogs, snails, crawfish, and insects. This grebe is an expert diver and swimmer, and is extremely skilled at capturing prey under water.

Supplemental Information

I'm always pleased to see this tiny waterfowl, especially during breeding season when the ring on its bill is apparent. One day as I crossed a bridge over a small stream of water, I glanced down and noticed a Pied-billed Grebe swimming upstream with a small fish in its bill. I was on a back road and no cars were coming, so I stopped to observe.

The little grebe was caught in the current and was swimming in place while simultaneously trying to swallow the fish. Eventually, I could see just the fish's tail sticking out of its mouth, when suddenly the whole fish was coughed into the air and snatched again by the determined bird. I watched for ten minutes while the grebe manipulated the fish first one way, then another. Finally, it managed to swallow the fish, and then drifted away downstream, giving in to the flow of the water.

Eared Grebe[*]
Podiceps nigricollis

Description: Black, crested head; red eye; dark back; breeding—
golden ear tufts; non-breeding—white neck and chin

The Eared Grebe measures twelve to fourteen inches long, and has a thin neck and a tailless appearance. The feet are placed far back toward the rump. Both sexes appear similar and in breeding plumage have a black, crested head and neck, golden ear tufts, brownish-black back, and rufous coloration below. The red iris is a very prominent attribute.

In winter, the Eared Grebe has a lighter gray face, and a white neck and breast that make it appear similar to the Horned Grebe. Its bill points upward, however, while that of the Horned Grebe points straight ahead.

Grebes are equipped with flat, lobed toes, which they use like propellers to maneuver efficiently through the water. These diving birds are most graceful in water but, because of their unique foot construction, are so clumsy on land that they usually avoid taking their feet out of water.

The Eared Grebe's utterance has been described as a squeaky *poo-eep* or *keryeep.* It is usually heard as it performs mating displays in the middle of a lake.

Habitat and Diet

The Eared Grebe is fairly common during the winter in the southern, warmer regions of the Southwest, but seldom breeds in this territory. It can be found on ponds, salt bays, and open lakes where emergent vegetation thrives.

The Eared Grebe is a diver, and it can either simply sink into the depths below or dive from the surface to obtain a variety of food choices such as fish, insects, crustaceans, frogs, and vegetable matter.

This common winter transient of the lowlands migrates at night. During the daytime, it is found on water sources bordered with reeds, in congregations large enough to accommodate many pairs.

Nesting and Mating Behaviors

Synchronization is a word to describe the behavior of the Eared Grebe. Not only does precise timing occur in the breeding process, as all

[*] Plate 1

young in the colony hatch at the same time, but also in the building of the nest, feeding, and even resting. When disturbed, every bird simultaneously disappears beneath the surface of the water and reappears out in the middle of the lake. When the danger has passed, they all dive under again, and suddenly appear on their nests.

These amazing birds choose nesting sites only a few feet apart, and both sexes construct the shallow, platform-type nests in a few hours. Although it appears fragile and sometimes even sinks slightly below the water, thus allowing the eggs to get wet, the nest is actually very substantial. It is made to rise and fall with the water level, and therefore is attached to vertical shafts of vegetation in such a fashion that allows it to float up and down the shaft without floating away. Even though the nest appears haphazard, it is constructed with foresight and deliberation.

The nest is lined with decaying vegetation, and the three or four whitish eggs are covered with algae to help conceal them as well as to maintain a constant temperature during the incubation period. Both sexes participate in the process as well as with the feeding and rearing of the young.

After the young are hatched, each parent takes part of the brood and goes its own way. Within about three weeks, the young are capable of taking care of themselves.

Supplemental Information

The Eared Grebe breeds in colonies and has its own specialized technique of self-preservation that assures its ongoing reproduction. In a finely tuned, synchronized fashion, each female in the colony lays eggs on the exact same timetable, thus allowing for the simultaneous hatching of the young. With so many eggs and so many young present at the same time, it is more likely that some will survive predation. The supply simply exceeds the demand, and the species can continue to thrive. The inner wisdom and unfolding of nature never cease to amaze me!

WESTERN GREBE[*]
Aechmophorus occidentalis

Description: Long, black-and-white neck; black crown extending
below eye; greenish-yellow bill

Not only is the Western Grebe the largest grebe in the Southwestern
lowlands, it is also the most regal-looking. Aptly nicknamed "Swan
Grebe," it is graced with a long, slender, slate-and-white neck. The entire
upper parts including the head are slate-black, while underparts are starkly contrasting white. A red eye is completely surrounded by dark
plumage, distinguishing it from the Clark's Grebe whose red eye is usually encircled with white feathers. The long, slender, sharply pointed bill is
greenish-yellow with a dark ridge along the top. Both sexes are similar
and measure twenty-two to twenty-nine inches long.

Although rarely seen in flight, an obvious white wing stripe may be
seen when it does fly. Usually it prefers staying in the middle of open
water where lobed toes enable it to swim quickly and effortlessly. These
water birds tend to remain in loose flocks during winter. Its call is a loud
creet-creet heard most often during breeding season.

Habitat and Diet

These graceful, aquatic birds are fairly common transient and winter
residents in the Southwestern lowlands, but may be seen year round on
the Colorado River. Lakes and sewage ponds offer protection in other
desert areas. As skillful divers, they obtain most food from the depths of
the water. A varied diet consists of aquatic vegetable matter, fish, crustaceans, insect larvae, and even frogs.

Nesting and Mating Behaviors

Western Grebes "dance" on the water in a breathtaking mating display. In pairs (sometimes of the same sex) they approach each other with
heads low, dip their bills in the water, then shake them to make a clicking
sound. Suddenly, in synchronization, they rise, arch their necks in an "S"
curve, and begin dancing across the water. Sometimes hundreds of pairs
may be seen displaying together.

[*] Plate 1

Western Grebes often nest in large colonies near waters bordered by aquatic vegetation along with other bird species such as herons, pelicans, and terns. The male brings material to the nesting site while the female does the actual construction. The nest floats to accommodate water level fluctuation, but is securely anchored to solid stalks. Both sexes share the task of incubating three to four bluish-white eggs for twenty-three days; then begin the task of feeding the young, and ultimately teaching them to feed themselves.

American White Pelican
Pelecanus erythrorhynchos

Description: White; black secondary and wing tips; large, yellow bill with expanding gular pouch; breeding—hard plate on orange bill

Bulky yet graceful, grotesque yet majestic, aggressive yet harmonious, this magnificent bird is full of paradoxes. Awkward on the ground, this large, bulky bird flies seemingly effortlessly once airborne. With a nine-and-one-half-foot wing span, its flight is a combination of flapping and sailing. Deep, powerful wingbeats are among the slowest of any bird species.

Buoyantly floating on the water's surface, the fifty-four- to seventy-inch-long White Pelican appears entirely white, but in flight the major wing feathers show black. Its huge bill is yellow-orange and measures up to eighteen inches in length. From the lower mandible an extendible pouch remains contracted and is used only as a "net" for catching fish. Fully flexed it reaches up to six inches in depth and will hold several quarts of water. In the breeding season a pale, yellow crest appears on the back of the head and a hard, plate-like projection extends from the upper mandible; both are shed with the fall molt.

The sexes are similar, and juveniles are dusky with gray bills. This large bird is usually silent, but in breeding season it may be heard making low, grunting sounds.

Habitat and Diet

The American White Pelican is a rare to uncommon transient in areas of the Southwestern lowlands where large, shallow bodies of water contain ample fish, its main diet. It is a year-round visitor along the Colorado River and at the Salton Sea, but no longer nests in either area.

Unlike the Brown Pelican, the American White Pelican does not dive from the air for fish. Instead it feeds by swimming jointly in a line with other pelicans, scooping up fish that swim near the water's surface into its extended pouch. This is a form of team hunting where pelicans are often seen extending their wings to shade the water from the sun, thus allowing better visibility of fish. Sometimes they encircle a school of fish, then slowly move in closer to scoop up the entrapped victims.

Nesting and Mating Behaviors

Moving northwest for breeding territories, the American White Pelican chooses large lakes with islands conducive to nesting. This conspicuous species needs the protection offered by remote islands because it nests on the ground and its bulky size restricts it from fast escapes.

Tight colonies contain nests as close as two feet from each other on bare ground, or on a mound consisting of pebbles, sand, or other debris found near the site. Both sexes incubate the one to three dull, white eggs which appear to be streaked with blood. They hatch after thirty days, then the adults are kept busy feeding the hungry youngsters by regurgitating a fishy soup the nestlings take directly from the parent's pouch. Gradually more solid food is made available until the youngsters are finally eating entire fish.

BROWN PELICAN*
Pelecanus occidentalis

Description: Large, brown body; white neck-front and head; back of neck chestnut; large, flat bill; non-breeding—head mostly white

This magnificent water bird with a comical appearance is really one of the most graceful large birds when in flight. It is fifty inches long and has a wingspan of six and one-half feet, making it slightly smaller than the American White Pelican.

The adults are alike in appearance. The glossy, gray-brown body displays white on the front of the neck and head, with a touch of yellow showing on the forehead. In its breeding plumage, the back of the neck is accented by a beautiful chestnut coloration. In winter plumage, the yel-

* Plate 2

low on the head is lighter, and the rest of the head and neck are entirely white. The immature is grayish brown above with whitish underparts changing slightly for several years until finally acquiring adult plumage.

The Brown Pelican has a flat bill, which often rests on the breast while the bird perches on a rock or post or floats high in the water. In flight the head is hunched back on the shoulders. Its gigantic throat pouch is extremely flexible and is retracted when the bird is in flight. However, under water the pouch expands to suck in small fish.

While flying, this robust waterbird characteristically alternates several flaps with a short glide as it flies in single file, or in V formation low over the water. Sometimes their wings actually touch the waves!

The only sounds heard in breeding colonies are made by the squealing nestlings. The adults are generally silent, except on very rare occasions when they might utter a barely audible croak.

Habitat and Diet

The Brown Pelican is seen on salt bays, on the ocean, and at beaches. It is widespread throughout the Gulf of California, and is seen occasionally inland in the Southwest.

The Brown Pelican's diet consists mainly of fish, which are seen from up to seventy feet above the water. With partially folded wings, the pelican immediately dives, bill first, and in a rotating fashion, hits the surface of the water with such a great force that the sound can actually be heard one-half mile away. This amazing bird is equipped with air sacs that cushion the impact and help it quickly surface, always facing upwind and ready for takeoff.

The large, expandable pouch is used as a scoop for prey, which are quickly swallowed after the pelican emerges from the water. The pouch is not used as storage and is retracted usually before takeoff.

Nesting and Mating Behaviors

The Brown Pelican always nests in colonies and very often is found with neighboring colonies of herons, egrets, and cormorants. The nests may be on the ground or in trees only a few feet apart. They are constructed of sticks, leaves, and grasses, and are lined with any available green vegetation. The female does the actual construction of the nest from material the male brings to her.

There are two or three white eggs, which are incubated by both parents. The yolk of these eggs is very unusual; it is deep orange rather than yellow. Both parents bring food to the ravenous youngsters until they learn the fine art of diving. They do not breed until three to five years of age.

Supplemental Information

One October evening while walking toward the sunset on a stretch of uninhabited beach in Puerto Penasco, my partner and I noticed a large flock of birds about two hundred yards ahead of us. They were hovering over the water, diving, and making loud, raucous noises. As we approached, a flock of Brown Pelicans moved closer to the shoreline. They did not seem to be concerned with our presence, and we eagerly watched while they proceeded with their feeding frenzy. Mature birds and juveniles alike were totally engrossed in capturing their dinner from a school of fish, some of which were trapped in a small tide pool. What entertainment these Brown Pelicans provided for the evening!

DOUBLE-CRESTED CORMORANT[*]
Phalacrocorax auritus

Description: Orange gular pouch, rounded at throat; shiny black plumage in adults; flies with kinked neck

The Double-crested Cormorant measures thirty to thirty-six inches long and is the main cormorant seen inland except for the Neotropical Cormorant, which occasionally crosses the Mexican border into the lower desert regions. The Neotropical is distinguished by its smaller size and pinnate gular pouch.

A black, shiny cloak adorns both adults, enunciating the large, orange, unfeathered throat pouch rounded near the neck. Also, look for the beautiful, piercing blue-green iris! In breeding season, two crests (not always visible) appear on each side of the head, hence its name. After nesting, however, the crests quickly disappear. First-year birds are brown above, have a brown iris, and are very pale on the breast.

This species has a distinctive silhouette dramatizing the long head, long tail, and cylindrical bill hooked at the tip. It flies with a kinked neck

* Plate 2

and swims low in open water, stretching its neck above the horizontal line forming an "S" shape. Cormorants' feathers are not completely water-proofed, so they must periodically leave the water, perch on open branches, and spread their wings to dry. Silence usually accompanies the cormorant except in the nesting colony, where it utters grunting sounds.

Habitat and Diet

The Double-crested Cormorant is a common resident along the Colorado River, Salton Sea, Picacho Reservoir, and Bosque del Apache National Wildlife Refuge (NWR). It is a rare transient and winter resident elsewhere on lakes, ponds, and rivers. This skilled diver secures most of its marine diet from beneath the water's surface.

Nesting and Mating Behaviors

At the beginning of mating season, the male swims near a likely mate and begins beating his wings against the water while jumping and diving. Sometimes both birds strew vegetation across the water, and occasionally the female twirls and spreads her wings. The male then flies to a nesting site with the female in close pursuit. They may re-use an old nest or build a new one of sticks forming a large platform; the nest is lined with softer materials. The female does the actual construction of materials the male brings to her. In about four days, the nest is ready for three to five pale blue eggs. Both adults incubate, brood, and feed the young.

AMERICAN BITTERN
Botaurus lentiginosus

Description: Brown streaking with black neck stripe; stubby tail; pointed wings; yellow, dagger-like bill

The elongated body of the American Bittern measures twenty-three to twenty-seven inches from the tip of its bill to the end of its short, stubby tail. Generally brown and buff, the body is streaked and dotted with cryptic markings that resemble a typical marshy habitat. A distinct feature is the black neck stripe, which extends from the base of the bill down each side of the throat. Upperparts are rich brown while underparts are tawny. A yellow iris and bill along with greenish-yellow legs and feet give this species a touch of color.

In flight, dark primaries and secondaries are conspicuous. The sexes are similar, while immatures lack the black throat stripes and are lighter overall. In breeding season, this monochromatic coloration is highlighted by bright greenish back plumage. Even with this adornment, the American Bittern is extremely hard to spot among the reeds lining the water's edge. Its defense is to freeze with its bill pointing upward, thus blending in with the weeds and stalks.

The American Bittern is usually very quiet, but when surprised it quickly departs, uttering a soft *kok-kok-kok*. During breeding season, however, the volume is turned up and the marshy territory resonates with a repeated phrase sounding like an old wooden pump. Gulping in air with amazing contortions resembling retching, it suddenly exhales with guttural sounds described as *pump-er-lunk*.

Habitat and Diet

The American Bittern is a rare transient and winter resident to the Southwestern lowlands where suitable habitat exists, namely marshy, boggy areas, or lakes with reeds. Needless to say, these areas are scarce in the desert but do exist mainly where habitat management has manipulated water levels to a sufficient status. The Picacho Reservoir, Bosque del Apache Wildlife Refuge, Salton Sea, Colorado River, and the Rio Grande are such areas.

The American Bittern is usually solitary and secretive. As a wading bird, it stalks prey in shallow water, or even more commonly waits motionless until an unsuspecting fish swims within the deadly reach of its bill. With a lightning fast thrust, dinner is served. Frogs, mice, insects, and crustaceans add variety to its diet.

Nesting and Mating Behaviors

The American Bittern is usually a solitary nester, but occasionally nests in loose colonies. In wet fields, swamps, and brackish marshes among cattails and bulrushes, this secretive heron nests on the ground or among reeds. With available dried grasses or reeds, the female constructs a platform-type nest, which appears to be part of the surroundings. Raising the young alone, she incubates three to seven olive-brown eggs for twenty-four to twenty-eight days beginning with the first eggs laid. Her first defense when approached is to sit motionless with neck outstretched and bill pointing skyward. If this camouflaged posture is not a successful deterrent, she resorts to aggression and uses her dagger-like bill with skill and precision. She feeds the young with the aid of a regurgitation process.

Least Bittern
Ixobrychus exilis

Description: Male–tiny size; dark green crown, back, and tail; buff underparts; female–chocolate-brown crown, back and tail; buff underparts

Hidden away among stalks and reeds, this secretive bittern is very difficult to spot. Smallest of the herons, the Least Bittern measures eleven to fourteen inches long, and is much slimmer and smaller than the American Bittern. The Least Bittern is the only member of the heron family in which the female differs from the male. She has a chocolate-brown crown, back, and tail, while the male displays greenish-black plumage on these areas. Both have two light stripes running down the back. Chestnut-colored plumage decorates the back of the neck and the outer edges of the inner secondaries. The wing tips are black, and the inner wing patches are tawny. The bill is pale yellow with a darker tip, the legs and feet are greenish-yellow, and the eye is yellow. In general, the underparts are buff with some streaking. Nuptial plumes on the side of the neck become obvious during breeding season. Immatures resemble the female, but have more streaking on the back and breast.

Nature has designed this species both in appearance and in disposition in such a way that it is observed by very few birders, but it may be surprisingly common in many areas. When approached, the Least Bittern freezes in an upright position, blending in perfectly with the surrounding vegetation. With bill pointed skyward, it is still able to rotate its eyes to see clearly.

Habitat and Diet

The Least Bittern is uncommon and may be found year round in marshy areas on ponds lined with cattails. The lower Colorado River Valley, Bosque del Apache Wildlife Refuge, Salton Sea, and Picacho Reservoir are prime choices for this species.

As a wader, it stalks food, or waits patiently until an unsuspecting creature moves within striking distance. Prey include fish, frogs, insects, and crustaceans.

Nesting and Mating Behaviors

The nest is a platform usually placed on bent stalks among dense aquatic vegetation. Unlike most species, the male does most of the construction, and he places the protected home two to three feet above the water. Sometimes he chooses an old nest of another species. Both sexes take turns incubating three to six smooth, pale bluish-green eggs for seventeen to twenty days starting with the first eggs laid. Also, both parents feed the young. The female stays closer to the nest, while the male hunts further away.

GREAT BLUE HERON*
Ardea herodias

Description: Long, slender, grayish body; yellow bill; black head stripes extending into plumes

Its large size makes the Great Blue Heron easily distinguishable from other herons. It measures forty-two to fifty-two inches long and is therefore the tallest wading bird in the Southwest. Its tremendous wing span reaches seven feet. Slightly longer and more lean than the Sandhill Crane, this blue-gray heron has whitish underparts with black streaking on the belly. It is white about the head, and a black stripe above the eye continues into plumes behind the head. In juveniles, chestnut patches appear on the forward part of the wing as well as on the thigh. Breeding adults have gray plumes extending from the black-and-white neck and chest.

Legs, neck, and the dagger-like bill are all very long. In flight, the Great Blue Heron folds its neck back on its shoulders and trails its feet horizontally behind its body. Upon takeoff, this heron flaps its wings heavily, but as it picks up speed, the wing beats become slow and deep.

* Plate 3

Herons are generally quiet unless disturbed or startled, then they utter deep, harsh croaks sounding like *grak* or *kraak*. They may also resonate in a deep, raucous *frahnk, frahnk, frahnk*. They breed in colonies, but are usually solitary the rest of the year.

Habitat and Diet

The Great Blue Heron is the water bird most often seen all over the Southwest. When possible, it chooses areas that are secluded and undisturbed, including marshes, wetlands, streams, and lakes. It may also be seen in more congested areas, however, such as lakes around golf courses, ponds, or any water source where there is an abundant supply of fish. At night, this heron prefers wetlands filled with tall trees, which provide safety for a rookerie, but during the daytime it is a common sight at almost any permanent water source.

In the winter, the Great Blue Heron is a resident of the lowlands, some remaining through the summer. In migratory flights or in search of feeding grounds, this heron is strong in flight. The Great Blue Heron may travel thirty miles round trip from its roosting site to its feeding ground.

Food consists mainly of fish, frogs, and crayfish, but it also occasionally takes snakes, small mammals, birds, and insects. The Great Blue Heron patiently stands in the edges of shallow water until an unsuspecting victim swims within striking range. Also, it carefully and silently stalks its prey, moving with slow, deliberate steps. At the appropriate moment, it strikes out with a lightning thrust of its bill and either stabs through the middle of prey or grabs it between its mandibles. It quickly swallows the meal whole, and an obvious lump may be seen as the meal slides down the long, skinny neck.

Nesting and Mating Behaviors

The majority of Great Blue Herons migrate to breeding territories early in the spring where they generally nest in colonies with other herons as well as with cormorants and ibises. Sometimes there are even several nests in one tree. The Great Blue Herons that choose to stay in the arid Southwestern lowlands, however, usually nest in isolated pairs.

The nest itself is usually constructed in a tree up to one hundred and thirty feet high. A pair may build a new nest, which is a simple flat platform appearing very flimsy, or they may refurbish an old nest. Either way, the male gathers all the sticks, which he leaves for the female to arrange. The large structure is lined with green leaves and small branches or twigs.

The female lays three to seven blue-green eggs, which are oval to long-oval with a fairly smooth shell. Both sexes share in the twenty-eight-day incubation process, and both take turns feeding the hatchlings while the other remains on guard to protect the young against birds of prey.

Courtship rituals are quite spectacular, especially when colonies contain hundreds of birds. The males strut about, defensively striking out with their bills at other competing males. The females excitedly cheer them on with loud croaking sounds. When pairs are formed, they dance in circles with wings flapping up and down and plumes widely spread while gracefully touching each other with their bills.

Supplemental Information

One noon in April after photographing all morning, I stopped by a lake to rest and have lunch. It was unseasonably warm, and the bird life had already gone under cover for a midday rest. As I approached the water, I could see people fishing from the edge of the bank, so I did not expect to see any wading birds.

I drove to the other side of the lake, and there in breeding plumage was a Great Blue Heron. I quickly forgot I was tired and that I needed lunch. Instead, I grabbed my camera and tripod, and eased my way toward the heron. Just as I focused my 800 mm lens, the Great Blue stabbed a sunfish right through its broad middle. The heron's beak had been opened while piercing the fish, and now it was having trouble trying to consume this delicacy without dropping it back into the water. By shaking its head, the Great Blue Heron finally tossed the fish into the air, and then gulped it down. I laughed as I saw the huge lump in the heron's long, skinny neck.

GREAT EGRET*
Casmerodius albus

Description: Large; white body; black legs and feet;
yellow bill

The Great Egret, formerly called the Common Egret, is a large heron next in size to the Great Blue Heron. It stands from thirty-seven to forty-

* Plate 3

one inches tall and appears very slender. The body is snow white with black legs and feet and a yellow bill. This is the opposite of the Snowy Egret with its black bill and yellow feet. The Great Egret is also nearly twice the size of both the Snowy Egret and the Cattle Egret, and is the most graceful of all herons. During the breeding season, the bill is orange with a dark ridge, and long, delicate plumes majestically extend from the head over the back.

While taking flight, a Great Egret starts out with its neck stretched outward and rapid wing movements; when it reaches a relaxed rate of speed, it folds its neck over its back in an S-shape and continues with slow, deep wingbeats, covering great distances with minimal flapping.

The voice is a low growling sound resembling a hoarse croak.

Habitat and Diet

The Great Egret breeds in all Southwestern states, but not frequently in the deserts and grasslands. In the latter situations it is more often just a winter resident. In the spring and early summer, however, main breeding territories include the Lower Colorado River Valley and the Salton Sea, with a few colonies found in other low elevations wherever water sources are permanent. It is uncommon at Bitter Lake.

As is typical of wading birds, the Great Egret is found at wetlands, marshes, ponds, and even irrigated fields. Its diet consists of fish, frogs, small snakes, insects, and even mice. When Great Egrets are in colonies, they often duel over fishing rights, making a raucous with each other in the water. When feeding alone, they appear quite stately as they quietly go about their business.

Nesting and Mating Behaviors

The nest may be solitary or built among large colonies of other herons, cormorants, ibises, and pelicans. Nests may be constructed just above the water in tules, or in treetops fifty feet high.

It is a rather flimsy platform type of nest, which is usually unlined. Sometimes an old nest is refurbished, which appears bulkier, and occasionally it is lined with leaves or moss. The diameter approximates two feet.

The three to five greenish-blue eggs are oval, with a smooth shell and no markings. Both sexes participate in the incubation of the eggs, which takes twenty-three to twenty-four days.

The adults perform a nest-relief ritual each time they take a turn at incubation. The bird who has just finished its turn fluffs out its plumes and stretches out its wings in a dance-like fashion. Ultimately, it picks up a stick and presents it to its mate, who eventually maneuvers to the nest and settles over the eggs, gracefully taking its turn.

The hungry nestlings know when the food is arriving and utter *kek-kek-kek-kek*. With great urgency, the young seizes the bill of the feeding parent, who then regurgitates food into the bill of the young bird.

Supplemental Information

The Great and Snowy egrets almost became extinct during the nineteenth century because their plumes were favorites for women's hats. These long aigrettes, which the Great Egret develops in the spring, were both its beauty and its demise. At that time, protest and legislation, including a bar on imports, and protection of nesting colonies saved this species from extinction. But what about the 1990s?

One day as I peacefully sat hidden in the reeds of a small lake watching a Great Egret preening its beautiful feathers, I realized this magnificent wading bird may not be any safer now than it had been in the past nineteenth century. It is not the confiscation of the bird itself that is presently the problem; it is the destruction of habitat that is increasingly threatening its existence. Now, we cannot blame the hat designers! Instead, we must look at our own motivation as we continue to clear more land, use more ground water, and build more homes around lakes.

SNOWY EGRET[*]
Egretta thula

Description: White body; yellow feet; black bill; fleshy yellow lores

Much smaller than the Great Egret, the Snowy Egret measures twenty to twenty-seven inches long. Snowy white plumage adorns this heron year round. A long, slender black bill and bright yellow feet appear just the opposite on the Great Egret (yellow bill and black feet). Additionally, the former has black legs and its eye and lores are yellow. The Cattle Egret differs with its yellow bill and yellow legs. The immature Little Blue

[*] Plate 3

Heron is also similar to the Snowy Egret, but has greenish legs, a two-toned bill, and dark tipped primaries. Spot the graceful Snowy Egret in flight and watch the head plumage spread apart as it touches down for landing. During breeding season the lores may turn burnished orange and the feet bright orange. Beautiful long plumes or aigrettes appear on the head, back, and breast. At one time, this species was hunted for the aigrettes, which are nuptial plumage growing on the back. These lacy, delicate plumes were used for "stylish" hats. Like the Great Egret, the Snowy Egret was hunted almost to extinction; now protected by law, this beautiful bird has made a remarkable comeback.

The sexes appear similar, and the juveniles lack breeding plumage and show a greenish-yellow stripe on the back of the legs. Some immatures have gray at the base of the bill. The voice of the Snowy Egret sounds like a low croak.

Habitat and Diet

The Snowy Egret may be found year round in the Colorado River Valley, Bitter Lake, Bosque del Apache NWR, and at the Salton Sea, in summer at Picacho Reservoir, and elsewhere in the Southwestern lowlands as a frequent migrant. It usually appears solitary, but occasionally is seen in small flocks. Look in areas with ponds, fresh and saltwater marshes, and rivers.

A wading bird, the Snowy Egret uses its feet to arouse small inhabitants from shallow waters, then snatches up prey with its bill. Food consists mainly of fish, but also includes other small forms of life such as shrimp, crabs, and grasshoppers and other available insects.

Nesting and Mating Behaviors

Nesting and mating behaviors of the Snowy Egret are among the most interesting of bird behaviors. Dressed in similar plumage, both sexes parade and woo the other. Face to face, crest upright, bodies bent forward as if bowing to each other, and wispy aigrettes waving behind each bird, they promenade together.

The nest is built in trees up to thirty feet above the ground. The platform-type nest is constructed by the female of materials the male brings for her usage. This process usually takes up to five days; then the female lays three to five smooth, unmarked, greenish-blue eggs. Both sexes incubate them for a total of twenty-two to twenty-three days. A nesting ritual continues throughout the whole process. When approaching the nest to take a turn at incubation, that adult greets the settled adult with bows and head motions displaying erected plumage, then they exchange places. When the young hatch, the parents take turns in feeding them regurgitated fish.

CATTLE EGRET*
Bubulcus ibis

Description: White with orangish highlights; yellow bill; yellow-green legs and feet

Smaller than the Great Egret, the Cattle Egret measures twenty inches tall, and appears stockier than both the Great and the Snowy egrets. The Cattle Egret is easily distinguished by its yellow bill and greenish-yellow legs and feet.

During the breeding season, the plumage of this small, white heron is highlighted with buff-orange coloration on the crown, breast, and back. Its legs and relatively short bill become a beautiful coral color.

Habitat and Diet

The Cattle Egret is an uncommon visitor in the Southwestern lowlands, but has been known to breed in California and Texas. It may be found in both freshwater and saltwater marshes and around ponds and swamps, and is often associated with cattle.

This squat egret originated in Africa, where it inhabits areas near elephants, camels, and water buffalo. It was first seen in Florida in 1952 and quickly spread to the Southwest. The first Cattle Egret was noticed in Tucson in 1969.

Why does this water bird associate with animals? Why does any bird choose a specific habitat? One major reason is for food. The Cattle Egret eats grasshoppers and other insects, which are attracted to the animals or are flushed out of the grasses by the grazing creatures. It sometimes actually rides on the backs of cattle, picking insects directly from the animals' hides. It is not totally dependent on this cohabitation for existence, how-

* Plate 4

ever, as it also feeds along the edges of water much like other egrets, stalking small fish or insects.

Nesting and Mating Behaviors

During mating season, the Cattle Egret grows buff-colored plumes, then usually nests in colonies. Some nest up to thirty feet above the ground in willows, cedars, and other available trees. In colonies where several species cohabitate, it is common that the larger species nest higher in a tree and the smaller species build lower down in the same vegetation. The Cattle Egret takes exception to this rule and nests wherever it pleases, often occupying spaces at the tops of trees.

It is also common for the male Cattle Egret to take sticks from nests of other species to be used by the female in its own nest. The male also collects other twigs and vines for the female to use in nest construction, which takes three to six days. Then she begins laying the two to five eggs, but may continue to add materials to the nest while taking turns with the male in incubating the eggs. The pale blue eggs are smooth with no marks, and hatch in twenty-three to twenty-five days.

Supplemental Information

Early one morning, I was out in an agricultural area waiting to catch the appropriate sunlight on the expressive posture of a singing Red-winged Blackbird. Finally, I was photographing to my heart's content when out of the corner of my eye I noticed a white water bird slinking along the edge of a reed-infested water canal.

At first I thought it was a Great Egret because I could see its yellow bill. I had already photographed one at great length so I continued with my original goal of photographing Red-winged Blackbirds. I kept glancing back at the egret, however, realizing that it appeared much smaller than a Great Egret. Finally, it crept out of the water's edge and through my binoculars I spotted the yellow feet.

I temporarily abandoned the Red-winged Blackbird and slowly and cautiously repositioned myself and my camera. The Cattle Egret crept along the edge of the water, shaking moss from its yellow feet while skillfully snatching bits of breakfast along the way. Finally, it flew closer to me and continued posing as it went on about its business of predation.

GREEN HERON*
Butorides striatus

Description: Glossy, blue-green back; chestnut head and neck;
yellow-orange legs

The Green Heron is the second smallest North American Heron,
measuring sixteen to twenty inches from the tip of its toes to the point of
its bill. The greenish-yellow legs—which turn to a deep orange in breeding plumage—appear short, and when the neck is pulled inward, this little
heron resembles a night heron in its stocky appearance.

It is not always easy to detect the green coloration on the back and
wings. Often it appears dark, and in flight may resemble a crow. In bright
sunlight, however, a blue-green gloss emanates from its back, and the
thick neck displays a deep chestnut hue. The immature Green Heron is
essentially all brown, with a streaked neck, breast, and sides.

This solitary heron often sits perfectly still, inconspicuously blending
with the surroundings. When alarmed, however, it reminds me of a roadrunner, raising the crest on its head and flicking its tail, creating comic
postures. The flight pattern of the Green Heron is typical of all herons; it
tucks in its neck and makes slow, deliberate wing strokes. The voice is a
loud *kyowk* or *skewk*.

Habitat and Diet

The Green Heron is a fairly common transient and winter resident in
the Southwestern lowlands, with some birds remaining in the area
throughout the summer. Although its habitat includes water sources such
as swampy areas, fresh streams, ponds, irrigation canals, and shorelines,
it chooses freshwater with trees for breeding habitat.

Dressed in inconspicuous plumage, this little heron hunts from a snag
just above the water's edge. Then, suddenly with a lightning-fast thrust of
the bill, it captures unsuspecting prey for a meal. Also, the Green Heron
may be seen intently and deliberately stalking prey through shallow
water, eating whatever it finds from frogs to fish.

* Plate 4

Nesting and Mating Behaviors

During the breeding ritual, the male crouches low and snaps his mandibles to attract attention. Next he flaunts his scapular plumes, hoping to attract the female. The pair may nest in a colony, but most often the Green Heron nests alone in pairs.

The nest site may be on the ground, but is most frequently in a tree from ten to twenty feet high. The male chooses the location and begins the construction. After pairing, the female builds while the male brings material to the nest site. Sometimes the finished platform-type abode is so flimsy, the eggs may be seen through the bottom. Both adults take turns incubating the four to five smooth, bluish-green eggs, which takes twenty days. When the young emerge from the eggs, both parents participate in the tedious tasks of feeding and rearing the young.

Supplementary Information

A vehicle is a tremendous aid in getting close to birds, and I often use my van as a blind from which I photograph. On one trip, as I slowly proceeded along the dirt road bordering Picacho Reservoir (Near Coolidge, Arizona), something caught my eye out in the shallow water full of stumps and snags. The silhouette of an immobile heron became visible, and because of size and body posture, I knew it was either a Least Bittern or a Green Heron. The dark coloration was the first clue, and through my binoculars I verified that it was the latter. While I observed its motionless pose, I bemoaned the fact that it was too far away to photograph, even with my giant lens.

I continued down the road, watching carefully for the surprise of the day (I call it my Crackerjack prize), and just around the corner it was waiting for me. Another Green Heron was standing in the shallow water near the bank, in perfect lighting. I quickly positioned my van and jumped in the back to photograph from the small, high window. The Green Heron was so intent with stalking its dinner it did not appear to attend to me in the least. I photographed and leisurely watched this incredible creature skillfully snatch minnow after minnow.

BLACK-CROWNED NIGHT-HERON*
Nycticorax nycticorax

Description: Black cap and back; white underparts; gray wings; dark bill; red eye; yellow legs and feet; immature– brownish with much streaking; yellow bill

Quite unlike the Great Blue Heron, the Black-crowned Night-heron is medium sized, measuring twenty-three to twenty-eight inches long, which is approximately one-half the size of the Great Blue. Both sexes of the Black-crowned Night-heron appear the same, having a stocky body, a short, thick neck, and a short bill. The body is whitish-gray, which sharply contrasts with the dark green-black crown and back. The wings and tail are gray, the large eyes are red, and the legs are yellow. During the breeding season, long white nuptial plumes appear, and the legs turn pink.

The immature bird is buff-brown with dark brown streaking below and light spots above. The eyes are yellow-orange. It resembles the American Bittern, but lacks dark neck stripes and wing-tips. The immature blends so well with the environment that it often goes unnoticed.

Although this heron may be seen singly, it is most often found in colonies. Its voice is a flat *quok,* which is most often heard at dusk. The genus name *nycticorax* means "raven of the night."

Habitat and Diet

Not only is the Black-crowned Night-heron present all over the Southwest, it is actually found worldwide, absent only in Australia. While this heron may be found around brackish marshes or even saltwater, it prefers freshwater areas with groves of shrubs, tall trees, reeds, and cattails.

The Black-crowned Night-heron is normally silent and fairly inactive during the daytime, when it is usually found in rookeries hidden among the inner branches of shrubs or trees. As its name suggests, it forages nocturnally and is most active at dusk and during the dark side of dawn. It may stand motionless, waiting for the precise moment to strike out at a passing fish, or slowly and cautiously stalk frogs and small crustaceans.

* Plate 4

Nesting and Mating Behaviors

This stocky heron nests in both small as well as large colonies often mixing in with other types of wading birds. It may nest on the ground or high up in a tree, and often the nests are very close together.

Both sexes participate in nest construction. Usually the male gathers the materials and the female places the incoming sticks or reeds to her own specifications, forming a platform that is sometimes very durable but occasionally rather flimsy. It takes two to five days to build a nest, which is ultimately lined with finer materials. The female lays three to five unmarked, oval-shaped, greenish-blue eggs, which are hatched in twenty-four to twenty-six days after being incubated by both sexes.

Although the adults hunt mainly at night, they feed their young both at night and during the day. Young nestlings are fed regurgitated liquids at first, then begin taking solid food from their parents' bills.

Supplemental Information

Each species of heron has its own unique mating display. The male Black-crowned Night-heron dances around the nesting area with his neck forward and his plumes fluffed. He bends down to his feet, uttering short buzzing sounds. Many females in the colony may approach and be driven away before one is encouraged to stay.

White-faced Ibis*
Plegadis chihi

Description: Glossy green and bronze body; long, decurved bill; adult breeding has white fringe on bare red face

At a distance or in poor light, the White-faced Ibis appears black. With closer observation and bright sunshine, however, this long-legged wader is a glossy delight. An overall bronze coloration is accented with greens and purples on the wings, rump, and tail, all illuminated with a metallic luster. The sexes are similar with a long neck; a long, reddish-colored, decurved bill; red facial skin with bordering white outlined during spring; reddish legs; and a red iris. In winter, the head and neck are streaked,

* Plate 5

and the facial skin, legs, and bill are dull gray. In this season it resembles the Glossy Ibis (which does not occur in the Southwest) but lacks the blue line from eye to bill. From the tip of its tail to the tip of the bill, it measures twenty inches long.

The breeding plumage of the White-faced Ibis inspired its name. A white facial fringe encircling the bill appears. Also the facial skin, bill, legs, and feet turn deep maroon. The young have green plumage with black legs and feet, and the iris is brown. Mature plumage begins with a glossy appearance after the first year.

The White-faced Ibis is a strong flier, usually joining others in a line alternately flapping and gliding as they speed toward their destination. Gregarious in nature, they are often heard quacking in flight. Around the nest, soft, guttural cooing suffices.

Habitat and Diet

The White-faced Ibis is an uncommon to common transient on lakes and ponds in the Southwestern lowlands. It prefers freshwater, but is also found in brackish or saltwater marshes and even in flooded fields. With long legs, it wades into shallow water and probes the muddy bottom with its sickle-shaped bill. Dining delights include fish, crayfish, earthworms, and frogs. This versatile species also frequents moist areas around lakes, meadows, or wet fields, feeding on insects, especially grasshoppers.

Nesting and Mating Behaviors

The White-faced Ibis often nests harmoniously in colonies with herons and egrets. The nest is a bulky, platform-type construction made of dead reeds and twigs, and well-lined with smaller stalks and grasses. Nests are usually among tall reeds over water, but are sometimes placed directly on the ground. The female lays two to seven smooth, unmarked, dark bluish-green eggs, which are incubated by both sexes for twenty-one to twenty-two days. Soft communication takes place between the two adults while changing turns at the brooding station. Both parents attend to the young nestlings.

GREATER WHITE-FRONTED GOOSE
Anser albifrons

Description: Brown body with scalloped black-and-white breast and flanks; white undertail coverts; white face; pink bill; orange legs

Awkward on the ground, but agile in the air, this medium-sized goose measures twenty-seven to thirty-four inches in length. The sexes are similar with a grayish-brown body and irregular, horizontal, black bars on the breast and belly, giving it the nickname "Speckle-belly." Another name is "Laughing Goose" because of its chuckling *kah-lah-a-luck* call.

The undertail coverts and rump show white, the bill is light pink, and the legs and feet are orange. A white band encircles the bill at its base, thus the name White-fronted. Immatures lack this band as well as the black markings on the underparts, but the white appears at the end of the first year; the black coloration is evident by the second year.

Habitat and Diet

The Greater White-fronted Goose migrates to the tundra of the Arctic during the breeding season, then in fall heads south again following the Pacific flyway. It is an occasional winter resident on various water sources in the Southwestern lowlands and is uncommon during migration periods.

From October to May it is found in marshy areas, lakes, or estuaries, where it feeds on aquatic vegetation including roots and seeds. All geese are grazers, supplementing their aquatic diets with grasses in close proximity to the safety of water. Additionally, stubble fields are always a favorite feeding ground.

Nesting and Mating Behaviors

The Greater White-fronted Goose is gone from its desert wintering ground by May when it makes a long journey northward to the Arctic, flying high in the sky in large flocks. Upon arrival, the female builds a nest in a shallow depression or directly on the wet tundra. Dry plants are used as the base, then she pulls down from her own breast for the lining. She lays four to eight creamy-white eggs and does all the incubation. Both adults feed and rear the young.

LESSER SNOW GOOSE[*]
Chen caerulescens

Description: White body; black-tipped wings; pink feet and bill
with black grinning patch

The Lesser Snow Goose, measuring twenty-seven to thirty-one inches
in length, has two color phases: the white phase, more prevalent in the
west, and the blue phase, which was formerly considered a distinct
species. The "Blue" has slowly spread into the west, but only appears in
the desert areas in small numbers compared to the large flocks of wintering, "White" Snow Geese.

The white phase Snow Goose has a pure white body and black wing
tips. Occasionally, on the head is a rusty wash, which is actually a stain
obtained in the Arctic feeding grounds. The bill and feet are pink. An
obvious black mark accentuates the pink bill and is called the "grinning
patch." This feature distinguishes it from the smaller Ross' Goose, which
is often seen mingling in flocks of Snow Geese. Immature birds are dusky
gray above and have a dark bill, legs, and feet.

The blue phase has a brown back and black wings with bluish wing
coverts. By the end of the first year, the immatures of both phases resemble the adults. In flocks, the Snow Geese call out in chorus with a loud,
nasally *how-wow*.

Habitat and Diet

Snow Geese congregate in large flocks on lakes, rivers, agricultural
fields, and wetlands during fall and winter, and are usually accompanied
by Ross' Geese. Habitat, weather, and food availability dictate their wintering grounds, knowledge of which seems to have been passed from
generation to generation.

Their food intake is primarily vegetable matter obtained both from
the water and on land. Geese are able to walk better than many other
waterfowl because their legs are set further forward. They graze on grain
left in the stubble fields, and in water they dabble for roots and seeds of
aquatic plants. Watch their comical acts as they submerge their heads
and necks, leaving their tail ends pointing toward the sky. During win-

[*] Plate 5

ter, Snow Geese gorge themselves in the marshes and fields in preparation for the "slim pickings" available to them when they first arrive in their breeding territory.

Nesting and Mating Behaviors

Far to the north on wet, barren tundra, the Snow Goose builds its nest in a scraped-out depression, near fresh water. Moss and down are used to line the crude construction where the female lays four to eight dull, white eggs. She does all the incubation, but the male helps in rearing and feeding the hatchlings. The young are covered with down and can swim within a day of hatching.

After the breeding season, Snow Geese molt, losing even their primary feathers, which leaves them flightless. Gathering in knots, they move along together for protection, often keeping to the safety of open water.

Ross' Goose
Chen rossii

Description: White body; black-tipped wings; dark-based, conical pink bill

The Ross' Goose looks like a miniature Snow Goose and measures twenty-one inches to twenty-five inches long. The "white phase" goose is white with black wing tips and reddish-pink legs, feet, and bill. Black coloration appears on the base of the bill, but not as extensive as the "grinning patch" worn by the Snow Goose. Close observation reveals a warty, purplish ridge on the side of the bill. A shorter neck and bill, rounded head, and rapid wingbeats also distinguish it from the latter. The sexes appear similar and the immatures are pale gray. There is also a very rare blue phase, which is similar to the blue phase of the Snow Goose. The call of the Ross' Goose is high and weak, sounding somewhat similar to a small barking dog.

Geese are extremely graceful in flight, but awkward on takeoff. To gain enough momentum with their heavy bodies, they appear to run on the surface of the water, propelling themselves with webbed feet and pounding wings that touch the water. Then suddenly, they are airborne.

Habitat and Diet

In the Southwest, the Ross' Goose winters on Salton Sea, the Colorado River, Bosque del Apache NWR, and other marshy areas along the Rio Grande. Suitable habitat always includes proximity to grasslands or grain-fields, where grazing enables it to obtain substantial amounts of food. The remaining portion consists of aquatic vegetation in marshy areas.

Geese migrate in large flocks of many family clans. The young learn migration routes by flying with their parents. The navigational abilities of birds continue to be a curiosity to humans, especially when routes are deliberate and repeated, like the one chosen by Ross' Geese. On the southward journey they make an acute westward turn near Great Falls, Montana, in order to cross the Rockies. How do they know where to turn? How do they store memory? It is exciting to recognize the gift of intelligence found in all life forms.

Nesting and Mating Behaviors

The Ross' Goose breeds in areas in the high Arctic, usually on islands of large lakes. Pair bonding is very strong, and some studies show it may last for a lifetime. In a shallow depression, the female places down plucked from her breast, then lays three to six white eggs. She does all of the incubation, then the male joins her to assist in feeding the young. After the breeding season the Ross' Goose molts, including primary feathers, thus leaving it flightless for several weeks. It gathers in knots for protection, keeping to the safety of open waters.

CANADA GOOSE*
Branta canadensis

Description: Gray body; black head and neck; white "chinstrap"

The Canada Goose is the most widespread goose in North America, and the most easily recognized as well. Because of various subspecies based on geographic locations, its size ranges from twenty-two to forty-five inches. The sexes are similar, but the female is smaller.

* Plate 6

Regardless of size, each goose exhibits the familiar long, black head and neck, highlighted with white cheek patches that form a "chinstrap." Its tail, bill, and feet are also black, while the tail coverts are contrasting white. Its breast is pale, grayish-brown. This large goose swims with its neck upright.

A Canada Goose is commonly called a "honker" because in flight the larger ones utter a deep honking sound called the "contact call."

Habitat and Diet

Most Canada Geese breed in the northern part of the continent, then many migrate southward as far as Mexico during winter. In the Southwestern lowlands, they may be seen on lakes, ponds, and marshes, as well as in grain fields from late October through March. Flocks travel long distances in a "V" formation with necks outstretched, usually "honking" loudly as they fly. They feed mainly on vegetation in lakes or ponds, but also graze on grass in nearby fields or pastures.

Nesting and Mating Behaviors

Canada Geese mate for life. The nest is usually made on the ground near water, and is typically a simple depression that the female lines with sticks, reeds, and various grasses. Occasionally it is constructed in bulrushes, stumps, or clumps of straw. As eggs are laid, she adds soft down plucked from her own breast to help keep the large eggs warm.

She lays four to eight large, white eggs, which are oval and fairly smooth; then incubates them for twenty-eight days. The male stays close to keep guard. The pair raises only one brood per year.

Supplemental Information

Even with their large size, Canada Geese are very graceful in the water and can easily move away from potential danger. On land, however, they are slow, waddling along on webbed feet.

One morning I was playing golf with some friends, and as we were planning our strategy for hitting over a lake, I noticed a small flock of Canada Geese swimming toward the shoreline. They climbed out on the bank and waddled over to the cart path. We hit our balls and continued down the path toward the geese.

Rather than retreating, as they do in water, the geese began hissing, and one even charged toward me. I jumped behind my pull-cart and quickly got out of its way. There was no doubt in my mind that it was their territory!

Green-winged Teal[*]
Anas crecca

Description: Glossy, green speculum; male—gray body; chestnut head; wide, green eyestripe; female—dark mottled upperparts lacking light patch; whitish belly; green speculum

The Green-winged Teal is one of the smallest ducks in the Southwest, measuring twelve and one-half to fifteen and one-half inches, which is about one-half the size of the Mallard. The male is gray with a chestnut head and a dark green stripe through the eye. A conspicuous vertical white mark appears on the shoulder. Cream-colored patches appear near the tail. The deep green, glossy speculum gives this bird its name. The small female is speckled with light- and dark-brown coloration, but she also has the iridescent green speculum.

When a group of ducks suddenly departs in unison from a lake, the smaller, faster ones are usually teals, who leap straight up and fly in tight formation. They flock closely together in the middle of a lake for safety in the daytime, but disperse during the night and feed more independently.

The female makes a high quacking sound, while the often-silent male makes a short whistling sound and sometimes a quiet peeping noise.

Habitat and Diet

The Green-winged Teal is common on open water during the winter months in the Southwest, and then heads north to its breeding territory with the first signs of spring. It is found on freshwater lakes, ponds, and marshes.

This teal feeds on seeds and pond weeds, often by diving and probing the vegetation on the bottom of the lake. They are amazing to watch as a group, at which time they dive and turn in perfect unison.

[*] Plate 6

Nesting and Mating Behaviors

In late winter, large flocks of Green-winged Teal break up into smaller groups containing one female and several males, all competing for her attention. The female ultimately chooses one male as her mate; all the rest are quickly driven away by the lucky suitor.

In early spring, the Green-winged Teal is called northward to its nesting ground. The nest is made in the midst of grass, weeds, and brush, always near water, and often at the base of shrubs. The depression or hollow is lined with grasses, leaves, twigs, and ultimately heavily layered with down, which the female pulls from her own breast.

The female incubates by herself and continually adds more down, which she uses to cover the ten to twelve whitish eggs each time she leaves the nest.

Supplemental Information

These small, quick teal are fun to watch as a group with their precise and deliberate formations. It is also fun to spot them during the breeding season. When disturbed, the female will fly straight up from the nest, but when she returns, she always lands away from it, slowly and cautiously making her way back.

MALLARD*
Anas platyrhynchos

Description: Male—green head; white collar, chestnut breast,
purplish-blue speculum; female—mottled brown;
dark crown; purplish-blue speculum

The Mallard is the best-known duck in the Southwest, and measures twenty to twenty-eight inches. In the breeding season and from fall through the winter months, the male has an iridescent green head with a white collar; a chestnut-colored breast; a white tail with curled, black feathers; a purplish-blue speculum; and a yellowish bill. The female has a mottled brown body with a dark crown and a purplish-blue speculum. Her bill is orange with dark patches, which differs from the lighter yellow bill of the male. Both have dark orange feet.

* Plate 6

When in flight the female displays a white bar on both sides of her speculum. During the molting season, the male looses his iridescent coloration, and both sexes exhibit the same mottled brown appearance. The distinguishing feature becomes the female's orange bill. The female is also slightly smaller than her male counterpart.

The Mallard flies fast, departing with a burst of energy in a vertical leap out of the water. Once in flight, the wingbeats slow to a powerful, rhythmic pace, and the wings seldom dip lower than the plane of the bird's body. Their webbed feet make Mallards equally efficient and graceful in the water as they are in the air.

The male is the quieter of the two sexes, uttering only a faint *yeeb* or *kwek,* while the female is very boisterous with her stereotypical quacking vocalization.

Habitat and Diet

Not only is the Mallard the best-known duck in the Southwest, it is also the most widespread duck throughout the Northern Hemisphere. It seldom breeds in the Southwestern lowlands, however, preferring to move to higher and cooler elevations. In winter, the Mallard tolerates cold, but cannot survive where water is entirely frozen, so it migrates to warmer elevations to find open water. It is found on lakes, ponds, marshes, bays, and wherever there are wetlands.

The Mallard is a dabbling duck and cannot disappear below the water's surface. It is often seen, however, with its head and neck under the water, bottom straight up, as it buoyantly stretches to reach plants growing below the surface. Alongside diving ducks, the Mallard appears rather comical.

Seeds of aquatic plants are the Mallard's primary food, but it also eats small fish, shrimp, crabs, mollusks, and aquatic insects. The Mallard has a special sieve-like bill that strains tiny animals and plant matter from the water. It also loves fresh grasses, and can be seen grazing where grasses abound close to water sources. Additionally, this species loves grain fields.

Nesting and Mating Behaviors

The mating ritual begins with the male swimming around the female with his feathers puffed up and head dipping in and out of the water. There is much acrobatic swimming as he suddenly breaks his long period of silence with whistling sounds. The female may follow several males around, quacking the whole time, and eventually chooses a single suitor by touching him with her bill.

The female not only chooses the male, the nesting site, and then constructs the nest, but she also chooses the actual nesting territory itself. Leaving the wintering flock of Mallards at the appropriate time, the mated pair actually returns to the birthplace of the female. Because she raises the hatchlings alone, she seems to prefer a familiar territory.

She builds the nest with reeds and grasses, carefully lining it with down. It is usually placed among reeds close to water, but occasionally in a pile of brush or even a tree. She lays eight to twelve buff-white eggs, which she incubates by herself.

For a while the male defends her against intruding pairs, but shortly after she begins incubation, he deserts her and gathers with other males to hide among the reeds and grasses to molt. He loses his flight feathers and therefore the ability to fly for a few weeks. During the molt, he develops the mottled brown camouflaged coloring similar to the female, which becomes his main protection until new flight feathers appear.

The female also loses her flight feathers, but she remains with the chicks. The downy, light yellow hatchlings follow their mother to water as soon as they are strong enough to walk.

Supplemental Information

It's fun to watch Mallards as they propel themselves through the water, jump straight up into flight, or waddle along on the ground. Observing them attempt to walk on thin ice is, without a doubt, a comical show. One winter morning a friend and I went birding and decided to stop at a partially frozen lake. Some Mallards were swimming in a thawed portion along the edge, but at our arrival they swam toward the middle and climbed up on the ice. They slipped and skidded, and even fell through the thinner portions. As we sat watching, even the slowest of their movements became comical. They finally gave it up and moved to more "fluid" water.

NORTHERN PINTAIL*
Anas acuta

Description: Male—dark-brown head; white neck; long, black,
pointed tail; female—mottled brown; shorter,
pointed tail

The male Northern Pintail measures twenty-five to twenty-nine inches,
and the smaller female twenty to twenty-two inches long. The male
appears very elegant with his long, slim neck; slender body; and long,
pointed tail. He exhibits a chocolate-brown head with a contrasting
white neck and underparts. His gray, streaked sides and back extend to a
conspicuous white patch adjacent to his black, pointed tail. A vertical
white stripe is very distinctive on his long neck, and his speculum is a
beautiful glossy brown and green. The female is a mottled brown with a
shorter pointed tail. Both have gray feet and bills.

The Northern Pintail sits high in the water with its tail angled upward.
When frightened, it quickly stretches its neck upward to scan for danger.
When taking off, this duck shoots straight out of the water without any
hesitation.

The male's call is a whistle and a high pitched *dreep-eeep,* and as is typical of ducks, the female makes a low quack.

Habitat and Diet

This abundant duck prefers open waters and gathers there in large
flocks during the winter months. It is also found on ponds, croplands,
stubble fields, sewage ponds, and open grasslands adjacent to water. It is
a transient and winter resident in the Southwestern lowlands.

The Northern Pintail is a dabbler and therefore feeds from the surface
of the water using its long, slender neck to reach wild celery and other
aquatic plants, as well as insects and mollusks. Feeding on land, it wad-
dles around to find grasses and seeds.

Nesting and Mating Behaviors

For the Northern Pintail of the Southwestern lowlands, pairing takes
place in late fall and winter. Then in early spring, the male follows the

* Plate 7

female to her breeding area. The Northern Pintail has the widest breeding range of all ducks and is perhaps North America's most abundant duck, though not as familiar to the casual observer as the Mallard.

The nest is a simple depression or hollow made among grasses, often far from water. It is dug by the female and lined with small sticks, grasses, or leaves, with a finishing touch of soft, warm down. The outside diameter is seven to fourteen inches, and the nest stands three to seven inches high.

The female broods the six to twelve oval-shaped, olive-green eggs by herself, a process that takes twenty-two to twenty-three days. Shortly after the chicks are hatched, they follow mom to the water. She defends them and feeds them without assistance from the male.

By July, the young are capable of flying. By late summer, the males—who have molted and are re-gaining winter plumage—begin to lead the migration southward with the females and immatures following.

Supplemental Information

In my opinion, the Northern Pintail is one of the most striking and elegant water birds in the Southwest. I love to watch its graceful aquatic skills. I was alarmed to learn, however, that fewer of these birds exist now than did a scant forty years ago.

According to the U.S. Fish and Wildlife Services, Northern Pintails have declined dramatically from 9.2 million in 1955 to 2.6 million in 1988. The loss of wetlands is the main cause, and it not only affects water birds such as the Northern Pintail, but also an overwhelming number of other birds. It is estimated that three-fourths of all bird species depend on wetlands for breeding, roosting, and feeding.

BLUE-WINGED TEAL
Anas discors

Description: Male—white face crescent; blue wing patch; female—
mottled brown; pale face spot; dark eye ring; blue
wing patch

The most distinguishing feature on the male Blue-winged Teal is the
white crescent-shaped patch between the dark eye and the ashy-colored
bill. His bluish-gray head and neck rest on a mottled brown upper body
and blend into the lighter, spotted chest. He has a chalky-blue wing
patch, which is most obvious in flight.

The female is mottled brown and beige over all, with her chin and
underparts showing lighter. Instead of the crescent, look for a pale face
spot and a dark line through her eye. She appears quite similar to the
female Cinnamon Teal, even in flight; both show blue wing patches, but
the Blue-winged Teal's bill is smaller and less spatulate. In fall plumage,
males resemble females, and the real confusion begins. The Blue-winged
Teal has a slightly smaller bill, and measures fourteen and one-half to sixteen inches long. Good luck in distinguishing the difference! The females
make a high quacking sound and the males produce a whistling sound or
one that sounds like *keck-keck-keck.*

Habitat and Diet

This little teal is an uncommon fall and spring transient throughout
the Southwestern lowlands, wintering south to Mexico, Central America, and South America. It is the first duck to migrate in fall, last to return
in spring, and least abundant of the three teals found in the Southwest.
The Blue-winged Teal prefers shallow portions of water rather than
large, deep, open areas. Its main food intake consists of vegetable matter
such as pondweed, grasses, and seeds, but it also eats snails, tadpoles,
and available insects.

Nesting and Mating Behaviors

The Blue-winged Teal chooses open regions of the Northwest for
breeding territory, but again prefers smaller, marshy areas rather than
large open lakes. The brooding site is near the water's edge but on dry

ground. The nest is made of dry grasses and stalks, then heavily lined with down. As more eggs are laid, more down is added. It is usually well hidden and even covered with surrounding vegetation. The female lays six to fifteen dull, white, unmarked eggs, which she incubates for about twenty-four days. She is very cautious when approaching her nest, never flying directly to it. Instead she lands a considerable distance away, then carefully sneaks through the thick vegetation. She covers the nest with down before leaving, both to conceal it and keep the eggs warm. She will not flush from the nest unless an intruder practically steps on her.

Cinnamon Teal*
Anas cyanoptera

Description: Male–cinnamon body; red eye; blue wing patch; long, broad bill; female–mottled brown body; dark eye; blue wing patch

This small duck measuring fifteen to seventeen inches is appropriately named for its beautiful bright cinnamon coloration. It has a large, light blue patch on the front of the wing, which in flight makes it resemble the Blue-winged Teal. Both sexes are similar, except the female's bill is slightly longer and she is tawnier in coloration.

The Cinnamon Teal is a very quiet duck except during courtship when the male utters a low chattering sound. The female is more vocal with her high quacking note.

It is a social duck and can often be seen chasing others over the water in playful displays. When startled, it may fly a short distance, making only a weak chattering sound or a *quack* from the female.

Habitat and Diet

The Cinnamon Teal is a very common spring and fall transient in the lower Southwestern deserts. The majority migrate to cooler, higher country for breeding purposes, but a few remain and reproduce at low desert lakes and marshes. Also, during the winter months they can often be found in vegetated, shallow ponds where they feed on tadpoles, minnows, and mollusks, as well as vegetation, grasses, and worms.

* Plate 7

Nesting and Mating Behaviors

As with many ducks, the Cinnamon Teal forms a pair bond months before the nesting season, but does not necessarily stay mated the entire year.

The nest is a simple hollow made in the reeds, bulrushes, or grasses and is carefully lined with down. It may be placed away from the water or possibly right over the water. The female lays six to twelve white or buff-colored eggs.

When off the nest, the hen assures the appropriate temperature of the incubating eggs by regulating them with a blanket of down, which she has gathered to line the crudely made nest.

Supplemental Information

Imprinting is a fascinating learning process and is especially prevalent in ducks. It takes place within a few hours after the young ducklings have hatched and is practically an irreversible process. Imprinting teaches the young which duck is the parent, thus protecting the hatchlings from following other moving forms in the water. Studies have shown that a duckling will imprint on the first animated form it sees. This learning process continues to be important for the duck later in life because it also plays a major role in mate selection.

NORTHERN SHOVELER*
Anas clypeata

Description: Shovel-shaped bill; male—green head and speculum; dark gray bill; chestnut sides and belly; blue wing patch; female—mottled brown; blue wing patch; grayish bill with orange edges

Decidedly smaller than the Mallard, the Northern Shoveler measures seventeen to twenty-two inches. It is appropriately named for its long, broad, spoon-shaped bill, which makes it appear to be tipping forward in the water, and gives the appearance that the wings are set back when flying. Sitting very low in the water while swimming, it keeps the shovel-shaped bill angled outward.

* Plate 7

The male has chestnut-colored sides and belly, while the lower neck and breast, as well as a patch in front of the black tail, show stark white. The breeding male has a glossy green head and speculum, a pale blue patch on the forewing, and orange feet.

The female is a mottled-brown color with a blue wing patch, orange feet, and a metallic-green speculum. Whereas the Mallard molts early in the fall, the Northern Shoveler stays in his dull summer plumage until February.

The male is silent except during mating season when he emits some rattling sounds. The vocal female quacks.

Habitat and Diet

The Northern Shoveler is an abundant transient as well as an abundant winter resident in freshwater marshes and ponds of the Southwestern deserts. In fact, their numbers are increasing due to a cooperative program among the game departments in Mexico, the United States, and Canada to protect breeding and wintering habitats, which has encouraged the ongoing survival of this and other game species, which are taken for food by some hunters and merely sport by others.

The diet of the Northern Shoveler consists of insects, tadpoles, minnows, mollusks, and occasionally seeds, which are filtered from the water through their bills in a sieve-like manner. Swimming in tight circles, churning the water with their "shovels," they skillfully scoop up these nutritious delicacies.

Nesting and Mating Behaviors

At the slightest hint of warmer weather, the Northern Shoveler migrates northward to its breeding territory. The courtship period lasts for a relatively short time in the spring, and the nest is immediately constructed. It is a very simple and shallow impression made in the tall grasses, under bushes, or hidden in weeds not far from water. Once it is lined with down, the female begins laying eight to twelve olive-green or grayish eggs.

The young do not develop the spoon-shaped bill until about two weeks of age, and then compared to their small bodies, it appears very conspicuous.

The Northern Shoveler is very temperature sensitive and is one of the first to migrate at the first signs of cold weather. It arrives in early fall in the lower, warmer elevations, and some even migrate 2,000 miles to winter in Hawaii!

Supplemental Information

Migration is an interesting phenomenon among many species, and it usually occurs when weather turns colder. Research tells us, however, that it is not the cold itself but the decline of food availability that triggers this behavior.

The same principle applies to some desert species when the weather becomes hot and dry, again prohibiting adequate food supplies. Some bird species move northward to higher, cooler, and wetter environments, which can better fulfill food needs during this period.

Because the Northern Shoveler moves at the first signs of weather changes, I can't help but wonder if it might be innately triggered in anticipation of its future needs.

GADWALL
Anas strepera

Description: Male—gray body; black rump and vent; brown head, white speculum; gray bill; female—mottled-brown body; white speculum; yellow feet; orange edges on gray bill

The Gadwall is the only dabbling duck with a white speculum, which is most visible in flight. Smaller than the Mallard, it measures eighteen and one-half to twenty-three inches long. The male is gray with a black rump and undertail coverts, and it displays both a light brown head and forewings.

The female Gadwall is similar to the female Mallard with mottled brown plumage, but the former's belly and speculum are white. Additionally, the female Gadwall's bill is gray and edged with orange. She utters a low, flat *quack* similar to the Mallard, while the male sounds like *kack-kack*.

Habitat and Diet

The Gadwall is a common transient and winter resident to the lowlands, where it is found on ponds, lakes, and rivers abounding with aquatic vegetation. Watch for "bottoms up" when it reaches downward under the surface in shallow water, stretching its neck for food growing on the bottom. When food sources near the surface of the water are scarce, this dabbler can also dive. Shoots of grasses, aquatic plant food, seeds, nuts, acorns, insects, mollusks, and even small fish are readily consumed. Being an opportunist, the Gadwall increases its chances for survival.

Nesting and Mating Behaviors

Most Gadwalls move to high mountain lakes for breeding, but small numbers stay in select portions of the desert. It chooses areas with tall, dense vegetation to build its nest, usually on land but near water. Grasses, roots, and reeds are used for the foundation, then the female plucks down from her breast for the lining. She lays seven to thirteen unmarked, creamy-white eggs and continually adds down until all have hatched.

American Wigeon[*]
Anas americana

Description: Male—brownish body; gray head; white crown; green facial patch; female—brown; dark back streaking; white wing patch

The American Wigeon measures eighteen to twenty-three inches and has been nicknamed "Baldpate" after the shiny white crown displayed by the male. The body is light pinkish-brown with a whitish belly, gray head, and a shiny green facial patch contrasting markedly with the white crown. A white patch is seen on the forewing in flight; with another placed near the black tail.

The female is deeper brown with darker streaks on her back. A white patch on the forewing distinguishes her from the Gadwall and Pintail. Both sexes have small bluish-gray bills with black tips.

In the air, the white patch on the forewing is easily noticed. It flies in tight flocks, and in winter gathers in large flocks. This duck rides high in the water, much like a coot, but is a surface feeder and does not dive.

[*] Plate 8

The male sounds a short whistle, and the female voices her needs with a loud croak.

Habitat and Diet

The American Wigeon is a common winter resident all over the Southwestern lowlands. It is found on lakes, marshes, bays, and far inland, where it can be seen grazing on grasses and weeds. It moves to higher, cooler areas for breeding.

Most diving and dabbling ducks do not compete for the same food source; the latter feeds from the surface and the former obviously feeds from the bottom of the lake. The American Wigeon challenges this procedure, however, by stealing food from diving ducks such as the Canvasback. Wild celery is a favorite, and it is not uncommon to find the birds playing tug-of-war for this delicacy.

Nesting and Mating Behaviors

The pairs bond only for a short duration, then the male leaves. The female incubates and cares for the young alone. The breeding season is later than for most ducks, with the first eggs being laid in early June.

The female makes her nest in a dry area away from the water. In a depression or hollow, she adds leaves, grasses, and much down, which she continually extracts from her own breast during the incubation process. The six to twelve eggs have a long-oval shape with a smooth, glossy, creamy white finish. Incubation takes twenty-three to twenty-four days.

Supplemental Information

My favorite sighting of the American Wigeon was on a small lake on the White Mountain Indian Reservation in east-central Arizona. The lake is available for fishing by special permit only, so few humans frequent the area. In this peaceful environment, I love to sit on the bank, listen to the quiet, and appreciate life. One afternoon I watched a pair of American Wigeons feeding along the mossy edges of the water. They were the only visible inhabitants on the lake that day, and they swam back and forth feeding to their hearts' content. I'll long treasure my own feelings of peace and plenty.

CANVASBACK
Aythya valisneria

Description: Male–red head; sloping forehead and bill; black bill; red eye; female–brownish body; dark breast and tail; dark eye; sloped forehead and bill

The Canvasback is often seen in large numbers on larger bodies of water where it can stay safely in the middle. It is the largest diving duck in the Southwest, measuring nineteen and one-half inches to twenty-four inches long. The drake has a red head and neck; a black breast, rump, and tail; and a white back and sides. This striking species is similar to the Redhead but has a red eye, black bill, and a long forehead sloping into the long bill. (The Redhead has a yellow eye, grayish bill with black tip, and a more rounded head.)

The female has a brown head and neck, buff-gray back and sides, and a darker breast and rump. Her belly is white. Juveniles and eclipse males resemble the female. Their profile is distinctive: The sloping forehead and long bill give them an angular look.

In migration, flocks travel in "V" formation, where they appear graceful and agile. Their wingbeats are strong and they fly faster than most ducks. Female Canvasbacks are usually quiet but occasionally utter a quacking sound. During breeding season, the male sounds somewhat like a cat with a *meow*-like sound.

Habitat and Diet

The Canvasback is an uncommon transient and winter resident to certain traditional ponds and lakes in the Southwestern lowlands. In winter, it tends to stay in the middle of open water. This species is prized by hunters for its flavorful flesh. When its diet consists of eelgrass or wild celery, the flavor is at its best, but this diving duck often eats other aquatic vegetation that does not guarantee its gourmet reputation. So, watch out hunters, you may be killing this beautiful species for naught.

Nesting and Mating Behaviors

The Canvasback leaves the lowlands in October to breed in states further north. It prefers lakes that are open and fairly inaccessible, surrounded by cattails and other dense aquatic vegetation.

The nest is usually placed over the water and is a semi-floating pile of dead plant material in the middle of growing vegetation. The female molds the nest into a deep basket, lined with dark gray down. She lays seven to twelve eggs, and sometimes other species add to the pile. Her eggs are slightly glossy and are bluish-olive in coloration, differing from the creamy-white of most duck eggs. She incubates the eggs, then rears and feeds them alone because the male deserts her after mating.

REDHEAD
Aythya americana

Description: Male—round, red head; yellow eye; black breast; gray back; female—brownish; light patch base of bill; dark eye

In breeding plumage, the drake has a red head and neck; a bluish-gray bill with a black tip; and a yellow eye. His back and sides are tawny-gray and his breast is black. (The Canvasback has a red eye; a long, sloping, black bill; and a long neck.)

The female is brown with a darker crown, with a light area under her chin and at the base of her bill. A light line extends behind her eye. This medium-sized duck measures eighteen to twenty-two inches long and is a strong flier usually in tight flocks low over water. Females are rather quiet, but males utter a loud *meow* during mating season.

Habitat and Diet

The Redhead is a fairly common transient and winter resident on lakes and ponds throughout the Southwestern lowlands. It dives for most food, including small fish and other aquatic life. Omnivorous, it is also fond of roots and shoots of aquatic plants. The decline of this species is due to loss of habitat, especially in its breeding territory.

Nesting and Mating Behaviors

Most Redheads leave the desert lowlands in April, but some nest at Bosque del Apache NWR, the Salton Sea and in the Colorado River Valley. It chooses large marshy areas that support cattails, bulrushes, and reeds. The nest is usually placed over water on floating vegetation, but it is sometimes placed on the ground near the water's edge. The female builds the nest in the shape of a deep basket using available dry matter in the area. The basket is supported by growing vegetation, which keeps it from floating away. Smaller pieces of cattail and down plucked from her breast line the cozy home.

In areas where many species of ducks nest in the same area, a form of parasitism occurs where one hen lays eggs in a nest belonging to another fowl of its own species, or sometimes even in that of a different species. The Redhead lays nine to fifteen pale, grayish-olive eggs, some of which may be placed in another nest. She incubates the brood for approximately twenty-four days, then begins the task of feeding and protecting the young hatchlings.

RING-NECKED DUCK*
Aythya collaris

Description: Male—black breast, back and tail; purple head; ringed bill; yellow eye; female—brown; white eye ring; ringed bill; dark eye

The Ring-necked Duck is decidedly smaller than the Mallard, measuring fifteen to eighteen inches. The head is almost triangularly shaped into a high dome resembling a crest.

In breeding plumage, the male has a black breast, back, and tail. The head is iridescent purple, the eye is yellow, and the bill is grayish-blue with a lighter ring near the tip of it. Gray sides display vertical white marks in front of the wings.

The female is brown with a dark eye, white eye ring, and light beige coloration on her face in back of the bill, which also has a ring around the tip of it. Both sexes have lobed feet for diving rather than the Mallard's webbed feet, which are used for surface feeding and swimming.

*Plate 8

A very similar species is the Lesser Scaup, which has a whitish back but lacks the vertical marks in front of the wings and the ring on the bill. The female Lesser Scaup has a darker head with a sharply defined white area at the base of the bill.

Directly overhead, it is difficult to discern the difference between the Ring-necked Duck and the Lesser Scaup, but when viewed from the topside it is easy to distinguish because the Ring-necked Duck is the only duck with a black back and gray wing stripes.

The male is relatively silent, except during courtship when he gives a soft whistling note.

Habitat and Diet

The Ring-necked Duck is a common transient throughout the Southwestern lowlands, and some stay throughout the winter months. They are quite frequently seen on marshes, ponds, small streams, or lakes. It is a freshwater diver that feeds on aquatic vegetation on the bottom of the lake. It winters near salt water, but stays on streams and marshes that feed into the salty sea.

The Ring-necked Duck is considered a game bird and is apparently very tasty. It is not hunted as often as other game birds, however, because this species does not gather in large flocks. Instead, it stays in small groups spreading out over smaller waterways, which is less desirable to hunters.

Nesting and Mating Behaviors

Nest building starts with the first egg laid. Initially, the nest may be constructed in a small depression in bent-over grasses and is lined with down. As more eggs are laid, the construction of the nest continues. More grasses or reeds are added on a daily basis. If the water level rises, the female continues to increase the height of the nest to prevent flooding. The nest may also serve as a raft or hammock-type structure.

There are six to fourteen eggs, but more typically eight to ten. These long-oval, olive-buff, unmarked eggs are laid one a day, with incubation beginning with the first one laid.

The female does all the incubation, which takes twenty-five to twenty-nine days. But unlike many male ducks, the Ring-necked male stays nearby for protection and accompanies the female when she is off the nest. Only one brood is common per year.

Supplemental Information

Nature's magnificent design never ceases to amaze me. Several species of water birds can co-exist in the same territory because of their different feeding styles. Ducks are either dabblers or divers, and obtain the majority of their food accordingly. Diving ducks, of which the Ring-necked Duck is one, have shorter and broader bills than the surface-feeding ducks. They use their powerful lobed toes to maneuver to depths of up to forty feet below the surface to find their food supply. Their legs are set far back on their bodies, making them powerful under water but very awkward on land.

Dabbling ducks jump vertically out of the water in flight, but diving ducks like the Ring-necked Duck must skit along the surface of the water to gain enough momentum to lift into the air.

Common Merganser
Mergus merganser

Description: Male–glossy, green head, no crest; thin, red bill; female–rufous, shaggy crest; thin, red bill; white breast

The Common Merganser is the largest of the mergansers, measuring twenty-two to twenty-seven inches long, but is very sleek with a slender bill. The male has a white breast and sides, with black-and-white wings. His head is smooth and iridescent green, contrasting sharply with the thin, hooked, red bill. The absence of a crest distinguishes him from the Red-breasted Merganser.

In this species, the female has the crest. Her head and neck are bright chestnut. The chin, lower neck and breast are white, while the upperparts are gray. Her bill is red like the male's, with nostrils nearly halfway down the bill. The upper mandible is serrated to aid in catching fish.

This species is fairly silent, but in the breeding season the female utters a low *qua-awk* while the male makes a guttural sound. Common Mergansers are fun to watch when they "run" across the water with wings flapping noisily while attempting to get their large bodies airborne.

Habitat and Diet

This sleek duck is an uncommon transient and winter resident on larger lakes and rivers in the Southwestern lowlands, preferring fresh water with an ample fish supply. Although large, the Common Merganser is an agile diver and pursues fish under water. Its long, narrow, cylindrical bill is equipped with saw-toothed edges, which allow it to capture sizable fish as well as other swimming prey such as tadpoles and insects.

Nesting and Mating Behaviors

The Common Merganser chooses unusual nesting sites for a duck; usually in a tree cavity, but also in holes of banks or cliffs. It will also use nesting boxes in appropriate habitat. The hollow is heavily lined with down. The female lays six to seventeen unmarked, ivory eggs, which she incubates approximately thirty-two days. She raises the chicks alone because by this point the drake has abandoned her.

RED-BREASTED MERGANSER
Mergus serrator

Description: Male—glossy green, shaggy crest; thin, red bill; red eye; female—brown crest; thin, red bill; brown breast; red eye

The Red-breasted Merganser is smaller than the Common Merganser, measuring nineteen to twenty-six inches long. Like the latter, it has a sleek body and a long, narrow bill with serrated "teeth" on the upper mandible. Unlike the male Common Merganser, the Red-breasted has a shaggy, glossy double crest. His head is iridescent green and sports a red eye and bill. His white plumage contrasts starkly with the dark head and black streaking on the brownish-red breast. Underparts show white, while the foreback and shoulders are intricately designed with black and white.

The female's head is cinnamon-brown with a shaggy double crest, but is lighter in coloration than that of the Common Merganser, which has a striking white chin patch. Her chin, foreneck, and underparts are grayish-white, and the rest of her body is grayish-brown. The eclipse male may be identified by his wing patterns, otherwise he resembles the female.

The Red-breasted Merganser is a quiet duck except in breeding season. The male's call is a *yeow-yeow* and the female's responds with *kaar.*

Habitat and Diet

The Red-breasted Merganser is an uncommon winter resident on inland lakes and ponds rich with its food supply, which consists mainly of fish. The long, thin serrated bill enables it to seize and consume fish of considerable size. Clear-water coves provide perfect opportunities for this agile hunter. Unlike the Common Merganser, the Red-breasted Merganser also takes to saltwater, and many winter on the Salton Sea.

Nesting and Mating Behaviors

The Red-breasted Merganser does not breed in the Southwestern lowlands, and leaves these areas in early spring. It chooses remote areas near water and places its nest on the ground among rocks, roots, or brush. Leaves, moss, and grasses are used for the simple base, then down is added for lining. Both sexes incubate the eggs, which takes about thirty days.

Ruddy Duck*
Oxyura jamaicensis

Description: Male—chestnut body; black cap; blue bill; female—
        dark, gray body; dark cheek line; bluish-gray bill

The Ruddy Duck is an easily recognized, small, chubby duck measuring fifteen to sixteen inches. In breeding plumage, the male wears a black cap on his otherwise deep chestnut body. The face and underparts are white, contrasting with a conspicuous, wide blue bill. He stays in this plumage from spring until the end of summer.

In winter, he is dark gray with white cheeks and a light blue-grayish bill. The female resembles the male in winter, except she has a dark line on her cheek. Both use their long tail as a rudder while swimming.

Overhead, the white face is conspicuous against the rusty red chest and stubby-looking body. The short wingspan gives it a bumble bee-type of flight, and the long tail becomes very obvious. The Ruddy Duck can

*Plate 8

often be seen flying close to the surface of the water, its short wings beating very rapidly.

This duck can often be seen swimming around, cocking its spiky tail vertically. Like many ducks, the male remains silent except during the mating season; then he may be heard making weak croaks or a sputtering sound described as *chic-ik-ik-ik-k-k-k-kurrr*. This is the only duck that cannot walk.

Habitat and Diet

The Ruddy Duck is a very common winter resident as well as a common transient. Occasionally it breeds at the lower elevations of the Southwest, but it usually retreats to the cooler heights during the spring and summer months. In both territories, this species can be found on lakes, ponds, and fresh marshes; and in winter on coastal salt bays.

The Ruddy Duck is a diving duck, but differs from other diving ducks in two ways: It is almost strictly vegetarian, and it feeds entirely from the bottom, even as young hatchlings. Other divers begin by feeding from the surface. The little Ruddy Duck, therefore, must find deep, clear water sources for feeding purposes.

Nesting and Mating Behaviors

During the courtship period, the male swims around with his crest raised and bobs his head up and down in quick, jerky motions. He kicks up sprays of water with his feet and skitters over the surface of the water. His small size allows him to move quickly, changing directions at whim, then stopping and cocking his spiky tail straight up.

While the Ruddy Duck feeds in deep water, it needs dense vegetation in shallow water for protection and nesting. The nest is a woven, basket-type structure made of cattails or bulrushes attached to growing plants seven or eight inches above the water's surface. It is more intricately constructed than the nests of many other ducks. The outside diameter is from eight to sixteen inches.

The female lays five to fifteen large, white, creamy, oval eggs. They are unmarked and rather rough. The female does all of the incubation, which takes twenty-five to twenty-six days.

Sometimes two or three females lay eggs in the same nest and then share in the task of herding thirty or more ducklings among the reeds in search of food. After a few weeks, the young may leave the safety of the marshes and gather together in large flocks on open water. Unlike many other male ducks, the Ruddy Duck remains with the female and helps with the raising of the young.

Supplemental Information

The Ruddy Duck has been known to engage in egg parasitism. This means that it occasionally lays one or more eggs in another bird's nest. Next time you are watching young ducklings, look closely. You might observe the results of this parasitism among a brood of chicks.

SORA
Porzana carolina

Description: Black face and throat; conical yellow bill; gray neck
            and breast; green legs; non-breeding—black fades

A short, yellow bill, and black face patch and bib make the Sora easily recognizable in breeding season. In winter plumage the black fades to gray. The sexes appear similar, with chicken-like bodies showing mottled brown on the back and gray on the throat, neck, and head. Black-and-white horizontal stripes appear on the belly, and the undertail covers are buff-white. This robin-sized rail measures eight to nine and three-quarters inches long.

This plump, secretive, wading bird has a short tail, which it cocks in expressive gestures. Although highly migratory, Soras are seldom seen in sustained flight, preferring to move about on the ground, slipping around under the cover of dense, marsh vegetation and flying only short distances when flushed. Migration is another matter, and once airborne, it chooses to travel under the cover of night. Rails are more often heard than seen, but the Sora is more easily detected than some because it often feeds at the edge of openings. Its voice suggests a whinny-like whistle descending in pitch and sounding like *wee-wi-wi-wi*. When alarmed, its call is an abrupt sound resembling *keek*. This call can be induced during field conditions by a simple clap of the hands.

Habitat and Diet

The Sora is an uncommon transient and winter resident in the desert lowlands on cattail-lined ponds and marshy areas. Migration occurs in September and May. This shy species spends the majority of its life slipping through dense shoreline vegetation in search of food, namely mollusks, insects, frogs, crustaceans, and aquatic vegetation. In late fall, the Sora feeds in a frenzy, gorging itself in preparation for a long migration flight as far as South America.

Nesting and Mating Behaviors

The Sora breeds in areas where food is readily available. Soggy, freshwater marshes or grassy meadows fit the bill. Dry materials, such as cattail stalks and grasses, are woven together into a little basket, which sits above the water level or is often located in an open meadow a short distance from the water. There are six to eighteen buff-colored eggs with brown spotting, incubated by both adults beginning with the first egg laid. Because the first eggs hatch before those laid later, one adult continues incubating while the other feeds and cares for the older siblings.

COMMON MOORHEN
Gallinula chloropus

Description: Breeding—red, frontal shield and bill; yellow-tipped bill; black head; white scalloping on flanks; non-breeding—brown facial shield; yellow-tipped bill

This active gallinule, formerly called the Common Gallinule, is a plump chicken-like bird measuring twelve to fifteen inches in length. From a distance it resembles the American Coot, but upon closer observation the bright red frontal shield and yellow-tipped red bill of the breeding plumage immediately distinguish it from the American Coot. (In immature birds, the red is replaced by brown, still differing from the stark white frontal shield of the coot.) Additional breeding plumage includes bright, greenish-yellow legs and feet with a red band showing above the ankle joint. Both sexes appear similar, with a black head and neck accompanied by slate-gray underparts. The back and wings are brown with conspicuous white scalloping and white undertail coverts. The juvenile is browner and has a light throat.

The Common Moorhen cocks its short tail in expressive postures and displays extremely long, slender toes while feeding among the grasses along the water's edge, or when running across the water's surface lightly stepping on lily pads, fluttering its wings for balance. It is an avid swimmer with lobed toes instead of webbed feet, and continuously bobs its head while swimming in deeper water. This water bird is very noisy, with a repertoire of sounds ranging from an explosive *kar-uck, kek, kek, kek, kek,* to a more despondent *tuka, tuka.*

Habitat and Diet

The Common Moorhen is an uncommon resident throughout the Southwestern lowlands where shallow ponds, streams, or marshes support cattails or reeds. Its hen-like bill picks at food, which includes both plant and animal matter such as mosquitoes, spiders, insect larvae, and worms, as well as available fruits and seeds.

Nesting and Mating Behaviors

The displaying behavior of a breeding male is quite fascinating. It may appear that he is dashing about unnoticed, but from somewhere in the shallow, reed-lined edges, a female is watching. Harsh utterances accompany his flashy show as he swims first in her direction then abruptly reverses his course. He flicks his stubby tail, flashing the white under tail-feathers, and cocks his head in various positions to display his red bill and frontal patch.

After coupling, a nest is built among stalks of vegetation in shallow water. It is a well-built, cup-shaped affair, often accompanied by a ramp leading from the nest to the water. It may also have a platform nearby for roosting purposes. Two to sixteen buff-colored eggs with dark spots are incubated by both sexes for nineteen to twenty-two days. The young can swim as soon as they hatch. For the first month the female gives them exquisite care, then leaves them to fend for themselves while she begins a second brood.

AMERICAN COOT*
Fulica americana

Description: Gray body; black head; white bill and frontal shield
with red, upper spot

The American Coot is a chicken-sized, duck-like bird that measures thirteen to sixteen inches long. It has a dark, slaty body with a blackish head
and neck. Both sexes have very similar markings with a divided ivory-colored patch under the tail. It is the only ducklike bird with an ivory-colored
bill and frontal shield showing a red upper spot. While swimming, a
pumping motion of the head is very characteristic of this species.

The coot uses the lobed toes to walk over lily pads and to maneuver
itself through the water. When frightened, this skilled aquatic bird may
dive abruptly, but most often it will skit over the water to a safe distance,
propelling itself with wings and feet.

In a similar fashion, it becomes airborne by "running" over the top of
the water to gain the necessary speed for takeoff. Because the tail is so
short and does not suffice for a rudder, the big feet are employed for this
purpose, trailing behind the tail. Even as slow as the American Coot
appears, it still can migrate for long distances.

Its voice is a plaintive call with much croaking and crackling.

Habitat and Diet

The American Coot is a common summer resident of the Southwestern lowlands and is easily found on lakes, marshes, and ponds, especially
where cattails and tules abound. It winters where waters do not freeze
over, and is even found on salt water where a supply of submerged vegetation abounds.

The American Coot feeds mainly by diving to the bottom. But it is also
a surface feeder, sometimes even leaving the water completely to graze
on vegetation surrounding lakes and ponds. Although the coot's diet
consists mainly of aquatic vegetation, this omnivorous bird also eats
insects, snails, worms, and small fish. Occasionally it will eat small
passerines.

*Plate 9

Nesting and Mating Behaviors

The nesting period is from late April through July, at which time this normally gregarious bird becomes even more aggressive. Both sexes participate in the building of the nest as well as with the incubation of the eggs. They also take turns defending their territory. When an intruder approaches, the American Coot rises up out of the water and slashes at the intruder with both feet and bill. The crackling, plaintive voice becomes explosive, with much wailing and clucking.

In his courtship display, the male fans his tail while swimming back and forth in front of the female. After coupling, the cup-shaped platform nest is built of grasses, usually on the edge of open water. It looks like a raft of vegetation and is attached to surrounding plants to keep it from floating away. The outside diameter is from fourteen to eighteen inches, while the inside diameter is approximately seven inches.

Usually there are eight to twelve eggs, although up to twenty-two have been found. The eggs are oval shaped with a smooth shell, a slight gloss, and are buff-colored with small dark brown dots covering the entire surface. Incubation takes twenty-three to twenty-four days.

Shortly after a chick is hatched, the down will dry out and it will swim away from the nest. The fledgling has a hairy appearance with an orange-red head and shoulders. The red-blue frontal shield seems to be a feeding signal for the parents.

Because incubation starts with the third or fourth egg laid, some chicks hatch ahead of others. It is the male who begins teaching them to feed in the marshes, while the female finishes incubation of the rest of the brood.

Supplemental Information

Birding is obviously a visual experience, evidenced by the vast numbers of binoculars purchased each year as well as by the many exposed rolls of film that I can account for personally! Additionally, it is a magnificent auditory experience.

Even in the middle of the day, when birding seems to be at a lull, I can almost always count on finding an American Coot feeding among the reeds of a Southwestern lake. Its loud, grating *kuk-kuk-kuk* or *ka-ha, ha-ha* breaks the silence, and I am reminded that I am not alone.

GREATER SANDHILL CRANE*
Grus canadensis

Description: Tall, grayish-tan body; red, heart-shaped cap on forehead

The Greater Sandhill Crane measures thirty-four to forty-eight inches in length, and although its upright, stately pose makes it appear tall, it is actually slightly shorter than the Great Blue Heron. The Sandhill Crane has a wingspread of six to seven feet and is a grayish-tan bird with an obvious red, heart-shaped cap on its forehead.

Splashes of rust appear on many adults while the immature birds appear brown all over. The eye is yellow, and the legs and feet are black. This long-legged, long-necked bird has a four- to five-inch dark gray bill, which appears short for the bird's great size.

The Sandhill Crane is extremely graceful both on the ground and in flight. It flies with its neck and legs outstretched, typical of all cranes. When the sights and sounds of hundreds of these incredible birds fill the air, it is no wonder that many spectators are touched with a spiritual presence not to be forgotten. When a flock is disturbed, or when flying in unison both at dawn and dusk, they join together uttering a chorus of *kroo-oo* or *gar-oo-a*. The higher-pitched voices are the juveniles, and the adults' cry is a significantly lower sound.

Habitat and Diet

The Greater Sandhill Crane winters in the Southwest from Southern California to western Texas, but is only seen in large flocks where suitable roosting sites, as well as food supplies, exist. These intriguing birds require shallow water with sandbars and sufficient open space to provide protection against predators.

Bosque del Apache National Wildlife Refuge represents the largest winter gathering of Sandhill Cranes in the southwestern region. In the early morning the Sandhill Cranes may be seen, as well as heard, flying from protected shallow waters to grain fields in the vicinity. Again, at sundown, they fill the sky with magnificent sights and sounds as they return to their traditional roost sites.

*Plate 9

While in the fields, these wary birds use their strong bills as probes to find grain and corn that have been scattered and buried under the topsoil, as well as insects. Here they are at risk because coyotes and other predators lurk among the cornstalks waiting for a chance to fulfill their own food needs. The flock itself is the main protection because some birds are always alert while others eat. As with all wildlife, the weakest of the species are usually the prey.

The Sandhill Crane is omnivorous. It is one species that actually will eat almost anything including insects, worms, snakes, small mammals, bird eggs and young birds of other species, seeds, grain, berries, etc. The young chicks, which require high protein as do almost all birds, primarily feed on insects and worms.

Nesting and Mating Behaviors

The Sandhill Crane graces the Southwestern lowlands with its presence only during the colder winter months, and returns to the Midwest and West for breeding purposes. It chooses a marshy habitat, preferably in isolated valleys and meadows. Although this bird roosts in colonies in the winter, it nests in isolated pairs.

The nesting site is selected in an open, flat area where predators can be easily seen before they ever get near the nest. The Sandhill Crane returns to the same breeding territory every year, and a territorial display is preformed by both sexes. A series of sounds, named the unison call, may be heard at this time, and by watching and listening carefully, one can easily distinguish the sexes. With heads tilted upward, the male calls once, while the female always calls twice.

The nest is made from dried reeds, rushes, sticks, or moss, and is built in or near shallow water. The outside diameter is from three to five feet depending on the availability of dried material in the area. The inside is a slight depression, where the one to three eggs are laid. They are oval with a smooth shell, and are olive colored with lavender-brownish spots.

Both sexes share the task of incubation, which takes twenty-eight to thirty-one days, and both also participate in the rearing of the young. Within a few hours of hatching, the first chick tries standing and walking on its long legs and soon joins the male, learning to acquire food while the female continues incubation of the remaining eggs.

Supplemental Information

Being in nature and photographing wildlife has always been an essential part of living for me. When I began to photograph birds seriously, however, it was as if another door was opened, one that would take me even further into an intimate and personal relationship with each species. While photographing, I feel a special connection with my subject and thus experience yet another aspect of my own being.

This is what I believe to be a spiritual awakening–a greater awareness of the inter-relatedness of all life. Each time I experience the presence of large numbers of Sandhill Cranes flying in the early dawn light and calling majestically to one another, I feel this magnificent connection!

KILLDEER*
Charadrius vociferus

Description: Two black bands on a white breast; brown above, white below; long legs

The Killdeer is an abundant shorebird in the Southwest. White underparts contrast starkly with the two black rings that extend from its lower breast to the top of its neck. These rings make it easily distinguishable from other plovers. The upperparts are a drab olive color. In flight, this robin-sized bird displays a rust-colored rump and white stripes on the wings. A longish tail is as obvious in flight, as the long legs are when this plover darts about the edges of a lake or stream.

This shorebird is extremely speedy on the ground and is fascinating to observe. It has three toes that point forward, but absolutely none in the back. With head tucked downward it runs, then stands straight upright to stop. A very fast flying species, it takes off with a burst of energy while continually crying the lament *killdeer.*

Habitat and Diet

The Killdeer can be found year round by rivers and lakes as well as around small water holes and even sometimes where water is practically non-existent. Hence, it fits very well into the Southwestern environment.

*Plate 10

Feeding almost entirely on insects, this active bird is often seen hurrying about jabbing its bill into the sand or under rocks.

Nesting and Mating Behavior

The Killdeer must guard its nest carefully because it is not built in a safe bush or tree out of reach of most predators. Instead, the nest is made on the bare ground in easy reach of any passerby. The Killdeer often chooses to lay eggs on a rocky terrain, however, which serves as clever camouflage. The nest is approximately six inches in diameter and is scraped down into the sand about one to one and one-half inches. There are usually four eggs in a clutch, and they are rather large and totally covered with buff brown spots. They blend perfectly with the gravel and rocks that make up the nest.

The male makes the nest by scratching several depressions in the ground. The female eventually chooses one that is right out in the open, allowing complete views in all directions. The incubation, which takes approximately twenty-five days, is done by both sexes.

Early one summer, a friend brought an egg to me, saying that her son had found it along the river. Apparently they had tried to search the trees for a nest, but were unable to find one that might have accommodated the egg. It was the large, pointed, splotchy egg of a Killdeer, and little did the boy know that he probably took it right from the subtly constructed nest itself.

Because the chicks are hatched right on the ground, in open reach of everything, nature has once again provided a special means for self-protection. The eggs are larger than most eggs of similar-sized birds because they take longer to hatch and necessarily have larger yolks to supply the developing chicks with nutrients. Because they are more mature when they are hatched, the majority of the young are able to take care of themselves within hours after hatching, but sometimes up to a full day. Because of nature's intricate planning, the chicks enter into the world and quickly escape their own vulnerable hatching site.

Supplemental Information

The Killdeer at one time came close to extinction because it was a favorite of many hunters. For the last several decades, however, this species has been protected from the hunter by law, and now it abounds in plentiful numbers. Because its diet consists mainly of insects, especially those that can be destructive to crops as well as to animals, the Killdeer is now recognized for its beneficial contribution. Once again, it is obvious that the intricacies of nature serve every detailed need for the balance of life itself.

BLACK-NECKED STILT*
Himantopus mexicanus

Description: Long, pink legs; needle-shaped bill; black neck and wings; white tail

The Black-necked Stilt is easily identified by the black upper head, neck, and back, which contrast sharply with the white throat, underneck, belly, and undertail coverts. Its long, needle-shaped bill is black. The eye is red and adorned with a white eye ring. In flight, extremely long, pink legs and feet trail behind, and whether wading or walking, the legs appear disproportionate to its size, for stilts have the longest legs in proportion to their bodies of any bird. Watch as it proceeds along with very measured steps bending spindly-looking legs backward while leaning forward to feed. The long bill makes it possible for this agile bird to reach prey. Considered a medium-sized shorebird, it measures thirteen to sixteen inches long.

The Black-necked Stilt is as graceful in flight as it is on the ground, and when landing, its beautiful wings are raised above the body momentarily before they are folded. It utters a yelping sound like *yip-yip, yip* or a long repeated series of *keek, keek*.

Habitat and Diet

The Black-necked Stilt breeds in limited areas of the Southwestern lowlands, otherwise it is a common transient on ponds, rivers, and lakes throughout the Sonoran Desert, where it chooses areas with shallow water and adjacent vegetation for feeding. This long-legged wader is very beneficial because it preys on large numbers of grasshoppers, diving beetles, and other insects.

*Plate 10

Nesting and Mating Behaviors

The nest is made either in a depression on the open ground or on a mound of mud where sticks are piled up above the water level. The female lays three to five smooth, buff-colored eggs blotched with brown or black. The adults take turns incubating them for about twenty-five days.

To distract a potential predator from the nest site, the Black-necked Stilt has an aerial style of feigning injury. Because long legs prevent it from flopping around on the ground, this crafty species mimics a wounded bird in flight, fluttering distractingly just above the ground. When the intruder comes closer, the stilt moves farther away from the nest to display, then ultimately flies away, re-approaching the nest when the danger has passed.

AMERICAN AVOCET*
Recurvirostra americana

Description: Black-and-white wings; long, thin, recurved bill; long, blue-gray legs; rusty head and neck in spring adult; non-breeding–gray neck

A large, gregarious shorebird, the striking American Avocet measures fifteen and one-half inches to twenty inches long from beak to tail. Black, white, gray, and cinnamon adorn this conspicuous wader. Its white body contrasts with the glossy, black stripes on the back and wings. In breeding plumage, the head, neck, and breast are cinnamon. In winter, these areas are gray and match its long, spindly looking legs and feet. Its dark, needle-sharp bill is recurved, more so in the female than the male. Juveniles appear with a light cinnamon coloration.

Sleek and graceful, the American Avocet is often found in large flocks feeding in shallow water and moving forward in lines, heads sweeping sideways in search of pray. Although typically waders, they do enter water and readily swim. When frightened, the American Avocet makes a sharp, repeated call sounding like *keek, keek, keek.*

*Plate 10

Habitat and Diet

The American Avocet is an uncommon to common transient in most of the Southwestern lowlands in April and May, and again in August through October. A few remain as summer residents. It prefers shallow lakes, river beds with sand bars, and wet meadows, but it may also be seen foraging in saltwater as well as freshwater marshes.

The unique feeding style of this striking bird makes appropriate use of the upturned bill. It wades into the water and touches the convex portion of its slender bill on the bottom. With mandibles slightly opened, it swings its head from side to side sweeping through the ooze in search of aquatic prey including insects, seeds, and small, shrimp-like crustaceans.

Nesting and Mating Behaviors

The American Avocet nests in colonies, but each pair has its own nest and territory. The nest is constructed by both sexes and may be scantily built on gravelly terrain, or more elaborately compiled of rootlets and debris placed in a shallow depression among low vegetation.

The three to five smooth, olive-colored eggs with darker splotches camouflage themselves in the chosen site. Both adults incubate the eggs for about twenty-three days. The young are capable of leaving the nest shortly after hatching.

GREATER YELLOWLEGS*
Tringa melanoleuca

Description: Long, yellow legs; slightly recurved, two-toned bill; white eye ring and superciliary; white rump and tail shown in flight

As you might suspect, this sandpiper has long, bright yellow legs. The long, slightly recurved bill is unmistakably longer than its head and is two toned: black at the tip and gray at the base. The sexes are similar, and in breeding plumage the throat and breast show streaking; the lower breast, sides, and belly are spotted and barred; and the upper parts are checkered with black, brown, gray, and white. The rump and tail are white,

*Plate 11

showing most conspicuously in flight, and its white head is streaked with dusky brown. Additionally, a white eye ring and white superciliary marking adorn the head. This large, thin, sandpiper measures twelve and one-half to fifteen inches long from beak to tail, compared to the smaller nine-and-one-half to eleven-inch-long Lesser Yellowlegs.

In winter plumage, the Greater Yellowlegs is a nearly identical but larger version of the non-breeding Lesser Yellowlegs, with the exception of its longer recurved bill and distinctive vocal characteristics. The darker coloration fades to gray and brownish-gray, while the underparts become white. In the Southwestern deserts, a single bird or small group may appear feeding along a shoreline. When approached it quickly takes flight, extending long legs beyond its tail then gracefully flying through the air with deliberate wing beats until gently touching the ground again. A clear three-whistled call, *whew-whew-whew,* easily distinguishes it from the soft, flat *tew-tew* of the Lesser Yellowlegs.

Habitat and Diet

The Greater Yellowlegs is a common transient and winter resident on lakes, ponds, and rivers in the Southwestern lowlands. Feeding in shallow pools, marshes, or estuaries, this wading bird finds minnows, insects, and other small forms of life available in or near the water. This food is obtained by aggressively sweeping its bill from side to side while progressing through the water. When feeding in a group, the Greater Yellowlegs will form a line and "round up" schools of minnows by driving them into a shallow, confined area for easy dining.

Nesting and Mating Behaviors

Most of the Greater Yellowlegs migrate into Canada for breeding purposes, choosing marshy areas protected by surrounding forests. They do not nest in the Southwestern United States. The nest is a mere depression in gravelly areas or among fallen logs. There is little or no lining added. The female usually lays four buff-tan eggs which are adorned with reddish-brown spots.

SOLITARY SANDPIPER[*]
Tringa solitaria

Description: Gray back with spotting; straight bill; white eye ring;
greenish legs; in flight—boldly barred white tail

The Solitary Sandpiper is the smallest of the sandpipers, measuring seven and one-half inches to nine inches long. In breeding plumage, its wings and back are dark grayish-brown with light spotting. Its head is lighter and displays a prominent white eye ring. Dark streaking adorns the lower throat, breast, and sides. A white tail with bold buffing contrasts with the white belly. The legs are olive green and the straight bill is dusky green. The sexes appear similar, and juveniles have faint streaking and slightly spotted gray backs. The molt to winter plumage finds the adult grayer and only faintly spotted above. As the name implies, it is often seen singly, but not always.

In flight this sandpiper displays dark wings and a flashy, barred tail. Graceful flight takes it easily and swiftly through the sky, and it often resembles a snipe. On the ground, the Solitary Sandpiper may be seen nodding and bowing its head.

The call of this small sandpiper is high pitched and clear. When flushed, it calls *pee-weet* or *bueet*.

Habitat and Diet

The Solitary Sandpiper is a fairly common transient throughout the Southwest on small lakes, ponds, and river sand bars. As it wades in shallow water, it disturbs tiny organisms with its feet, quickly snatching them with its rather long bill. Prey include aquatic insects and small mollusks, as well as land insects such as grasshoppers and moths—sometimes even catching these delicacies on the wing.

Nesting and Mating Behaviors

The Solitary Sandpiper does not nest in the Southwestern lowlands. It travels to the northern wilderness and breeds near the water's edge. Unique to shorebirds, it nests in trees, absconding abandoned nests of

[*]Plate 11

robins and blackbirds. Four pale, green eggs covered with brown spots soon become four small feathered creatures demanding food from the attending parent.

Willet*
Catoptrophorus semipalmatus

Description: Sandy-gray; long legged; straight, stout bill; flight—
             bold black and white wing patterns; partially
             webbed feet; breeding—mottled plumage; non-
             breeding—plain

The Willet appears very ordinary with an overall sandy-gray coloration. In breeding plumage, dark spots and specks appear on the upperparts and the breast is mottled brown. When flushed, startling black-and-white wings and a white tail patch will catch your attention, as well as its loud cries of *peet-weet* or *peet-weet-weet*. The long bill and legs are grayish-blue, and there is a darker tip on the bill. The brown iris is enhanced by a white eye ring. Look closely, because its feet are partially webbed. The sexes are similar and are often seen resting in a hunched position either in pairs or in flocks. This large shorebird measures fourteen to seventeen inches long and is thicker-bodied than the Greater Yellowlegs.

Habitat and Diet

The Willet is an uncommon to common migrant throughout much of the Southwest on ponds, lakes, and rivers. As a shorebird, it feeds in shallow water taking mollusks, fiddler crabs, crayfish, small fish, insects, grass roots, and seeds. Although generally a loner when feeding, it may appear in flocks at other times.

Nesting and Mating Behaviors

During mating season, the male flaps his bold black-and-white wings while displaying for the female. Both are very vocal with cries of *kuk-kuk-kuk-kuk-kuk*.

The female chooses the nesting site, and although in a colony, the nests are quite some distance apart. A slight depression in soft, sandy soil

*Plate 11

is sparsely lined with grasses and weeds, and is typically hidden among dense grasses. Three or four smooth, buff eggs with brown splotches are incubated by the female for twenty-two to twenty-nine days.

SPOTTED SANDPIPER
Actitis macularia

Description: Constant teetering; breeding–spotted underparts; yellow-orange bill; non-breeding–plain underparts; greenish-gray bill

The Spotted Sandpiper is small, measuring seven and one-half to eight inches long, and is easily identified in breeding plumage. As its name depicts, white underparts are heavily spotted with dark brown from chin to tail. Its upperparts are gray-brown, while short legs and feet sport bright fleshy-pink or yellow coloration. The bill is yellow to orange with a dark tip. A vertical, dark stripe crosses through the white eye ring and is accompanied by a white superciliary marking.

The sexes are similarly adorned. In winter, a faded version of plumage prevails. The spots disappear, the bill and legs fade to a duller, dusky-yellow version, and the upperparts are lighter grayish brown.

Regardless of season, this sandpiper may be identified by obvious teetering movements. When approached, the Spotted Sandpiper runs along the shore, stops and wags its tail up and down, then proceeds a bit further and repeats the same bobbing behavior. If pursued further it flies, usually returning to the same area when danger has passed.

The Spotted Sandpiper is not found in flocks. Its call is a loud *peet-weet*, often repeated.

Habitat and Diet

The Spotted Sandpiper is a common transient and an uncommon winter resident on ponds, lakes, and rivers, especially the Colorado River.

Although this small sandpiper will dive into the water, it is a wading bird that feeds in shallow water by flushing prey from the sandy bottom with its feet. Teetering back and forth with every step, it feeds on crustaceans, fish, and insects.

Nesting and Mating Behaviors

Leaving the lowlands in April and May, this species prefers to breed in higher elevations. In pastures, prairies, or near freshwater ponds, both sexes build the crude nest in a shallow depression in gravel or grassy areas away from the shore. The female lays three to five smooth, buff-colored eggs covered with brown blotches. Fairly unique in the bird world, the male does the incubation. The downy young can swim and often do so to flee when danger approaches.

WHIMBREL
Numenius phaeopus

Description: Large; decurved bill; conspicuous head stripes

This large, brown shorebird measures fifteen to eighteen inches from the tip of its rather heavy-looking, decurved bill to the tip of its toes, and is smaller than the superficially similar Long-billed Curlew. Bold crown stripes and a substantially shorter bill (only four inches long) also distinguish the Whimbrel from the former. Mottled brown upperparts fade into light gray-brown plumage underneath, with both sexes appearing similar. The legs are steely bluish-gray in color.

In small flocks, Whimbrels may be seen flying over land in a "V" formation similar to ducks and geese, but over water they usually form single lines. Sometimes one is seen flying singly, circling high in the air. This curlew is fairly noisy, making a whistling sound like *whi whi whi whi whi.*

Habitat and Diet

Although the Whimbrel is a common migrant on the Salton Sea, it is a rare and casual fall and spring transient elsewhere on desert lakes, ponds, and rivers. Its migratory routes are mainly down the east and west coastlines, but there is a scattering flight through the interior.

While feeding in the shallows, this shorebird often stands stork-like on one leg while capturing small insects with its stout bill. Another favorite food is shellfish, which is obtained by thrusting its decurved bill deep into mud to extract the morsel. Crabs, spiders, beetles, worms, and berries complete its dietary needs. Look for Whimbrels feeding among dowitchers and other smaller wading birds.

Nesting and Mating Behaviors

For breeding purposes, the Whimbrel migrates to the far north to breed in open tundra areas. A shallow depression is lined with grasses, then the female lays four olive-colored eggs blotched with brown. Both adults share the responsibility of incubating and brooding, and become extremely aggressive with intruders. Screaming loudly, they thrust themselves at the approaching perpetrators.

LONG-BILLED CURLEW*
Numenius americanus

Description:　Cinnamon brown; long, decurved bill; lacks head stripes

The largest of shorebirds, the Long-billed Curlew measures twenty to twenty-six inches long and is easily identified by its extremely, long, thin, decurved bill. (The Whimbrel is smaller with a shorter bill and has distinctive bold crown stripes, which are absent on the Long-billed Curlew.) The upperparts of the Long-billed Curlew are cinnamon brown with darker mottling, while the underparts are buff colored with cinnamon streaking on the head and neck. The underwings show cinnamon, and the long legs and feet are grayish blue. The dusky-yellow bill with a dark tip appears almost as long as the body. A buff-colored eye rings surrounds the brown iris.

Long-billed Curlews are social birds, feeding, roosting, and migrating in flocks. Like its bill, its voice is far-reaching and emphatic, sounding like *wit-wit, wit-wit, wit-wit, wit-wit.* An additional cry sounds almost like its name *cuurrleeeewwww.*

Habitat and Diet

The Long-billed Curlew is an uncommon transient throughout the deserts and grassland areas, especially in agricultural fields along the Colorado River. It is drawn to open fields and grasslands, where it picks large numbers of insects from among the grasses with its long, sickle-shaped bill. Agriculturists welcome this natural exterminator whose diet

*Plate 12

includes locusts and grasshoppers, which are harmful to crops. Additionally, this skilled hunter uses its bill as a forceps to extract meat from shellfish, which exist along beaches and tidal flats.

Nesting and Mating Behaviors

Breeding areas include both upland and aquatic locations north of the hot deserts. There may be many nests in the same vicinity, each consisting of a grassy hollow sparsely lined with grasses and forbs. Both sexes take turns incubating the four or five glossy, olive-colored eggs, with brown and lavender spots, for twenty-one days. When a nest is disturbed, many birds from the scattered colony fly over the intruder with loud cries. Colonization, a form of group protection, assures survival of the species.

MARBLED GODWIT
Limosa fedoa

Description: Marbled cinnamon brown; long, recurved bill; vermiculated underparts

This large, sixteen- to twenty-inch-long shorebird resembles the Long-billed Curlew in coloration, but has a slightly recurved bill instead of the sickle-shaped bill of the curlew. The upperparts are a marbled cinnamon-brown, while the underparts are a lighter finely vermiculated buff coloration. The bill is fleshy-orange with a dark tip, while the legs and feet are grayish-blue. A white eyebrow appears above the dark eye. A winter bird has only faint markings on its underneck, breast, and belly. The sexes appear similar, and juveniles are similar to winter birds.

This is a very noisy bird when disturbed, or when it arrives in breeding territory. It identifies itself with a loud voice calling out its own name: *godwit, godwit!*

Habitat and Diet

The Marbled Godwit is a rare to uncommon spring transient and fairly common fall transient at lakes, ponds, agricultural areas, and along the Colorado River.

Along with fish and crustaceans, this long-legged wading bird eats many insects, especially grasshoppers.

Nesting and Mating Behaviors

The Marbled Godwit flies north to breed, and although it chooses an area in the vicinity of some slough, it actually nests in a dry area on a grassy prairie. Conspicuous displays of aerial flights and noisy exchanges fill the air on its breeding territory in late May or early June.

In the midst of short grass, a slight depression is made and then sparsely filled with grasses. Three to five buff-olive eggs with a sprinkling of brown spots are very conspicuous in the open nest. A short period after hatching, the young already display gregarious and noisy behaviors, running around on the prairie calling *godwit, godwit.*

WESTERN SANDPIPER
Calidris mauri

Description: Rust on crown and scapulars; rusty ear patches (breeding); slightly decurved bill; black legs

In breeding plumage, the Western Sandpiper has rusty-red scapulars, a back crown, and ear patches. Brown streaking appears on the white neck, breast, and flanks. The legs and feet are black as is the stout bill, which curves downward ever so slightly. Females have longer bills than males, otherwise both sexes are similar in markings. Both measure six to seven inches long.

Winter birds fade into light brown above and white below, and are almost indistinguishable from the Semipalmated Sandpiper (a casual transient to the desert areas) except by voice. The Western has a squeaky, high note sounding like *keep* while the Semipalmated makes a harsh sound like *cherk.* Juveniles are similar to wintering adults but have a rusty edge on the scapular.

Habitat and Diet

The Western Sandpiper is a common transient in many areas of the Southwestern lowlands because it migrates up and down the Pacific Coast, venturing to the interior where it frequents ponds and lakes as well as sewage ponds. On coastal beaches, these birds feed at low tide on tiny crustaceans and insects. When an intruder approaches, they fly in flocks and return to the beach when the danger has passed.

Nesting and Mating Behaviors

The Western Sandpiper breeds on the coastal tundra of Alaska, where many gather in flocks and display themselves in flight and song until pairs settle down to the task of reproduction. On an area of dry tundra, a slight depression is made where the female lays four creamy eggs covered with reddish-brown splotches. The chicks hatch before the middle of June, and by the end of July they are already heading southward.

LEAST SANDPIPER[*]
Calidris minutilla

Description: Breeding—short, thin, black bill; yellow legs; streaky bib; non-breeding—brown breast band

The Least Sandpiper, the Semipalmated Sandpiper, and the Western Sandpiper are often called "peeps." The Least Sandpiper, smallest of the trio, measures five to six and one-half inches long. Otherwise, in winter plumage all three appear very similar. The short, thin, black bill and straw-yellow legs and feet distinguish the Least Sandpiper from the other two.

In breeding plumage it is mottled with sooty brown on the neck and upperparts, while the light brown breast is streaked with darker brown. In winter plumage this peep fades to dusky gray above and white below. Juveniles have a rufous tinge on the upperparts with streaky breasts and white bellies.

The Least Sandpiper is relatively tame and will allow a close approach before fleeing. It flies in tight flocks with synchronized rhythm, turning and twisting through the sky. Its call is a high *kreet* or *kreep.*

Habitat and Diet

This smallest of North American shorebirds prefers wet, muddy, or grassy areas as well as salt marshes. It is a common to abundant transient and an uncommon winter resident on some ponds and lakes, where it forages for small crustaceans and insects both along the shoreline as well as in shallow water.

[*]Plate 12

Nesting and Mating Behaviors

The Least Sandpiper migrates to the far northern part of the continent to breed near water. With leaves and grasses, it lines a shallow depression in northern moss. The female lays four buff eggs spotted with chestnut coloration. When the eggs hatch, little buff-colored balls of downy life emerge.

LONG-BILLED DOWITCHER
Limnodromus scolopaceus

Description: Long, straight bill; rusty underparts (breeding); black tail with thin bars; white back in flight

The Long-billed Dowitcher is a medium-sized, plump, and very long-billed sandpiper measuring eleven to twelve and one-half inches from the tip of its straight bill to the tip of its tail. The Short-billed Dowitcher is very similar in plumage, and its bill is nearly the same length, making identification difficult, especially in winter plumage. In breeding plumage, there is heavier streaking and spotting on the throat and upper breast of the Long-billed Dowitcher. The underparts are rufous from the top of the breast to the lower belly. The upperparts are dark with hints of rust. Dusky yellow legs, brown eyes, and a dark streak from the bill through and behind the eye adorn both species.

Winter finds the Long-billed Dowitcher faded to dark gray upperparts, light gray underparts and white belly. The dark crown of spring also turns to gray. In flight a white stripe is revealed down the middle of the back.

Dowitchers are usually seen wading in shallow water. Feeding flocks continually chatter, and the flight call is a distinctive *keek.*

Habitat and Diet

The Long-billed Dowitcher is a common transient throughout the Southwestern lowlands. It winters sparingly near ponds, lakes, and especially along the Colorado River and Salton Sea. This dowitcher is seen farther inland than the Short-billed because it prefers pond habitats; the latter frequents tidal mud flats.

Along with minnows, crustaceans, and worms, the dowitcher's diet includes several species of destructive insects including grasshoppers and diving beetles.

Nesting and Mating Behaviors

The Long-billed Dowitcher migrates to the Alaskan tundra to breed. As noisy as they are in non-breeding season, one can well imagine the raucousness on mating territory. From the middle of May until early June, the mating cries break the silence as males fly in acrobatic fashion chasing females.

Silence accompanies nesting activities. A slight depression is made on the ground and then is scantily lined with grasses and leaves. Three to four grayish-white eggs spotted with lavender and brown are the beginning of a new life cycle.

COMMON SNIPE
Gallinago gallinago

Description: Boldly patterned body; head stripes; cinnamon tail

The Common Snipe is a short, stocky shorebird with a long, straight, stout bill. It is boldly and intricately marked with brown, black, cinnamon, and white. A large head with distinctive stripes and cinnamon tail distinguish it from other shorebirds. Dark brown, mottled upperparts are highlighted with bold, white stripes. The buff breast and flanks are barred and spotted with dark brown, contrasting sharply with the white belly. Its legs and feet are dull greenish-yellow like the bill, which is tipped black.

Most sandpipers are fairly tame and are easily seen out in the open. The Common Snipe, however, is rather secretive and finds security in low vegetation where camouflaged plumage blends this bird with the surroundings. When flushed, it makes a raspy sound like *ahak* then flies to safety with a zigzag flight pattern. It often returns to the same locale when the danger has passed. Watch for the long, pointed wings to unfold from the rather short, squatty body.

Habitat and Diet

The Common Snipe is a common transient and winter resident at ponds and lakes of the Southwestern lowlands, choosing areas with vegetation for concealment. With its stout bill, it probes into wet soil for worms, snails, small crustaceans, and aquatic insect larvae.

Nesting and Mating Behaviors

The Common Snipe does not breed in the Southwestern lowlands, and migrates from this habitat in late April or early May. On breeding grounds, it performs an exquisite courtship flight, sailing high in the sky, darting about in wide circles. Suddenly it rapidly dives toward the earth and makes a vibrating sound with the outer tail feathers while additionally projecting a vocal cackling sound. This is called a winnowing performance and goes on for several minutes.

The grass-lined nest is a depression in marshy ground, which supports three or four buff eggs with chestnut-colored streaks and dots. The young are precocial—they are not cared for in the nest by the adults. Instead they are able to run about only a short time after hatching, so feeding takes place outside the nest.

WILSON'S PHALAROPE
Phalaropus tricolor

Description: Long, thin bill; light body plumage; black face and
                neck stripe; dark wings; female larger, brighter
                plumage on neck and wings

Phalaropes have reversed nature's typical trends, giving the female more sriking plumage as well as aggressive courtship behaviors. The largest representative of this group is the Wilson's Phalarope, which measures eight to ten inches long; the female is the larger bird. Both sexes display a long, straight, slender, black bill, and long, slender legs with marginal webs on the toes. The tail is short and rounded.

The breeding female sports a bold, black line extending from the base of the bill through the eye and down the neck to merge with a chestnut wash, which covers her breast. Her wings are dark and her gray back is highlighted with chestnut stripes. Her crown is gray while her chin and underparts are starkly white.

The breeding male's plumage is somewhat similar, but with less intensity. His crown, back, and neck stripe appear brown, and he has only a light wash on his chest. In winter, both sexes fade to light gray above and white below. Only a hint of face markings remain. Immatures are brown above with buffy underparts and a slight eye line. The call is a raspy *wruk*.

Habitat and Diet

The Wilson's Phalarope is a common transient and winter resident on ponds, lakes, and rivers throughout the Southwestern deserts. This species feeds aggressively and creatively. Sitting high in the water with its neck in a vertical position, it suddenly begins whirling in circles on the water's surface, which stirs up the bottom of shallow areas causing mosquito larvae, insects, crustaceans, and mollusks to surface for easing picking. One Wilson's Phalarope was observed spinning a total of 247 cycles. What a miracle to catch prey after that many turns!

Another, more conventional way of feeding is to submerge the long bill, then swing it side to side similar to the American Avocet. Unlike the latter, however, the phalarope's straight bill probes into mud for hidden treasures.

Nesting and Mating Behaviors

The female is the aggressive pursuer in the mating game. Sometimes even two females chase a male while swelling their necks and making nasal sounds. Finally, the male succumbs to one of them and a bond occurs. She selects a nesting site, but the building is totally up to the male. In a depression in the ground, he adds moss and grasses. When the nest is ready, the female lays three or four slightly glossy, buff eggs covered with brown dots; she then leaves the male alone to incubate, feed, and rear the young. The females unite in flocks and wait for the males who re-join them when their fatherly duties are completed.

RED-NECKED PHALAROPE
Phalaropus lobatus

Description: Chestnut neck; white throat and belly; rufous, striped back; thin bill; female brighter; non-breeding—lacks chestnut coloration

In the aviary world, few females are adorned with brighter colors than males. The phalaropes are one family that carries this distinction. The female Red-necked Phalarope sports bright, rusty plumage on her throat and neck, and contrasting white on her chin and underparts. Dark gray head plumage extends onto her back where rusty strips add distinct highlights. The male is less intense with brown tinges, less rufous coloration on his neck, and a lighter gray head plumage with a white patch behind his eye. Juveniles are similar to the male, but have buff-red stripes.

Spinning in water like buoyant tops, the phalaropes are easy to identify by behavior. In breeding plumage specific identifications are easy, but winter finds this species less flamboyant, making the task a bit more challenging. In non-breeding season, both sexes appear in medium-gray upper plumage with two white stripes, white underneath, and a bold, gray mark behind the eye. The white crown gives way to a gray nape and neck.

Smaller than the Wilson's Phalarope, the Red-necked measures six and one-half to eight inches long; the female is the larger of the sexes. Like the Wilson's, the bill is thin, but appears much shorter, about the length of the head. Although this species appears very active, it is rather quiet vocally except on breeding territory where low nasal sounds may be heard.

Habitat and Diet

Although typically a sea voyager, the Red-necked Phalarope appears inland, especially during migration periods. In the desert lowlands it may be seen uncommonly in fall, and rarely in spring on ponds, lakes, and rivers.

While swimming in shallow water, the energetic phalarope suddenly begins turning in tight circles, spinning again and again. This action is not really a dance, but a unique way to stir up food from the muddy bottom. Insects, mollusks, and crustaceans are the targeted food sources, and may be taken while wading as well as swimming. Again in a circular fashion, the phalarope treads the bottom so that prey is flushed to the surface for easy picking.

Nesting and Mating Behaviors

Not only is the female the brighter of the sexes, she is also more aggressive during courting and defending breeding territory. A polyandrous species, she may mate with two or more males and lay a clutch of eggs for each. After she chooses a nesting site, the male builds the nest without her assistance. The female lays four buff-olive eggs heavily spotted with brown, then leaves the male alone to incubate them; then he feeds the young and teaches them to fend for themselves. She unites with other females and waits for the males to rejoin her when the young have matured.

HEERMANN'S GULL*
Larus heermanni

Description: Dark gray body; white head; black wings and tail;
red bill; non-breeding–brownish overall

The Heermann's Gull is a medium-sized gull, measuring eighteen to
twenty-one inches long, and is the easiest western gull to identify. The
male and female are both dark gray with a white head during the breeding season; during the non-breeding season, the Heermann's Gull's
white head becomes mottled with gray. The wings and tail are slate black
and the bill is red. The immature Heermann's appears essentially dark
with a lighter throat, and the bill is a brownish color with a reddish tip.

Because of the famous novella *Jonathan Livingston Seagull,* one often
associates a peaceful, free image with gulls, which are perhaps the most
common of all sea birds. Upon observing gulls for any length of time,
however, it becomes obvious that they are very aggressive and even
appear ill-tempered when interacting with one another. Gulls live in
colonies and aggressively compete for mates as well as food, and will
even eat the eggs of their own species. Nikolaas Tinbergen, a naturalist
who has spent many hours observing gulls, writes, "A gullery is no city of
friends. It is indeed a city of thieves and murderers." This aggressive
behavior, however, has assured them of survival from outside predation.

Habitat and Diet

The Heermann's Gull is only an occasional visitor to the inland waters
of the Southwest, preferring instead coastal waters, islands, and beaches.
Where the desert meets the sea is a beautiful sight in and of itself, but it is
greatly enhanced by the presence of the Heermann's Gull.

It finds most of its food by scavenging the beaches for fish, shellfish,
and small mammals. This gull also robs fish from pelicans, consumes
eggs, and even eats young nestlings of its own species. This cannibalism
is another example of the gull's aggressive nature.

*Plate 13

Nesting and Mating Behaviors

Young, unmated gulls, or gulls whose partners have died, participate in courting dances until a new mate is chosen. A male first secures his territory in early spring by running all others out of the area. The females fly over the colony, finally choosing one specific territory. After some posturing or dancing, she approaches a male and pecks at his bill. If he accepts her, he regurgitates food and offers it to her. In this way, gulls begin a partnership thought to be for life.

The Gulf of California and the west coast of Baja California serve as the main breeding areas of the Heermann's Gull. Its nest is a simple hollow scraped in the sand near other nests. The female lays two or three greenish eggs with brown spots. Both sexes take turns with the incubation, and both must continually be on guard for outside predators, as well as predation within the colony. Both adults also aid in the feeding and rearing of the young. Gulls begin breeding the second year after leaving the nest.

Supplemental Information

I have to admit that I am one of those individuals who loves the story of *Jonathan Livingston Seagull,* even though I know the true aggressive nature of gulls. The story represents freedom and suggests that anything is possible if we believe in ourselves. I believe that each entity of life has its individual purpose and therefore contributes back to the whole, simply by being itself.

Although the Heermann's Gull is not the actual gull portrayed as Jonathan, it certainly is the one that maintains its individuality as did Jonathan Livingston Seagull. Most migratory birds in the Northern Hemisphere travel south for the winter and northward for breeding purposes. The Heermann's Gull does exactly the opposite, migrating northward to spend the winter.

RING-BILLED GULL*
Larus delawarensis

Description: Black ring on yellow bill; light gray mantle; red eye
ring; yellow legs; non-breeding–streaked head and
nape

The adult Ring-billed Gull (three years old) is white with a gray mantle
(slightly lighter than that of the similar California Gull), and has a black
subterminal ring on the otherwise yellow bill and a distinctive red eye-
ring. Similar to the California Gull, it displays yellow legs and feet with
white spots on the black wing tips. Slightly smaller than the aforemen-
tioned species, it measures eighteen to twenty-one inches long. Adults in
winter plumage have brown streaking on their heads, while juveniles are
mottled brown with dusky legs and dark bills. From years one through
three, the immatures gradually change coloration, eventually taking on
the plumage of the adult.

The Ring-billed Gull has a higher-pitched voice than the California
Gull, resonating with a shrill *ky-eow*.

Habitat and Diet

This gull is a fairly common to uncommon transient and winter resident along the Colorado River and the Salton Sea, but is a rare transient
elsewhere on ponds and lakes. It is the most frequent visitor to inland
areas of the Southwest.

Gulls eat a variety of food consisting of fish, small dead mammals,
worms, debris from garbage piles, and plenty of insects. Swooping and
squealing, these agile gulls often seize insects on the wing. As scavengers,
they are very beneficial because they help clean the beaches and shorelines of lakes.

Nesting and Mating Behaviors

The Ring-billed Gull leaves the desert wintering territories to breed at
inland lakes near the coast of Northern California and on Great Salt

*Plate 13

Lake. Ring-billed Gulls and California Gulls generally nest together in large colonies along with pelicans, herons, and cormorants. The nest is usually a pile of debris built on the ground but occasionally is placed in a low tree. Three buff eggs with dark splotches are incubated by both adults for three weeks. The hatchlings wander away from the nest in just a few days.

CALIFORNIA GULL
Larus californicus

Description: Dark gray mantle; one red, one black spot on lower mandible; greenish legs and feet; non-breeding– streaked head and breast

The adult California Gull measures twenty to twenty-three inches long, appearing slightly larger than the similar Ring-billed Gull. Its gray mantle is darker than that of the latter, and a small black dot with a slightly larger, vermilion dot adorn the tip of its yellow bill. There is no ring like that of the Ring-billed; however, winter and immature birds have a two-toned bill. The gray wings sport black tips and spots, and the legs and feet are greenish-yellow. In winter plumage, the pure-white body shows brown streaking on the head. First-year birds are brown with pinkish legs and feet, and sport a black-tipped bill. The voice is a harsh, repetitive *kee-yah.*

Habitat and Diet

The California Gull is a fairly common to uncommon migrant along the Colorado River and on the Salton Sea and is a rare transient at other inland ponds and lakes. Additionally, it winters on the Salton Sea and on inland lakes with shallow areas. It is usually found with the Ring-billed Gull.

Like most gulls, the California Gull eats almost anything from fish to insects to scraps of human food left on the beaches. It even eats small, dead mammals.

Nesting and Mating Behaviors

Thousands of California Gulls nest at Great Salt Lake north of the hot, desert areas. They nest in large colonies along with pelicans, herons, and cormorants. The nesting sites are often only two feet from each other. A depression in the sand is lined with weeds, sticks, grasses, and even rubbish. The female lays two to three pale-olive eggs with brown spots. The eggs hatch in about three weeks, and the young leave the nest in only a few days. The nests are conspicuous, so the main defense against intruders is a joint effort. A deafening clamor fills the air as hordes of gulls run a predator out of their territory.

Supplemental Information

The California Gull is the infamous "savior" of agriculture in Utah in 1848. Throngs of crickets had begun devouring crops, when out of the blue horizon vast numbers of California Gulls dropped from the skies to feast on the abundant pests.

CASPIAN TERN
Sterna caspia

Description: Summer—thick, red bill with black near tip; black cap; short, forked tail; winter—dusky cap

The Caspian Tern is the largest tern in North America, measuring nineteen to twenty-three inches long. It is pure white with a gray mantle similar to some gulls, but has a more pointed bill, longer, pointed wings, and a forked tail. This stocky tern has a thick, red bill and shows a black cap in breeding season, which fades to streaked, dusky coloration in winter. (The Royal tern is similar but smaller, has more orange on the thinner bill, and displays a white crown most of the year.)

The sexes are similar and the juvenile Caspian Tern resembles the adult in winter plumage. The call of this graceful bird is a low, harsh, *kraa-uh* or *ca-arr*, or repeated *kaks*.

Habitat and Diet

The Caspian Tern is a casual transient and summer resident on inland ponds and lakes, which differs from the similar Royal Tern who seldom goes inland. In winter, the Caspian Tern is often seen resting on sandbars with other species of tern. Characteristic of all terns, the Caspian feeds on fish and hunts by hovering, then plunging for prey. Because of this technique, terns have been nicknamed "strikers."

Nesting and Mating Behaviors

The Caspian Tern breeds on mainland beaches, inland lake islands, or along rivers. The mating ritual is typical of terns and is quite elaborate. The male plunges for a fish which he then lays in front of the female. If she chooses to accept the gift, the male picks it up again, flying high into the air. She follows him in an aerial courtship flight.

Nesting in colonies near gulls, pelicans, herons, and cormorants, the Caspian Tern usually builds its nest in a shallow depression in the sand, adding only small bits of available material. Occasionally, this gregarious tern is more elaborate and makes a larger depression, adding more sticks, shells, and rubbish. The breeding area is sometimes densely populated, with nests only a few feet apart.

The female lays one to four rough, buff-colored eggs irregularly spotted with brown. Both adults take turns incubating the eggs for twenty days. The hatchlings are able to leave the nest in only a few days and to even enter the water, but they are dependent upon their parents until they learn to fly. The parents are very protective and keep the young from wandering away from the nest by pouncing on them, pecking them, sometimes even killing them! Eventually with time and maturation, the young learn to dive and fish for themselves.

FORSTER'S TERN
Sterna forsteri

Description: Summer—black cap; black-tipped, orange bill; slim forked tail; winter—black eye, earpatch, and bill

The Forster's Tern has a light-gray mantle, black cap and nape, orange legs and feet, and reddish-orange bill with a black tip. The gray tail is deeply forked and edged in white. In winter plumage, the black cap fades to gray and only a black eye and ear patch remain. Additionally, the reddish-orange bill turns black. Smaller than the Caspian Tern, the Forster's Tern measures fourteen to fifteen inches long. The juvenile is similar to the adult but has a dark eye and ear patch and a streaked head. Terns are gull-like, but thinner.

As this graceful tern flies over water, its sharp bill always points downward while keen eyes scan the surface for fish. The Forster's Tern utters two different sounds, both with a nasal quality: One is low-pitched and sounds like *ky-yarr,* and the other is more harsh resembling *za-a-ap.*

Habitat and Diet

The Forster's Tern is the one most often seen on inland lakes and ponds of the Southwest. It is a rare to uncommon transient, most often appearing in fall.

This agile tern flits over the water searching for available fish. When one is spotted, it hovers, waiting for the precise moment, then plunges into the water to snatch the unaware victim with its long, thin bill.

Nesting and Mating Behaviors

The Forster's Tern moves farther north to breed on inland lakes and marshes, as well as coastal salt marshes. This species differs from the Caspian Tern in nesting behaviors by avoiding crowded colonies. It is sociable, however, and breeds in the same vicinity as other terns. The nests are a floating mass of vegetation with a small depression with limited materials added. Sometimes inland nests are placed on a muskrat house.

The female lays two to five smooth, olive or pinkish eggs covered with small brown spots. Both adults incubate the eggs for twenty-three to twenty-four days, then share the tasks of raising the young.

Section 2

LAND BIRDS/NON-PASSERINES

NON-PASSERINE land birds consist of several families including birds of prey (vultures, raptors, owls), gallinaceous birds, doves, cuckoos, nightjars, swifts, hummingbirds, kingfishers, and woodpeckers.

Black Vulture*
Turkey Vulture*
Osprey*
Bald Eagle*
Northern Harrier
Sharp-shinned Hawk
Cooper's Hawk*
Harris' Hawk*
Swainson's Hawk*
Red-tailed Hawk*
Ferruginous Hawk
Rough-legged Hawk
Golden Eagle
Crested Caracara*
American Kestrel*
Peregrine Falcon*
Prairie Falcon
Common Barn Owl
Western Screech-owl*

Great Horned Owl*
Ferruginous Pygmy-owl
Elf Owl*
Burrowing Owl*
Long-eared Owl
Short-eared Owl
Ring-necked Pheasant*
Wild Turkey*
Scaled Quail
Gambel's Quail*
California Quail
White-winged Dove*
Mourning Dove*
Inca Dove*
Common Ground Dove
Yellow-billed Cuckoo
Greater Roadrunner*
Lesser Nighthawk
Common Nighthawk

Common Poorwill
Buff-collared Nightjar
Vaux's Swift
White-throated Swift
Black-chinned
    Hummingbird
Anna's Hummingbird
Costa's Hummingbird
Rufous Hummingbird
Belted Kingfisher*
Green Kingfisher*
Acorn Woodpecker*
Gila Woodpecker*
Red-naped Sapsucker*
Ladder-backed
    Woodpecker
Gilded Flicker*

*See color section

BLACK VULTURE*
Coragyps atratus

Description: Black body; white underwing patches; short,
square tail

Somewhat smaller than the Turkey Vulture, the Black Vulture measures twenty-three to twenty-seven inches long with a wing span between forty-nine and fifty-four inches. The sexes are alike in plumage as well as in size.

As the name depicts, it is entirely black, except for a white patch near the underside of the wing tips. The neck appears long with a featherless head that appears more gray in adults. The immatures have black heads and fewer wrinkles. The iris is a dark brown color.

The legs are longer and whiter than the Turkey Vulture's, and the tail is square and short, barely extending beyond the wings. In flight, the legs usually trail behind. In general, the Black Vulture is blacker, stockier, shorter tailed, and more broad winged than the Turkey Vulture.

In the air the Black Vulture can easily be distinguished from the Turkey Vulture, even from great distances, because while soaring it resorts to frequent rapid wing beats with shorter gliding periods, and the white wing tips are conspicuous.

The Black Vulture is usually silent, but when threatened or annoyed it makes a grunting noise or a hissing sound.

Habitat and Diet

The Black Vulture is not as common as the Turkey Vulture, and tends to stay in the lower elevations, avoiding higher mountains. It frequents food sources such as slaughter houses or dumps, especially where little attention is spent in burying the disposed rubbish. As a scavenger, it is most beneficial in the order of nature because its main diet consists of decaying meat.

The Black Vulture does not have a pronounced sense of smell as does the Turkey Vulture, and therefore depends on sight alone to locate its next meal. Through communal hunting, this species maximizes the potential for finding food. In a soaring network, flocks scan the countryside for fresh carrion. As one spots a food source, it signals the others by its descending flight, and soon all are sharing in the feast.

*Plate 13

Nesting and Mating Behaviors

There is seldom a nest at all, as these vultures usually lay their eggs right on the bare ground. Occasionally they use a hollow log or deposit the eggs under a large boulder or downed tree. Sometimes the nest area is surrounded with shiny trash, such as glass or aluminum lids.

There are one to three eggs, typically two, which are oval to long-oval, bluish white, and heavily blotched with lavender around the larger end. Both sexes participate in the incubation of the eggs, which takes between twenty-eight and forty-one days. The Black Vulture chicks are buff colored, while those of the Turkey Vulture are white.

Supplemental Information

In spite of their smaller size, Black Vultures will dominate over Turkey Vultures while competing for carrion. They may even follow Turkey Vultures and then descend in greater numbers to appropriate the carcass for themselves.

The wing structure of the Black Vulture is heavier than that of the Turkey Vulture, and as a result the former needs stronger air thermals to aid in lifting it off the ground. As a result, hunting does not begin until the warmer, mid-morning currents beckon it upward. Then it may be seen soaring even higher than the Turkey Vulture.

TURKEY VULTURE*
Cathartes aura

Description: Dark body; red head; long tail

The Turkey Vulture is one of the largest birds of prey, measuring two and one-half to three feet from the head to the tip of the tail feathers. From a distance it appears to be jet black, but upon closer observation it becomes obvious that the Turkey Vulture is two-toned. The front of the underwing is darker than the back portion. Its bald head is bright red, like the Wild Turkey, but leg feathers are white with contrasting yellow feet. The gigantic wing spread reaches six feet, making it comparable in size to an eagle.

*Plate 14

Although relatively slow moving on the ground, the Turkey Vulture can ultimately gain great speeds in flight. It is often seen soaring effortlessly, riding the uplifting air currents at will. The long, extended wings are bent on a slight "V" form above the back.

The Turkey Vulture is one of the quietest birds in the desert. In fact, it has no song whatsoever. Occasionally a hissing sort of sound may be uttered, but only when cornered or threatened.

Habitat and Diet

The Turkey Vulture is a bird of prey and feeds mainly on carrion. This bird is a common summer resident all over the Southwest, and a few remain throughout the year. The main flocks come to the desert in March and begin to thin out in October.

While other birds of prey attack and kill with the use of extremely sharp claws, the vulture is unique in that it does not have to kill at all. This large bird sometimes hunts small prey, but because of weak talons, its main food source is decaying carcasses. Because it does not have to kill, the Turkey Vulture's claws are much shorter than those of other birds of prey. The relatively dull talons are used mainly to hold down carrion flesh so that it can be ripped into bite-size pieces by the extremely sharp beak.

The Turkey Vulture has keen eyesight and can spot prey while circling from high above. Unlike any other bird, it has long been thought that the Turkey Vulture also has a well developed sense of smell, which aids greatly in the search for carrion. It is truly amazing how quickly it is attracted to dead animals.

The Turkey Vulture, which is often called a buzzard, is indeed a scavenger and, due to its barbarous eating habits, is viewed by many as a filthy, repulsive creature. This vulture, however, definitely has its useful place in the ecological system by ridding the environment of decaying animals that could spread disease.

Nesting and Mating Behaviors

The nest is simply a crude shelter found in rocks, logs, cliffs, and sometimes right on the ground. There are one to three white eggs with brown splotches, which incubate in approximately thirty days.

Both sexes aid in the incubation, as well as in the feeding and rearing of the young. This is quite a chore because of the large size of the young and the fact that they do not leave the nest until approximately ten weeks after incubation.

Supplemental Information

The Turkey Vulture can easily be seen along highways where it is attracted to rabbits and other animals that have been killed by automobiles. I will never forget an incident that involved a closer view of the vulture than had ever been intended. I was twelve years old and riding on a bus with other children while on a 4-H excursion. A dead rabbit was on the road ahead, and several Turkey Vultures were meticulously attending to their dinner. We approached so rapidly that one of them did not have an opportunity to lift its large body to safety. The next instant the heavy bird hurtled itself into the windshield of the bus, shattering bits of glass all over the front seat passengers, including me! The vulture was killed upon impact, but we passengers escaped with minor cuts.

OSPREY*
Pandion haliaetus

Description: Dark upperparts; white below; white head; dark
eye stripe

The Osprey is the only raptor that hovers above the water and plunges feet first into it. This large "fish hawk" is twenty-one to twenty-four and one-half inches long and has a wing span of four and one-half to six feet. Although smaller than the Bald Eagle, its dark and white appearance is somewhat similar.

The head is white with a black cheek patch extending through the eyes. The body is dark brown above and has more white below than any other hawk. The male has a pure white breast, while the female wears a necklace of dark-brown streaking. It also has a black patch under the wrist joint. The Osprey flies with a crook in its long, pointed wings. Both sexes are similar, but the female is larger; the immature appears scaly.

The Osprey's voice is described as a high, whistled *k-yewk, k-yewk, k-yewk*. It may also be heard making squealing sounds, especially during breeding season.

*Plate 14

Habitat and Diet

In the Southwestern lowlands, the Osprey is occasionally seen as a transient in the spring and fall, and a few remain year round. All birds choose habitats that fulfill their dietary needs, and so the Osprey is found where fish are abundant in rivers, lakes, and along coasts.

This raptor has been called the "fish hawk" because its diet consists entirely of fish. Unlike other raptors, the Osprey has rough scaly pads on its toes to help hold slippery fish. In addition, a reversible front toe enables it to grasp the fish with a sharp claw on each side of its prey.

Ospreys may be seen high in a tree above a water source scanning for fish, or they may hover closely to the surface. They can spot a fish from distances up to one hundred feet, and will plunge feet first, often disappearing under the water to grasp prey. Upon surfacing, this dynamo immediately rises from the water and flies to a perch or to its nest, turning the fish in mid-air to align with its aerodynamic position . . . headfirst!

Nesting and Mating Behaviors

Ospreys build nests high in trees, or perhaps in cactus on the coastal deserts. They will also build on nesting platforms constructed especially for their use, and even nest occasionally on the ground. They often nest in loose colonies, but are also found solitarily.

The nest is a large bulky mass constructed of sticks and lined with grasses, vines, sod, rope, and various other objects. The nest is used year after year and gets bigger each season. The female lays three or four light cinnamon-colored eggs blotched with reddish brown. She singly undertakes the task of incubation, which takes about thirty-five days.

When the eggs hatch, the male brings food to the nest and the female tears it in small pieces for the nestlings until they are old enough to help themselves. Then both parents hunt and bring food to the nest while the nestlings take turns standing on the fish and tearing away bite-size pieces.

When the young first start fishing for themselves, it appears as if diving comes naturally to them. They miss more often than the adults, however, so some practice is necessary for them to hone their natural catching skills.

Supplemental Information

One August morning just as the sun peaked over a canyon wall, I sat hidden in the trees photographing the activity in an Osprey's nest. The bulky structure was in the top of a hundred-foot-tall tree that extended upward from the edge of a creek on the canyon floor. Sitting halfway up the side of the canyon, I had a perfect view of both the creek flowing below me and the awesome nest straight across from me.

I had made several trips to this site to watch the young in their various stages of maturation and to observe the adults bringing fish to the nestlings. After several weeks, it was hard to tell the young from the adults, except for a slightly scaly appearance exhibited by the juveniles.

This particular morning, only one young Osprey occupied the nest. Stretching its wings as it had been doing all week, it suddenly took flight and glided down the canyon, following the flow of the creek. I lost sight of it among the trees, so I scurried along the edge of the canyon wall hoping to catch another glimpse of the immature bird. Finally, I spotted the Osprey in the top branch of a dead tree. Appearing to be hanging on for dear life, the young fledgling was crying out as if asking what to do next. The adults flew overhead giving encouragement. I watched for half an hour, but the adventuresome youth had apparently been warned to stay still. I finally left so that my presence would not continue to hinder this new pilot's flight lessons.

BALD EAGLE*
Haliaeetus leucocephalus

Description: Large body; white head, neck, tail; yellow beak

The Bald Eagle, truly a magnificent bird, measures from thirty to forty-five inches in length, and has a wingspan reaching seven or eight feet! Besides its size, the adult is easily recognized by its white head, neck, and tail, which contrast sharply with its brownish-black body and massive, yellow beak. Both sexes are similar, but the female is larger.

The immature Bald Eagle resembles the Golden Eagle, with brown coloration and a dark beak. With each annual molt, however, the Bald Eagle's head and tail gradually turn whiter until it reaches its pure, adult plumage in three to five years.

The Bald Eagle soars with its wings horizontal and makes a rather soft screeching for so powerful a bird. The weak, high-pitched cry sounds like *kleek-kik-ik-ik-ik-ik.*

*Plate 15

Habitat and Diet

Even though the Bald Eagle is our national emblem, many scientists fear for its future. It has recently been removed from the endangered species' list and occurs all over the United States in open areas, forests, or mountains near large lakes where fish abound. It is abundant only in Alaska. This great bird is uncommon in the Southwestern lowlands during winter, with some pairs breeding in the lower elevations of central Arizona.

The Bald Eagle continues to be a threatened species because fish is the primary food choice, many of which are contaminated with pesticides and other pollutants. Although the poison may not kill an adult, it results in a chemical deficiency in the shell of the eggs. As a result, many eggs never hatch. Even though this eagle is a powerful bird, it often is a lazy hunter, and will scavenge for dead food, rather than hunt for fresh fish. Occasionally a Bald Eagle supplements its fish diet with a rodent or a bird.

Sometimes this magnificent raptor resorts to piracy and will harass an Osprey until it drops the fish it is carrying. In mid-air, the eagle snatches the falling prey with its own talons, then speeds away looking for a perch where it can consume its loot.

Nesting and Mating Behaviors

Bald Eagles mate for life, staying together until one dies. They nest when they are three to five years old, usually constructing in a fork at the top of a large tree or occasionally on a cliff. Both birds construct the massive structure of large sticks and branches, and then line it with fresh twigs, forbs, and grasses. They refurbish the same nest year after year, enlarging it each season. Some have been measured at ten feet across and twenty feet deep. Because of the immense weight, a massive nest occasionally falls, taking the tree with it. Sometimes Bald Eagles build two nests, which are used in alternate seasons.

There are from one to three eggs, which are incubated by both sexes. After the eggs have hatched, the male brings food to the nest, but the female actually distributes it to the eaglets. When it is time for the young to fly (approximately 12 weeks), the adults simply quit bringing food to the nest. Instead, they offer it from some distance away, thus "encouraging" the young to take wing.

Supplemental Information

It really is a special treat to see the Bald Eagle. It was chosen for our national emblem because it symbolizes courage and strength. In the Southwest, I have seen it perching on various snags by the edges of lakes, watching for the opportune moment to swoop down and snatch a fish from the water's surface. Only in Alaska, however, have I seen large numbers of Bald Eagles, and it was there that I was able to see the eaglets on the nest. Because there are so few in the Southwest, it is especially important to respect their nesting territories so that they are not jeopardized.

NORTHERN HARRIER
Circus cyaneus

Description: White rump in flight; disk-shaped face; female dark brown; male gray

The Northern Harrier is easily distinguished from other raptors by its white rump patch, which flashes conspicuously as this hawk hovers low over the earth in search of prey. A slim body, long, yellow-orange legs, a long tail, and a dark crown clinch the identification. The owl-like, disk-shaped face is another distinctive characteristic. This raptor measures seventeen and one-half to twenty-four inches long and has a wing span stretching to forty-two inches.

In many hawk species the sexes appear similar in coloration, but the Northern Harrier is one exception. The female is noticeably larger, which is typical of all raptors. She displays dark brown feathers on her upperparts, but the male is gray. Underneath she is creamy-white with obvious brown streaks, and he is mostly white with some rufous spots. Her long tail consists of white and brown alternating bands, while those of the male are a subtle white and gray. The male has black on the wingtips and his iris is bright yellow; the female's iris is brownish-yellow. The immature Northern Harrier resembles the female, but appears more rust colored. They all choose to roost on the ground, and while perching, the long wings fold back over the tail.

Habitat and Diet

The Northern Harrier is a common winter resident in the Southwestern lowlands. It loves open country and glides low over grasslands close to water, over freshwater or saltwater marshes, or hovers over wet meadows. With wings positioned in a slight "V" shape, this agile hawk glides effortlessly and amazingly low over its hunting territory. When prey is spotted, the Northern Harrier hovers momentarily, then quickly pounces on the unsuspecting creature—a mammal, frog, snake, fish, bird, or almost any small creature that happens to be visible.

The Northern Harrier flies quietly and can locate prey by sound, which is similar to the owl's hunting technique. It often hunts late into dusk, sometimes even competing with the owl. A hunting territory might have a radius of five miles, and the kill is usually eaten on the ground.

Nesting and Mating Behaviors

The courtship ritual of the Northern Harrier is especially fascinating and begins in its favorite arena—the sky. Tumbling and somersaulting through the air, a male may suddenly turn skyward and climb with tremendous speed, only to parachute downward in perfect form. After the air display, he gracefully alights on the earth to continue the mating ritual. The Northern Harrier is the only polygamous North American raptor. One male may mate with as many as three different females.

The nest is usually placed on the ground, but a saucer-shaped structure is occasionally positioned over shallow water. It consists of reeds, grasses, and sticks, and may be flimsy or extremely well-made. The female does the actual construction and incubation, while the male hunts and brings food to the nest.

The three to seven eggs are bluish-white and hatch in about four weeks. The nestlings stay in the nest for another five weeks while both adults feed and care for them. Once the nestlings fledge and become independent, they may wander for hundreds of miles.

Supplemental Information

Climbing skyward, the Northern Harrier flashed its white rump patch in our direction, and in unison, my little birding group proclaimed, "Northern Harrier!" It had been perched on the heavy, dry stem of an overturned tumbleweed, and we had not yet made positive identification until it flew. We followed it with our binoculars as it gracefully glided over the grassy terrain in what appeared to be an effortless manner. Back and forth it went, flying purposefully low over its territory.

We had been birding around a reservoir all morning, and were content to sit quietly in the now-sparse shade of a large mesquite tree. Behind us, we could hear the calls of the busy, Yellow-headed Blackbirds and the occasional quacking of a female Mallard. Patience and quietness often bring wonderful surprises, and we weren't disappointed that day. The Northern Harrier we had been watching flew in our direction, then hovered momentarily in plain sight and pounced directly on a mouse that was scurrying through the thick grasses. We watched this amazing raptor eat its dinner, fur and all!

SHARP-SHINNED HAWK
Accipiter striatus

Description: Square tail; rounded head; dull gray crown

Small, shy, and secretive, the Sharp-shinned Hawk is fast and deadly when hunting prey. It is very difficult to distinguish this accipiter from the somewhat larger Cooper's Hawk because it has similar markings. Measuring ten to fourteen inches in length, it compares in size to the Mourning Dove. The female is the larger of the species and is similar in size to the smaller male Cooper's Hawk, so distinguishing between the species by size alone is doubtful. It is best to obtain two distinguishing features in order to make a correct identification.

Accipiters are short-winged, long-tailed, and long-legged raptors. The Sharp-shinned is bluish-gray above and has white underparts barred with cinnamon coloration. The tail is square on the edges, and may be notched. (The Cooper's is rounded.) In flight its head appears relatively small (the Cooper's appears large), and on a perching bird, the head appears more rounded (squarish on Cooper's). The crown of the Sharp-shinned is lighter and does not show a contrasting line, which is more apparent on the Cooper's hawk. The Sharp-shinned Hawk's eyes are intensely yellow-orange. Its voice is more shrill than the Cooper's and sounds like *ke-ke-ke-ke.*

Habitat and Diet

The Sharp-shinned is a woodland hawk that commonly winters in the Southwestern lowlands where sufficiently wooded areas offer it protection. It feeds almost exclusively on birds, but occasionally consumes small mammals as well. Because of its choice of food and its amazing bursts of speed, this small hawk has been named pigeon hawk, sparrow hawk, bird hawk, chicken hawk, bullet hawk and little blue darter.

The Sharp-shinned Hawk eats any bird from the size of warblers to larger doves, flickers, and thrashers. One study showed that nearly ninety-six percent of food intake consists of bird species, and the remaining four percent is mammals and insects.

Nesting and Mating Behaviors

Returning to higher elevations for breeding, the Sharp-shinned Hawk most often chooses a tall, coniferous tree as a nesting site, but occasionally deciduous trees suffice. Both sexes build the large platform of sticks, placing them near the trunk. They prefer a new nest each year, but occasionally renovate an old one. It may be unlined, or sparsely lined with stems or bark.

The three to five eggs are smooth, pale blue with brown blotching. The female does most of the incubation while the male brings her food, but he occasionally takes his turn as well; the whole process takes about thirty-five days. Both adults will ferociously drive away intruders. The young fledge after two months and soon begin to learn the arduous task of hunting for themselves.

COOPER'S HAWK*
Accipiter cooperii

Description: Long, rounded tail; short, rounded wings; dark brown crown

The Cooper's Hawk, slightly smaller than the Common Crow, measures fourteen to twenty inches long. This accipiter has a wing span of thirty to thirty-six inches, thus appearing relatively short in comparison to

*Plate 15

the larger buteos. As a group, accipiters have short wings, long tails, and quick, aggressive flight, while those raptors classified as buteos are larger, with heavier bodies, long, broad wings, and short tails that allow them to soar with ease.

The wings and tail of the Cooper's Hawk have rounded tips, which distinguish it from the otherwise similar Sharp-shinned Hawk, whose tail is conspicuously square-tipped. The former also has a blackish crown, which is lacking in the smaller Sharp-shinned.

Both sexes have similar markings, but the female is considerably larger as is characteristic of all raptors. The adult Cooper's Hawk is blue-gray on its back with a rusty breast. There is a broad white tip on the tail, and the underparts are barred with white. The immature Cooper's is brown with streaking below.

A hawk's eyes are extremely sophisticated and can change focus very rapidly, the way a human being can with a highly refined pair of binoculars. A Cooper's Hawk is able to adapt its vision rapidly and acutely, while it flashes through the bushes and into the undergrowth in pursuit of prey, usually other birds.

Habitat and Diet

The Cooper's Hawk is a year-round resident all over the Southwest and prefers open woodlands, river groves, canyons, and mature forests. This accipiter does not usually ride the high air currents in search of prey as do the larger buteos, but waits inconspicuously in the cover of trees or shrubs, waiting for prey to appear. When a likely victim surfaces, it flies with amazing speed using stiff, strong wingbeats, and may even continue after its prey on foot. It usually prefers small birds, but also eats small mammals, and in the desert it consumes many lizards.

Nesting and Mating Behaviors

The Cooper's Hawk is an early nester and usually builds a new nest every year, although occasionally it will refurbish an old one. It chooses a spot high in the upper branches of a tall tree thus assuring protection from ground predators.

The nest is approximately twenty-six inches in diameter and six inches high, and can often be easily spotted in early spring because it is constructed before the leaves of the tree bud forth to camouflage it. The nest is made of small sticks carefully woven together and lined with chips. Both sexes share the construction tasks.

There are four or five bluish-white eggs, which are laid in one- or two-day intervals. The female does the majority of the incubation, but the male occasionally takes a turn with the twenty-four-day task.

The young are extremely dependent on the adults and stay in the nest longer than many birds. While the young mature slowly, the adults keep extremely busy in securing enough food for the ravenous nestlings. Once the young hawks leave the nest, the adults begin the tedious undertaking of educating them in the fine art of predation.

Supplemental Information

Living in the midst of saguaros, palos verdes, and mesquites, I am blessed with daily sightings of many desert birds. Among them, I occasionally get a quick glimpse of a Cooper's Hawk as it suddenly blasts out of the trees along the wash and snatches up an unsuspecting bird feeding in an open area. Once one landed on my birdbath, and as I watched the raptor's vigilant composure, I reflected about its reputation, which some describe as "ferocious and destructive."

A closer look at the types of birds taken for prey strongly indicates that the aggressive actions of the Cooper's Hawk are simply one step in a larger plan of the ecological system. By killing off the weaker individuals in a species, that species of bird becomes stronger through the survival of the fittest.

HARRIS' HAWK[*]
Parabuteo unicinctus

Description: Black body; white rump and tail tip; chestnut thighs and shoulder patches

This long-legged, long-tailed buteo measures from seventeen to twenty-nine inches in length with a wing span of three and one-half to three and three-quarters feet. The sexes are similar in markings, but the female is much larger.

The flashy white rump and white band at the tip of the tail are conspicuously displayed on this black hawk. Distinctive chestnut patches high-

*Plate 16

light the shoulders and thighs. Its legs are pale orange and the eye appears dark brown. Its underwings display dark gray flight feathers and chestnut coverts, and its wings are somewhat paddle-shaped. While perching, the wingtips reach halfway down the tail.

The immature Harris' Hawk appears pale with light streaking on the dark body, but the rusty shoulder patches are already present. Its chestnut thighs are barred with white. The conspicuous white patch at the base of the tail distinguishes it from the similar Red-shouldered Hawk. The two species do not occur together, however, except in some areas of Texas.

This medium-sized buteo is more energetic in flight than larger raptors, moving with quicker and more shallow wingbeats. Its call is an *iirrr* sound that quickly changes into a prolonged scream when its territory becomes threatened.

Harris' Hawks are very communal and may be seen in groups of ten or twelve, especially in the fall and winter.

Habitat and Diet

The Harris' Hawk can be found in mesquite and palo verde-lined washes, in saguaro deserts, and where cottonwoods abound along the banks of streams. In the Southwest it is a fairly common year-round resident.

Its diet consists primarily of small mammals such as rats, ground squirrels, and rabbits, but it will also eat lizards, small snakes, and various small birds.

The Harris' Hawk can be a lone hunter, but it is unique in that it also hunts in groups. This sophisticated hunting style is more successful than hunting alone, producing a meal with almost every outing.

Nesting and Mating Behaviors

The Harris' Hawk builds a nest of sticks and weeds in bushes five feet off the ground or in saguaros or trees up to fifty feet tall. The nest is lined with leaves, grass, small roots, and even bark. The female lays from two to four whitish eggs, lightly spotted with brown or lavender, and does all of the incubation. The male brings her food and when the young are hatched, he continues to furnish food for the entire family. Polyandry occurs among some Harris' Hawks, whereby the larger female simultaneously accepts two males as mates.

Supplemental Information

While hiking in the Tucson Mountains, I was almost to the top of a small ridge when I heard the screaming cry of a hawk. I stopped to listen and heard a second scream, which seemed to be over the ridge and further to my right. Silence followed and I proceeded upward hoping to see what was causing the raucousness. From the top I could see two Harris' Hawks with what appeared to be a cottontail. A third Harris' was perched in the top of a mesquite, ready to jump down for its share. Cooperative hunting had been successful once again.

Swainson's Hawk*
Buteo swainsoni

Description: Dark head and back; wings extend beyond tail; white throat; brown bib

This diurnal raptor of the Southwestern deserts and grasslands is a buteo like the Red-tailed Hawk; however, its broad wings are more pointed and it is slightly smaller, measuring nineteen to twenty-two inches. The female is larger as is common with all raptors, otherwise the sexes are similar in markings.

Hawks can be difficult to identify because the same species may appear in a variety of plumages, as they replace their feathers on an annual basis. In addition, they may have a light and dark morph, which challenges the birder even further.

Typically, an adult Swainson's Hawk has a dark head and back with a reddish upper breast, which contrasts with the light-colored lower breast and belly. In the dark morph, the wings, including the flight feathers, are dark throughout. In the light morph, two distinctive tones under the wings are apparent, along with a large white throat patch.

The adult Swainson's Hawk has a long tail, which is barred below and a dark terminal band. It takes two years to reach adult plumage; then the hawk tends to mate with another hawk of the same color morph.

While soaring on the air currents, the wings are held slightly above horizontal, and the wingspread itself is from four to five feet. The Swainson's Hawk can often be seen practically motionless while it rides the

*Plate 16

uplifting air currents. In flight, this broad-winged buteo is much slower than the smaller, more streamlined accipiter.

Like many raptors, it is usually silent except during the mating and nesting season. During this period, it may be heard making a shrill, plaintive whistle that sounds like a drawn-out *keeeeer*.

Habitat and Diet

The Swainson's Hawk is a frequent summer resident of the plains and grasslands of the Southwestern lowlands, and is usually fairly obvious. Often in large flocks, it migrates to the open range country in April, then leaves again in September and October to winter in South America.

Hunting from perches near the ground as well as from soaring positions high above the terrain, this hawk constantly searches for prey. It seems to prefer small rodents when they are available, but also eats many insects, including large populations of grasshoppers and locusts. Just prior to fall migration, they may be seen flocking together in groups, sometimes in the thousands, gorging themselves on fields of grasshoppers in preparation for their long flight.

Nesting and Mating Behaviors

The nest is a bulky mass of sticks in a saguaro cactus, a tree, a yucca, or even on a cliff. The completed structure may range from six to thirty feet above the ground, and is often lined with green sprigs from surrounding foliage or grasses when available. The outside diameter is approximately forty-five inches and the height nears ten inches. Often an old nest is renovated and re-used rather than starting a new one.

There are usually two to four oval eggs with a rather smooth shell that is often spotted. The female does the incubation while the male brings food to her.

The Swainson's Hawk is very protective of its nest, especially after the young have hatched. If disturbed prior to hatching, the parents may abandon the nest. When the young emerge, the adults' defensive behaviors are much more aggressive, and they may attack an intruder.

Supplemental Information

The Swainson's Hawk is one of the most prevalent hawks during summer in the Sulphur Springs Valley in Southeastern Arizona where I grew up. On our ranch each summer, we moved the majority of our cattle from the Mule Mountains, their winter pasture, to the grassy valley floor. Swainson's Hawks perched on mesquites or posts watching for the moment a small mammal would show itself through the grasses. From horseback I could watch them snatch prey and then carry it to a nearby perch to be consumed on the spot. It seemed as though they followed us because our activity flushed many rodents.

Red-tailed Hawk*
Buteo jamaicensis

Description: Reddish tail; dark-streaked belly band; dark head and upperparts

The Red-tailed Hawk is a large raptor measuring from twenty to twenty-five inches in length. It is dark on the upperparts, contrasted with some lighter streaking. The breast is a reversal, showing mostly white with some dark streaks forming a band across the belly. As the name indicates, the most distinguishing characteristic is the reddish-brown coloration on the topside of the tail, which can be easily seen as the Hawk spreads its broad, rounded rudder in flight. The ends of the wings are black, making a handsome silhouette against the sky. The wingspan reaches from four to four and one-half feet. The female is almost a third larger than the male.

The Red-tailed Hawk is one of the most common large hawks in the Southwest and belongs to the largest group of hawks called buteos. Slower-moving than the accipiters, the buteos are typically seen soaring so gracefully and effortlessly on air currents thousands of feet up. They have very broad wings that make them somewhat slower in attacking their prey.

Nature has designed the Red-tailed Hawk with absolute precision. Its eyes are extremely developed to spot prey while on the move and often from great heights. It is frequently seen perching high on a saguaro or on a high-wire pole, and is constantly surveying the land for a possible food source.

*Plate 17

Habitat and Diet

The Red-tailed Hawk is found in a variety of habitats from the deserts and grasslands, to farmlands and wooded areas. Its diet mainly consists of mice, rats, rabbits, and occasionally reptiles and birds. Due to its slower approach, this hawk typically takes the weakest of birds.

In the hunting process, the Red-tailed Hawk must first find the prey, which sometimes takes hours, then make its attack, which happens in a matter of minutes. Considering that all raptorial birds make more attempts than actual kills, it is easily understood why the majority of the day is spent in continual search for prey.

Once prey is discovered, the Red-tailed Hawk attacks quickly, grasping the victim with its talons. The force of impact causes the toes to grip instantly, thus sinking the talons into the prey, killing it immediately. There are three toes pointing forward and one backward. In unison they function as strongly as a vise grip. If the prey is relatively small, it is carried to a higher perch to be eaten. If the prey is too large to be carried off, it is eaten on the spot.

The strong, sharply honed beak is not used in the actual killing, but is used instead to tear the meat into bite-sized pieces. Because the Red-tailed Hawk removes some of the fur before ingesting the flesh, the feet are used for holding the prey while the hooked beak rips away the fur and tears at the meat. Any fur that is swallowed is later regurgitated in the form of a hard pellet. When reptilian and avian prey are taken, scales and feathers are likewise coughed up in pellets.

Nesting and Mating Behaviors

The breeding season starts in mid-February. The nest is a large, bulky platform placed high in a tree, in the arms of a saguaro, or sometimes on a rocky cliff ledge. The nest is often used year after year, with only slight remodeling. It is made of sticks and lined with various kinds of roots. Each year small, green branches are added by both sexes.

The female lays one to four slightly marbled eggs, which she incubates for approximately thirty days. The male spends his time foraging for food, both for himself and for the female. The pair is monogamous, mating for life.

When first hatched, the young are blind and extremely dependent. The female feeds them very small pieces of meat she tears away with her beak.

As the young mature, the female must also go in search of prey for the ravenous youngsters; they may stay in the nest from one to four months.

The young hawks begin their predatory training by first learning to tear away bite-sized peices of flesh from prey brought to the nest by their parents. Later they begin stretching their wings and flying from perch to perch. They are fed by their parents longer than many species of birds because it takes time to develop the muscle coordination essential to successful hunting and time for their eyes to develop keen vision. The voice develops into a harsh descending scream, and within four months the young Red-tailed Hawks are ready to start their own ventures in hunting and surviving.

Supplemental Information

Hidden away in my blind, I spent many fun hours observing a pair of Red-tailed Hawks bringing fresh, green branches to their nest, incubating their eggs, and rearing their young. If I were not concealed, the adults would leave the nest and perch on other saguaros farther away while they watched my every move with their keen eyes. Once tucked quietly away in my blind, they would return to the nest and bring food to their young. I watched them bring in small rabbits and rodents, but most often they brought snakes. The reptile would still be squirming around in the nest, but the female would finally get it under control with her talons and begin tearing bites of flesh, which she fed to her ravenous youngsters.

FERRUGINOUS HAWK
Buteo regalis

Description: Large body; rufous above, light below; chestnut "V" formed by pantaloons; white on upper base of primaries in flight; rusty-tipped white tail

The name "regalis" is fitting for this largest North American buteo who is occasionally mistaken for an eagle. The light morphs greatly outnumber the dark morphs in the Southwest, but "ferruginous" aptly describes the rusty back and leggings of both phases. This hawk measures twenty-two and one-half to twenty-five inches long and has an impressive wingspan of fifty-six inches. From below, you can easily see the rufous wrist patches, black-tipped primaries, and the chestnut "V" formed by the dark leggings. The head is usually pale, and the white tail is often tipped with light rusty plumage. Notice the unusually large gape.

Immatures are dark brown above, light below including leggings, which may have rusty spots. Young birds lack the rufous wing patches as well as the rusty flair on the tip of the tail. The dark morph (seldom seen in desert areas) is dark below as well as above; it slightly resembles the Rough-legged Hawk, but lacks the dark tipped tail.

This solemn bird of prey usually perches low near areas abounding with food sources. Less vocal than many hawks during non-breeding season, it becomes quite robust on its breeding grounds. To defend territory, the Ferruginous Hawk flies overhead screaming like a gull with loud, descending notes resembling *kre-ah*.

Habitat and Diet

This buteo is an uncommon winter resident in the dry, open country. Food availability draws this regal-looking raptor to grasslands and agricultural areas where it consumes both insects and rodents. Before the prairie dog was chemically eradicated, it was the favored food. Now, ground squirrels are the first choice, which has prompted locals to name the raptor "squirrel hawk." Additionally, many rabbits and rats are consumed as are insects, especially grasshoppers.

Group hunting is best demonstrated by the Harris' Hawk, but the Ferruginous has its own team style of catching prey. One bird positions itself between the rodent and its home while the other makes the actual kill. This intelligent creature may also perch near a digging badger, then snatch rodents that have been disturbed by its "assistant."

Nesting and Mating Behaviors

By the end of April, the deserts are void of Ferruginous Hawks. In higher elevations this magnificent raptor builds a nest from six to sixty feet high in a tree, on a rocky cliff, or even on the barren ground if other sites are not available. Nests are often re-used year after year. Both sexes build or add material, which may increase the nest size to more than three feet in height. Built mainly of sticks, this monstrosity often contains cow dung, roots, and dried grasses.

The female lays three to five creamy-white eggs with brown blotches. Both sexes take turns with the incubation process, which takes from twenty-eight to thirty-three days; then both hunt and feed the young.

Rough-legged Hawk
Buteo lagopus

Description: Light morph: barred leg feathers; dark eyes; black trailing edges of underwing; light "U" between breast and belly; white tail base with dark subterminal band; large dark wrist marks on underwings; dark belly band

The Rough-legged Hawk has two morphs with many variations within each group. The sexes sport different plumage, and the immatures add to the confusion. In the Southwestern lowlands, the light morph is the phase most frequently seen. The adult male has grayish-brown plumage with light mottling above, and is white below with dark markings on his breast. His head is light brown with streaking, the iris is dark, and a dark eyeline contrasts with the lighter head. His white tail has a dark subterminal band making the white base and the tip more obvious.

This species measures nineteen to twenty-four inches long. The female, which is the larger of the sexes, appears browner, displays heavier breast markings, and often sports a belly band. Both sexes display a creamy "U" between the breast and belly. Many of the birds in the desert areas seem to be immatures who have a single, dark, subterminal tail band and lighter heads.

The less-common dark phase birds are distinguished as follows: The male appears black with a lighter nape, and his dark tail sports three or four slender, white bands. The female is dark brown with a lighter nape, and her tail is dark on top, light underneath, and sports a dark terminal band.

This big bird of prey with feathered legs flies with slow, deliberate wing beats and may be seen hovering above prey. Seldom heard in desert wintering territory unless alarmed, it becomes more vocal on breeding grounds. Territorial screeches sound like *kee-we-uk,* but around the nest a more subdued *mew* is sufficient.

Habitat and Diet

The Rough-legged Hawk is a rare to uncommon winter resident in the Southwestern lowlands. Look for it in desert grasslands and agricultural areas in the same vicinity as Ferruginous Hawks.

This graceful raptor is diurnal as are all hawks, but comes the closest to crossing the line into nighttime hunting. Crepuscular light finds this avid hunter in the open countryside hoping for the first—or perhaps the last—opportunity to seize prey. Feeding almost entirely on small rodents such as mice and ground squirrels, it will occasionally add a small bird to its dietary smorgasbord. On breeding grounds, lemmings and ptarmigans become the targeted prey.

Nesting and Mating Behaviors

By late March or early April, the Rough-legged Hawk has disappeared from the lowlands. A long journey northward takes it to higher latitudes where it nests in the upland tundra.

The nest is usually constructed in a large tree, but may also be located on a mossy cliff. Sticks, grasses, and weeds are woven into a bulky but well-constructed platform, then lined with smaller, fibrous materials. There are two to six buff-white eggs with dark brown splotches. It is an arduous task to rear the young, teach them to hunt, and begin the long journey southward before the next winter.

Golden Eagle
Aguila chrysaetos

Description: Large, brown, feathered legs, faintly banded tail; golden nape on adults

The largest Southwestern bird of prey is the Golden Eagle. With a wingspan of seven to seven and one-half feet, this graceful creature measures thirty to forty-one inches in length, and the female is the larger.

The golden coloration appears as a wash over the otherwise dark brown body. Legs and cere show yellow, while the deeply set eyes are brown, similar in coloration to its large, sharp claws. The immense beak is bone-colored with a dark, decurved, pointed tip. The legs are feathered to the toes, and the tail is faintly banded.

A high soaring species, the Golden Eagle may be mistaken for a Turkey Vulture. Take another look. They both glide with wings slightly uplifted, but the eagle has a distinctively longer neck and tail. Immatures in flight show white wing patches and white at the base of the tail.

Habitat and Diet

In the United States, the Golden Eagle's breeding territory is now restricted almost entirely to the mountainous regions of the West. In non-breeding season, however, it may be seen in almost any habitat—including the Southwestern deserts, where it is most often found in winter.

As a diurnal bird of prey, it feeds chiefly on rabbits and ground squirrels, but also eats birds, snakes, and even carrion.

Southwestern populations are declining partially because of shooting, but mainly because of the evergrowing problem of habitat destruction due to human encroachment.

Nesting and Mating Behaviors

The nest may be constructed high in a tree, but is most often placed on an inaccessible, rocky cliff with a commanding view. Often several nests are built and are used alternately from year to year. New sticks are added each season until the nest reaches five to six feet in diameter and approximately four to five feet high. In addition to sticks, the bulky aerie contains roots, stems, and unfortunately even human rubbish; then it is lined with grasses, fresh leaves, and lichens.

The normal clutch consists of two eggs, which are white with brown and gray spots. Incubation is done chiefly by the female, it begins with the first egg laid and continues for forty to forty-five days. The young do not fledge until they reach a minimum age of eleven weeks. Both parents hunt and care for the nestlings.

CRESTED CARACARA*
Polyborus plancus

Description: Black body; white neck; black crest; red face; bluish bill, white barred tail with black tip

The Crested Caracara is a long-legged bird of prey measuring twenty to twenty-five inches in length. It is occasionally seen around vultures, with whom it shares large carrion. Both sexes have similar markings, which feature a black cap and crest, and white cheeks and throat that emphasize the bare-skinned, red face and eye ring. Its bluish beak has a sharp hook at the tip which enables this vulture-like bird to rip through the tough hide of an animal in order to feed on the exposed flesh.

The white neck speckles into a black body, boldly contrasting with numerous black and white tail bars, the terminal one being black and noticeably wider. Long, yellow, unfeathered legs enable this lanky-looking bird to run quickly along the ground. In flight it displays a long, outstretched neck, white chest, black belly, and large, white wing patches on the extremities. It soars with wings held flat. The immature is browner with streaking on the underparts, and the facial skin is gray to pink.

Although the Crested Caracara is usually silent, it emits a crackle-like call when excited. With head thrown backward and crest erect, this bird of prey utters a raucous cry sounding similar to its name—*caracara.* It also has a single note that can be described as *"wuck."*

Habitat and Diet

The Crested Caracara is a neotropical species reaching its northernmost limits in the Southwestern deserts. It inhabits semi-open country with desert scrub, mesquite, and tall cacti. In this type of environment, I have seen it flying for long distances above highways, apparently looking for roadside kills.

Primarily a carrion eater, this vulture-like member of the falcon family is an aggressive feeder, using its long, yellow legs to lash out at hungry vultures, sometimes pirating food straight from their beaks. Often, the Black Vulture surrenders its portion to avoid scraping with the feisty caracara. Additionally, the Crested Caracara preys on reptiles, amphib-

*Plate 17

ians, insects, and small mammals, including an occasional bird. A rapid runner, it skillfully hunts on foot.

Nesting and Mating Behaviors

Unlike a falcon, the caracara builds its own nest; both sexes share in the task. The bulky, loosely constructed nest of sticks and briars is placed in a tree or cactus a safe distance off the ground, up to fifty feet high. In the scantily lined bowl, the female lays two or three whitish eggs with brown blotches. Both adults take turns incubating the eggs for about twenty-eight days. The young hatchlings appear with buffy down plumage highlighted with brown caps, shoulders, thighs, and rumps.

Supplemental Information

The national bird of Mexico, the Crested Caracara is displayed on its flag and is known as the "Mexican Eagle." It is also embossed on the peso with a squirming rattlesnake in its beak.

AMERICAN KESTREL*
Falco sparverius

Description: Two black face stripes; rufous black; male–blue wings, female–rufous wings

The American Kestrel is the smallest falcon of the desert, and it is also the most common. It is sometimes called the Sparrow Hawk, but it measures from nine to twelve inches, which is actually more comparable to the size of a jay. The wingspan is one and three-quarters to two feet, and the female is the larger of the species, as is typical of other raptors.

The American Kestrel beautifully displays a distinctive white face with a double mustache, and black mark behind the ear. It has a rufous back, crown, and tail, which is emphasized by dark brown bands with the one at the tip showing darkest. The male has gray-blue wings, while the female's are dark rufous; and she has heavier streaking on the buff-colored breast. The nape is also buff-colored, while the leg feathers are creamy to reddish. The young soon take on the characteristics of the same-sex parent.

*Plate 18

The notched bill and powerful feet are characteristic of all falcons, and so are the long, narrow, pointed wings. Although it can frequently be seen hovering over prey while rapidly beating its wings like a kingfisher, the American Kestrel is also very quick in actual flight. While perching in an upright manner, it occasionally jerks its long tail.

The American Kestrel is extremely vocal compared to other birds of prey. Its shrill call can often be heard before the little falcon can actually be seen. It utters a rapid, high-pitched sound alternating *klee, klee, klee,* with *killy, killy, killy, killy.*

Habitat and Diet

Numbers of American Kestrels increase as year-round residents are joined by winter residents. They can be found in a wide range of habitats, hunting from high exposed perches, such as power poles, wires, and along the edge of wooded areas but usually close to open pastures, meadows, and fields.

The American Kestrel feeds primarily on insects, especially grasshoppers and crickets. Prey also includes small birds, lizards, snakes, and rodents. Hovering with rapidly beating wings and tail fanned outward, it suddenly pounces on its victim, flicking its tail vigorously upon landing.

During the fall and winter, females are often seen hunting in open areas more often than males. Also, in winter the sexes divide the habitats, with the female obtaining the better areas.

Nesting and Mating

In the spring and summer, the American Kestrel can often be seen around dead trees on the edges of open fields because its most common nesting sight is in either natural tree cavities or abandoned woodpecker holes. In the desert, it nests in holes in saguaro cacti made by the Gila Woodpecker or the Gilded Flicker. It has also been found nesting in the eaves of buildings and in nesting boxes.

In the desert, the male American Kestrel offers food to the female as part of the courtship ritual. Although the female does the majority of the incubation, the male has also been seen occasionally aiding in this process, which is unusual in raptors. The three to five eggs are buff to pinkish white, and lightly covered with brown dots. Incubation takes twenty-nine to thirty-one days.

Supplemental Information

I was sitting at the edge of a meadow one fall day, feeling the warmth of the sun and watching the grasses sway gently with the breeze. A pair of American Kestrels, still accompanied by a juvenile, were feeding on insects. Grasshoppers and crickets seemed to be the menu that day, and I was overwhelmed at the numbers captured. Later, I learned that the American Kestrel has a high metabolic rate and requires enormous amounts of food intake in proportion to its size. It has been estimated that this small falcon eats as many as two hundred and ninety mice per year. As grasshoppers and crickets are its favorite food choices, just imagine how many of these creatures must be consumed!

Peregrine Falcon*
Falco peregrinus

Description: Black "helmet" with sideburns; bluish-gray above; light with bars underneath; pointed wings; slender tail; plain underwings

This sixteen- to twenty-inch-long dynamo is fast and deadly. Its long, pointed tail, broad wings, and quick wing beats are typical of falcons, and the Peregrine Falcon hunts other bird species, often ferociously knocking them right out of the sky.

The dark head, nape, and malar stripes make it appear that this falcon is wearing a helmet. Adults are slate-gray above and light underneath with spots and bars. Immatures are brown above with heavily streaked, lighter underparts. From below, the absence of dark wing linings and axillars distinguish it from the Prairie Falcon.

There are three forms of the Peregrine Falcon: The *tundrius* is the smallest, and displays a white breast; the *anatum* shows a light cinnamon tinge underneath; the *pealei* is darkest and largest with dark streaks on the breast.

Loud, repeated cries of *hak, hak, hak, hak* warn intruders to stay away from breeding territories. Additionally, *we'chew, we'chew* may be heard. At other times of the year this species is fairly quiet.

*Plate 18

Habitat and Diet

The Peregrine Falcon is a rare but increasingly more common transient and resident in the Southwestern lowlands, and prefers areas near rocky cliffs and permanent water sources. Those migrating here for the winter do so in pursuit of other migratory birds, upon which this falcon feeds exclusively.

Most prey is taken in mid-air. Sharp talons automatically clench upon impact, usually causing instant death. After this occurs, the Peregrine Falcon immediately begins stripping feathers from its victim, and often arrives on a perch with a completely plucked bird. Another hunting technique is to shoot downward in a power dive to knock its victim out of the sky. Following the stunned species to the ground, it finishes the kill and begins devouring the flesh. Shorebirds and waterfowl are favorites, but ground birds and passerines are eaten as well.

Nesting and Mating Behaviors

The Peregrine Falcon does not build its own nest, but always claims one with a commanding view. Inaccessible, rocky cliffs are primary choices, but occasionally an old nest constructed by another raptor or a ledge of a building will suffice. Similar to other raptors, a pair may return to the same site year after year.

The female lays three to five creamy-white eggs heavily covered with brown blotches, and does the majority of the incubation for thirty-two to thirty-five days. Both adults participate in the tasks of feeding the nestlings and teaching them to fly and hunt for themselves.

PRAIRIE FALCON
Falco mexicanus

Description: Pale brown above; creamy underparts, brown streaking or spotting; white area between narrow mustache and dark ear patch; dark axilars

The Prairie Falcon measures seventeen to twenty inches long and has a forty-two-inch wing span. The female is the larger bird, and the sexes appear similar in plumage. Pale, sandy upperparts are decorated with brown mottling, while creamy underparts are streaked or dotted with darker brown patterns. The narrow mustache and a dark ear patch are separated by white plumage, making the dark areas appear like two teardrops. Look for dark patches on the underwings when it flies, and also notice its slender build. Light leg feathers are barred or spotted, and the long tail may show faint bands. Immatures appear darker above and with more streaking below, but show fewer spots.

This remarkable bird darts low over the countryside with incredible speed, hovering occasionally to have a better look at food possibilities; then either quickly strikes its prey or simply continues on its way. This speedster can overtake any bird of similar size, and is actually faster than the more aggressive Peregrine Falcon.

Usually silent except when alarmed, the Prairie Falcon is most vocal on its breeding territory. If you hear *kree-kree-kree,* you are probably too close to the nest.

Habitat and Diet

The Prairie Falcon usually chooses more arid habitat than the Peregrine Falcon, so it is more common in the Southwestern deserts. It is a rare to uncommon resident of grasslands, agricultural areas, and canyons with rocky cliffs. Numbers increase during winter and migration periods. It does not appear comfortable around people, so it does not choose to nest on buildings in towns as the Peregrine will occasionally do.

Whereas the Peregrine Falcon feeds almost exclusively on birds, the Prairie Falcon seems to prefer small mammals, but additionally eats birds as well as insects. Some birds are taken in mid-air, but most prey is captured on the ground. From a perch or from high in the sky, the Prairie Falcon boldly streaks after prey, seizing the chosen victim with deadly, sharp talons.

Nesting and Mating Behaviors

The arid climate of the Southwest, especially on high, inaccessible cliffs, makes ideal habitat for the breeding Prairie Falcon. This species does not build a nest, but rather lays eggs on bare ground among grains of small gravel, or sometimes occupies an old, abandoned nest. It has many choices for nesting sites because it breeds earlier than most other raptors.

The female lays two to six creamy-white eggs heavily covered with brown splotches. She does most of the incubation, which takes twenty-nine to thirty-three days, while the male hunts and brings food to her. When the eggs hatch, both adults jointly rear the young.

COMMON BARN OWL
Tyto alba

Description: Large, tuftless head; heart-shaped face; pale underparts

The Barn Owl is the lightest colored, medium-sized owl of the Southwest, measuring fourteen to twenty inches in length with a wing span of forty-four inches. A white, heart-shaped face with small, dark, piercing eyes and a large, tuftless head give it the appearance of a monkey and distinguish it from all other owls. It is even commonly called "monkey-faced owl."

The back is mottled cinnamon-buff while the underparts are pale. The bill is dull yellow and the legs are long and feathered. The larger and darker bird is the female.

The voice of the Barn Owl is an intense, rasping hiss sounding like *kschh*. When frightened, it snaps its bill to make a clicking sound.

Habitat and Diet

Although not often seen, the Barn Owl is fairly common throughout the Southwestern lowlands. It roosts in groves of trees, but hunts throughout the deserts, grasslands, and adjoining farmlands. This nocturnal bird of prey often hunts by sound alone on moonless nights. Studies show that it can locate and obtain living prey repetitiously and unerringly using only auditory faculties.

Because its favorite food seems to be rats and mice, the Barn Owl is extremely beneficial to humankind. It devours the entire rodent, but can't digest fur and bones; so it periodically regurgitates the residue in the form of pellets which can be found around the nesting area and under its roost.

Nesting and Mating Behaviors

Barn Owls form pair bonds, probably for life, returning to the same breeding territory year after year. The nest may be made in a natural tree cavity, but also in barns (hence, its common name), abandoned mine shafts, old wells, or on cliffs. There is no actual nest constructed, so the eggs are laid on a foundation of disgorged pellets.

The female lays three to eleven elliptical, white eggs at intervals of two to three days, and does the incubation while the male hunts and brings food to her. There is no synchronized hatching, so the first nestling may be two weeks older than the last one hatched. The ravenous youngsters keep both adults busy, who hunt all night long to satisfy their demands.

Western Screech-owl*
Otus kennicotti

Description: Small body; ear tufts; yellow eyes; dark bill

The Western Screech-owl is a common, widespread owl, approximately seven to ten inches long, only slightly larger than the tiny Elf Owl. The most obvious distinguishing feature, other than size, is the "horned" effect possessed by the Western Screech-Owl. It has even been nicknamed the "Little Horned Owl." Yellow eyes are accompanied by a dark bill, and overall gray plumage includes black streaking on the underparts.

As with nearly all birds, the Western Screech-owl is most vocal during the mating season, but can be heard any time of the year. Mainly nocturnal, it is more easily heard than seen. Although this owl has been named "screech-owl," its call does not sound like a screech at all: It is more like a chatter and has been described by some birders as sounding like a bouncing ping-pong ball.

Habitat and Diet

The Western Screech-owl is a permanent resident in the Southwest and can be found among saguaros, in riparian vegetation, or in open grasslands. It prefers open spaces for nocturnal hunting.

*Plate 18

This small owl's diet consists of a variety of insects, as well as arachnids, birds, and an assortment of small mammals. If available, crayfish, fish, and some small reptiles are savored.

Nesting and Mating Behaviors

The Western Screech-owl does not build its own nest, but rather moves into a saguaro hole or cavity in a tree. It will also set up housekeeping in commercial birdhouses, if the entrance hole is large enough. The four or five eggs are plain white, as are all owl eggs, but those of the Western Screech-owl are distinctly smaller than most.

Mid-April is the height of the nesting season, and the adults begin incubation immediately after the first egg is laid. Additional eggs are laid two or three days apart. Although the female does most of the incubation, the male hunts for both of them. During the daytime, they may both be found snuggled together in the particular cavity they have chosen for their nest, but once the young have hatched, the adults usually roost outside but nearby the cavity.

Supplemental Information

One September I spent several days in an old ranch house that had been void of people for four years. The birds and wildlife in the vicinity became accustomed to moving about at their free will without the intrusion of human beings. The first evening on the darker side of dusk, I let my little dog out in the yard. In a matter of minutes, I could hear a ruckus and ran outside to see what was occurring. My first concern was that my dog might have run into some skunks. There were none to be seen, nor to be smelled, thank goodness. My dog had been intimidated by something, however, and she was hunkered down on the ground. As I approached her, the ruckus recurred, and there in a large mulberry tree above us sat a Western Screech-owl scolding us for intruding into "its" yard. The bobbing of this little owl's head, as it continued chattering at us, served as a warning for me, and I soon retreated back into the house with my dog. Her hunkering behavior suggested that she had already been dive-bombed once, and I didn't want to take a chance on being the second victim!

GREAT HORNED OWL*
Bubo virginianus

Description: Large body; wide-set ear tufts; white throat;
yellow eyes

This magnificent owl is the largest and most powerful of the nocturnal raptors in the Southwest. Its body length is eighteen to twenty-five inches, while its enormous wing span reaches from forty-five to sixty inches. In flight, the Great Horned Owl is comparable in size to many of the larger hawks.

Its name very accurately includes the large ear tufts that appear conspicuously on its head, giving the illusion of horns. In addition to these tufts, the large, yellow eyes make the Great Horned Owl's face look like that of a sophisticated cat. For this reason, it has even been nicknamed the "cat owl."

The throat of the Great Horned Owl is white, and the underparts display many horizontal bars. Feathers cover the lower legs and even part of its toes. As with all owls, it has three toes in front and one behind. If necessary, one of the front toes can be moved to the back to aid in grasping prey while the owl is tearing away edible pieces with its strong, curved beak. Also, as is common for most birds of prey, the female is the larger of the sexes.

Habitat and Diet

The Great Horned Owl can be found in almost any kind of habitat as long as there is sufficient shelter and a continual food supply. It hunts rabbits, rodents, and small birds.

This large owl has powerful feet for snatching up prey: Even the rodents that move about under the cover of night are not safe from this valuable predator. Along with its highly perfected vision, the Great Horned Owl has a built-in hearing mechanism that allows it to zero in on barely audible sounds made by moving prey. It sometimes hunts by sound alone.

The owl dives at prey and attacks with sharp talons. Although the act is ferocious, it all happens very quickly and very quietly. The wings and

*Plate 19

body are equipped with soft feathers that muffle the sound of motion. The silent attack often surprises the victim.

Nesting and Mating Behavior

The Great Horned Owl is one of the first large birds to nest in early spring, and the young are hatched during the last throes of winter. The maturing owlets need extra time to perfect their hunting skills before the next winter makes their food supply scarce.

Owls do not usually construct their own nests. Because they begin to rear their young so early, they have their pick of the previous season's sites, even those built by other raptors. If it cannot find a convenient nest constructed in a sagauro, tree, or thorny bush, the Great Horned Owl will lay eggs directly upon a rocky cliff or in a concealed pile of rocks.

There are usually two or three white, unmarked eggs with relatively coarse shells, which take approximately four weeks to incubate. Both sexes aid in incubation, but the majority is done by the female while the male brings her food. Both contribute to the feeding and rearing of the owlets.

Supplemental Information

I am very fortunate to have been able to observe the Great Horned Owl many times. For several years, one roosted in the large Arizona Cypress tree right outside my bedroom window on the ranch where I grew up. The whole owl family would show up in the summertime, and I loved watching them camouflage themselves next to the cypress' heavy trunk, which was hidden by dense outer needles. The immature owls already displayed the confidence and sophistication demonstrated by the adults. They would look straight at me, displaying the calmness and seeming wisdom of the larger birds.

Because the Great Horned Owl is a nocturnal hunter, I would often go out by the cypress tree at dusk and watch the magnificent bird lift off to begin surveillance for its survival. At dawn this magnificent creature would return from nightly forays, and from my bedroom I could again hear it land in the tree, disturbing other birds who had roosted there throughout the night. I would know that, as the owl's hours of adventures were ending, it was time for mine to begin.

FERRUGINOUS PYGMY-OWL
Glaucidium brasilianum

Description: Small size; rusty tail with dusky tail bars; brown-streaked breast; streaked forehead and crown

The Ferruginous Pygmy-owl measures six and one-half to seven inches long, only slightly larger than the Elf Owl. The former's long, rusty tail quickly identifies it, however, and dusky cross bars further distinguish it from another cousin, the Northern Pygmy-owl. Additionally, The Ferruginous Pygmy-owl displays a white-streaked crown, grayish-brown upperparts, and brown streaking on the breast. Two black spots appear on the nape, giving it the appearance of eyes in the back of its head.

Most owls are nocturnal creatures, moving about under the cover of night. The diurnal Ferruginous Pygmy-owl is one exception and is not at all impeded by the brilliance of the desert sun, but rather takes advantage of its luring effects on prey.

In appropriate locations during spring, listen for this vocal owl during the day, even though it calls more frequently at night. The male compulsively and incessantly makes short, rapid sounds like *took took took*. He has been heard calling for hours on end. Once this precious little owl has selected a nighttime perch, it stays there until dawn.

Diet and Habitat

The Ferruginous Pygmy-owl is a neotropical species, but crosses the Mexican border to reach its northern limits in southern Arizona where it has become very rare. From Tucson westward to the Ajo Mountains of Organ Pipe Cactus National Monument, it is a permanent resident in mesquite thickets and mainly where saguaros abound.

This owl is a diurnal hunter and is often mobbed by small birds, sometimes to their own demise because the Ferruginous Pygmy-owl feeds on aviary species. It also preys on lizards, insects, mice, and other small mammals, even some larger than itself.

Nesting and Mating Behaviors

The Ferruginous Pygmy-owl nests in old woodpecker holes, especially those cavities made in the saguaro cactus. No time is wasted on the nest, not even to add any lining. The female lays three to four white eggs on the barren floor of the cavity, then incubates them by herself while the male hunts and brings her food. Both adults assist in feeding and rearing the young.

ELF OWL*
Micrathene whitneyi

Description: Small body; no ear tufts; white eyebrows; short tail

Owls are often visualized as large predators who hunt and kill their prey in the darkness of night. Regularly, photographs depict the owl as a harsh survivor with a snake or bloody rodent in its talons. For the Pima Indians, the owl is a symbol of death. This imagery is appropriate for many of the larger owls, but diminish the size of the predator as well as the size of the prey, and the image appears slightly different.

The smallest North American Owl is the five- to six-inch Elf Owl. It has large, yellow eyes, white eyebrows, white streaks on its wings above the shoulders, and buff-colored underparts striped with rust. Notice the relatively small head with no ear tufts, and a short tail that aligns with the end of the wings. The wingspan extends to approximately fifteen inches.

Habitat and Diet

The Elf Owl is very abundant in the desert, especially in the saguaro forests, but is also readily found within wooded canyons. It chooses these areas for its summer home, then moves farther south for the winter.

This tiniest of predators feeds almost entirely on insects—especially crickets, moths, and beetles—but also feeds on scorpions, centipedes, and occasionally small reptiles. The Elf Owl hides in saguaro "boots" or tree cavities during the day and begins its search for food at dusk. It may be seen in the early twilight hours or at pre-dawn, silhouetted on a perch or branch from which it darts after any available insect.

Nesting and Mating Behavior

This small, sparrow-sized owl nests in saguaro cavities made by the Gila Woodpecker, or in the holes in trees made by other woodpeckers.

*Plate 19

The female lays three to five white eggs and does the entire incubation by herself. The male brings her food at night, and they both participate in feeding and rearing the young.

Supplemental Information

The ever-so-precious Elf Owl stole my heart the first time I saw it, and has continued to touch me each time I have had the wonderful opportunity to observe it. One encounter was on a backpack trip in Arizona's Aravaipa Canyon. We were sitting around the campfire at dusk when the little owl suddenly appeared in a small meadow. It darted after insects until the darkness hid it from our diurnal eyes. Because owls are very habitual creatures, we stationed ourselves at the same spot the next few nights with the expectancy of children. We were not disappointed. The Elf Owl offered nightly entertainment.

Since I now live in the middle of a saguaro desert, I am treated with the presence of Elf Owls every summer. I hear them nightly in the spring and early summer, which is their mating and nesting season. I often see glimpses of them close to my windows as they are apparently "exterminating" the bugs that have been attracted by the lights in my house.

BURROWING OWL*
Athene cunicularia

Description: Long, lanky legs; no ear tufts; yellow eyes

Most owls are nocturnal and therefore are difficult to see with total clarity, but the Burrowing Owl is diurnal. It is about fourteen inches tall, is buff brown on its back with a lighter-colored breast, and has striped brown-and-white tail feathers. This lanky owl has long, featherless legs, and wings as long as its body.

Because the Burrowing Own cannot move its large yellow eyes within the eye sockets, the entire head revolves in order to view the surroundings. These head movements give this distinct little owl a lot of character. While one was observing me, it was also trying to keep an eye on something behind the burrow. It turned its head so quickly that the motion itself was practically impossible to detect. The busy owl simply

*Plate 19

appeared at one moment to have large yellow eyes and at the next moment to have none.

The Burrowing Owl's long wings make it appear very graceful in flight. From a distance, it has an undulating flight pattern similar to the woodpecker.

Habitat and Diet

Prior to the 1920s, the Burrowing Owl was abundant all over the Southwest. Since that time, the Federal Rodent Control Operation poisoned numerous prairie dogs, and as a result came the loss of the majority of our Burrowing Owls. They are still fairly abundant around Yuma and the Salton Sea. Also, a few are still seen around Tucson, Phoenix, and other more remote areas in Arizona and New Mexico.

The Burrowing Owl is an avid hunter and keeps an abundant supply of food in the channels of its burrow, especially during nesting season. It is very active on moonlit nights, but principally feeds in the early morning and late evening hours.

Just as one can tell a great deal about a person by his garbage, so one can quickly tell the eating habits of the Burrowing Owl. Almost every burrow I have found has had mounds of trash deposited outside the entrance. Remains of frogs, clams, crawdads, insects, snails, and various bones of small vertebrates made its diet obvious.

Nesting and Mating Behaviors

As the name implies, the Burrowing Owl nests in a burrow. However, it does not dig its own, but takes up residence in those made by prairie dogs, squirrels, foxes, and skunks. Most other owls simply move into a home totally constructed by some other creature, but the Burrowing Owl spends a great deal of effort remodeling the chosen site. It uses sharp talons to scratch the dirt from inside of the entrance, thus forming a small mound to be used for surveillance purposes.

The nesting area itself is lined with weeds, grasses, manure, and a various assortment of trash. The prime nesting season is in May, when the female lays from five to nine round, white eggs, which hatch in about four weeks. Both sexes share, not only in the task of incubation, but also in the feeding and rearing of the owlets.

Supplemental Information

Observing Burrowing Owls is very exciting. On one occasion when I was driving along a canal, I spotted a burrow on the opposite side. Sure enough, there in the entrance posed a long-legged owl. As I approached, it bobbed its head up and down, and then crouched close to the ground in front of a mound of dirt, trying to hide from me. As I pressed closer, it flew to a safer distance to watch me.

Further down the canal I found a stretch that contained many burrows on both sides. There I found about a dozen owls in front of the entrances as well as along the embankments. Burrowing Owls live in colonies, and I was excited to see three of the little "sentinels" saunter out of the same hole. When my intrusion got too close for their comfort, they would bob up and down, often in opposite direction, as if they could not get their dance steps together. What a joy they were to watch!

LONG-EARED OWL
Asio otus

Description: Slender body; dark, vertical bars on throat and breast; long, narrow ear tufts close together

Perching stiffly upright near the trunk of a tree during daylight hours, the Long-eared Owl with its cryptic coloration resembles a branch or stub and may go unnoticed. It only hunts at night, so spotting this bird of prey takes special effort. Measuring thirteen to sixteen inches long, this nocturnal owl is most similar to the Great Horned Owl, but much smaller. The chest markings are in a vertical pattern rather than the horizontal bars characteristic of the Great Horned Owl. Additionally, the more slender Long-eared Owl lacks the white throat bib.

Dark "ear" tufts—which are simply feathers and not really ears at all—are placed close together and are usually conspicuous except during flight when they are folded back. A rusty facial disk enhances the intense, lemon-yellow eyes.

At night during breeding season, listen for the long *hooo's*, sometimes uttered singly, other times in pairs. Its flight appears somewhat uncertain and wavering, yet silently powerful.

Habitat and Diet

The Long-eared Owl is a rare winter and summer resident, even nesting occasionally in mesquites or saguaros. Look for it in mesquite bosques, desert scrub, or along dry washes.

As a nocturnal bird of prey, this skillful hunter feeds mainly on mice. Additionally, it eats other small rodents and will resort to small birds when the former are not available.

Nesting and Mating Behaviors

Typical of most owls, the Long-eared Owl does not usually build its own nest. Because it is one of the earliest breeders, it has many choices and usually settles for an abandoned raven's or hawk's nest. If the stick structure is lined at all, it will contain scarce amounts of grasses, fresh green branches, or feathers.

Every other day, the female lays up to eight eggs, with four or five constituting a normal clutch size. The male does not incubate, but roosts nearby and brings food to the female. The first egg hatches in twenty-one days, and the last one may hatch ten days later. Both parents protect and feed the young; then as maturation demands, they slowly begin teaching the refined skills of nighttime hunting.

SHORT-EARED OWL
Asio flammeus

Description: Medium-sized body; short ear tufts; dark, vertical streaking; dark wrist patches in flight

Unlike most owls of comparable size, the Short-eared Owl is partially diurnal and nests and roosts on the ground. This thirteen- to seventeen-inch-long bird of prey displays large, buffy wing patches and propels itself through the sky with erratic but silent wingbeats. The wingspan reaches three and one-half feet. The "ears" are only tufts of feathers, and are usually inconspicuous. Paler than the Long-eared Owl, the Short-eared has similar mottled brown markings on the upperparts, with vertical streaks extending from the throat and breast down to the belly. Additionally, its face mask is lighter, revealing large, yellow eyes encircled with black plumage. In flight, dark wrist patches are visible on the underwings.

Although the Short-eared Owl is most active at dawn and dusk, it may also be seen during daylight hours, especially on cloudy days. When maturing youngsters begin demanding more food, the parents are forced to accommodate them, often with diurnal hunting. The call is mainly heard during breeding season, and is a sharp and emphatic bark described as *ke-yow*.

Habitat and Diet

This nearly cosmopolitan owl does not often visit the driest portions of the desert, but is a rare transient and winter resident in grasslands and agricultural areas. It is attracted there by mice and other small rodents. Circling low over the earth's surface, a Short-eared Owl may hunt entirely by sound, especially if prey is moving about under the protection of vegetation. Once a victim is discovered, the skillful hunter hovers momentarily, then pounces on the unsuspecting rodent, sinking sharp talons into the delicate flesh. When mice and other rodents are scarce, the Short-eared Owl will eat insects and small birds, especially sparrows.

Nesting and Mating Behaviors

Only a winter resident, the Short-eared Owl is absent in the desert lowlands by mid-March. It moves northward to nest in habitat consisting of meadows, marshes, or forest clearings where it nests on the ground. Uncharacteristic of owls, this one builds its own nest. A slight depression is haphazardly filled with sticks, then scarcely lined with grasses and a few feathers. Every other day an egg is laid, with the total varying between three and eight. The female incubates them while the male hunts and brings food to her. In twenty-one days, the first eggs begin to hatch. Both parents hunt to feed the young and teach them the necessary skills to survive on their own.

RING-NECKED PHEASANT*
Phasianus colchicus

Description: Male—iridescent array of colors; red wattles; white neck ring; long pointed tail. Female—brown with dark mottling; shorter, pointed wings

Dressed in spectacular, iridescent plumage, the male Ring-necked Pheasant appears generally bronze with greens, blues, purples, and reds accentuating his long, sleek body. His glossy head and ear tufts are green or purple, emphasized by the white ring around his neck (occasionally lacking). He has a greenish rump, pale grayish-blue wing coverts, and a red face and wattles. The legs and beak are yellow, and a long, pointed, sweeping tail completes his elegant attire.

The female, following nature's protective plan, is buff overall with dark mottled markings. She has a white line curving under her eye, and her tail is shorter than the male's. She measures twenty-one to twenty-five inches from the tip of her tail to the end of her beak, while the larger male is thirty to thirty-six inches long.

This striking ground bird is a fast runner, bursting into flight almost vertically when a potential enemy approaches. The noisy departure can be startling due to strong, rapid beating of short, rounded wings, which sustain flight for only a short distance. For protection, the Ring-necked Pheasant roosts in trees.

The male's loud, territorial call sounds like *kork-kok* with an emphasis on the first note. He stretches upward and makes a whirring sound with his wings as he crows. Both sexes may be heard giving a hoarse alarm call.

Habitat and Diet

The Ring-necked Pheasant is not endemic to the United States: It was imported here from Asia. One of the several attempts to acclimate it to this country finally succeeded in 1880. Adaptation to a new environment is a slow process, and although the desert is not a frequent habitat of choice, some Ring-necked Pheasants have found favorable conditions where agriculture, especially cultivated grain fields, are interspersed with grasslands, brushy growth, and berry-growing shrubs adjacent to marshy

*Plate 20

areas. Bosque del Apache National Wildlife Refuge and Salton Sea National Wildlife Refuge are great examples. The hardy, gallinaceous pheasant thrives on seeds, insects, and young, tender plants.

Nesting and Mating Behaviors

The Ring-necked Pheasant usually lives in harems where the females exclusively rear the young. The nest is made directly on the ground in a natural, grassy depression, or in a scraped-out hollow casually lined with leaves, grasses, and feathers, and encircled by protective vegetation.

Six to fifteen brownish-olive colored, unmarked eggs are laid in each nest, not always by the same female. Sometime eggs are even dropped right on the ground in the feeding areas.

The female incubates the eggs for twenty-three to twenty-five days. She is slow to fledge when approached, but at the last minute she bursts into flight, landing a short distance away hoping to attract attention to herself, thus distracting a predator from the eggs. The young hatchlings roost on the ground initially, but soon join the adults to sleep in the protective arms of nearby trees.

WILD TURKEY*
Meleagris gallopavo

Description: Dark, iridescent body; bald, blue head; red wattles

The Wild Turkey is divided into "subspecies" and given a variety of names, strictly to describe each in geographic terms. Each one differs slightly, but not enough to be considered a separate species. The most common subspecies of the Southwestern lowlands, the "Rio Grande Turkey," is found mainly in the higher deserts of Texas and New Mexico.

The Wild Turkey is more streamlined than the stereotypical domestic variety, as the former has a longer neck and more slender body with a long tail and long legs. The gobbler measures approximately forty-eight inches high, while the smaller hen is about thirty-six inches high. Its bald, bluish head contrasts with the red wattles—fleshy growths hanging from the throat area. When the male is in courtship or threatening another male, the wattles become noticeably brighter red. The slender body is dusky brown with a magnificent iridescent bronze sheen.

*Plate 20

The sexes are very similar, but generally the gobbler is larger, has a darker and more iridescent body, a lighter head, and a beard. The beard alone is not enough for a safe identification of sex, however, as some females also have beards. Extending from the middle of the chest, like the male's beard, it has a coarse texture similar to a horse's tail. At close range, one can also notice that the male has spurs, which are stiff horn-like growths just a few inches above the foot. The hen clucks to gather her brood, while both sexes make gobbling calls similar to that of the domestic turkey.

Habitat and Diet

Although the Wild Turkey typically inhabits woods, mountain forests, and wooded swamps, the Rio Grande Turkey finds brushy protection where it has access to open grassy areas as well as corn and grain fields. Wild Turkeys in higher elevations forage for acorns, ponderosa pine seeds, berries, etc., but the Rio Grande Turkey depends largely on grass seeds, insects, grain, and green forage for its diet.

Trees and brushy areas are essential for the Wild Turkey for roosting sites. Although ground predators are discouraged at this height, the Wild Turkey is not totally safe from predation. The Great Horned Owl is the greatest threat, and under cover of night it silently moves with lightning speed, sinking its sharp talons deep into the turkey's back. During the daytime, turkeys must not only watch for coyotes, bobcats, and other ground predators, but must also keep a vigil for aerial attacks from eagles. In addition, with an ever-increasing number of human predators, it is no wonder that the Wild Turkey is a wary bird.

Nesting and Mating Behaviors

The mating ritual is a sight to behold, as the male fans his beautiful tail, puffs his body feathers to appear plump, presses his head against his body, expands his wattles, intensifying their redness, and struts about in short, stiff steps. The wing feathers brush against the ground making a *schhhhhhh* sound, further intensified by a similar sound he makes by expelling air. Soon, a repertoire of sounds described as *schhhhhhhhh-vrrrrrrrrrrrrrrrromp-gobble-gobble-gobble-gobble* fill the air.

While promenading, the gobblers actually pay more attention to each other than to the hens. Finally, by squatting or uttering a *yelp*, the female signals a male that she accepts him. The male is polygamous and gathers a harem of hens.

Nesting begins in March and April, and the hatching period for the Rio Grande Turkey is May and June. The female makes the nest on dry ground in a shallow depression of grass or leaves, often under the protective cover of mesquite, lantana, prickly pear, or larger clumps of grass. Here she lays eight to fifteen eggs, which are a buffy white with a smooth shell showing reddish-brown spots. Eggs measure two to two and one-half inches long. The hen does the incubation without the aid of the male, and when she leaves the nest, she covers the eggs with leaves for protection and warmth. Incubation takes twenty-eight days. Soon after hatching, the poults are moving about in search of their own food.

Supplemental Information

As a ground bird, the Wild Turkey seldom ventures far from some source of protective cover. Although it does fly and is even fairly fast and graceful for such a hulking bird, it usually chooses to run from potential danger.

One morning I observed a flock of turkeys strutting through a stretch of barren ground to reach a field of dried corn stalks. They had come from the protection of a dense mesquite bosque and were about halfway to their destination when one wary turkey spotted a coyote lurking by the edge of the cornfield. That turkey immediately took flight, but the rest of the flock retreated on foot with amazing speed until reaching the protection of the mesquites. It has been estimated that a Wild Turkey can run up to eighteen miles per hour.

SCALED QUAIL
Callipepla squamata

Description: Scaly appearance; bushy, white crest

Similarly marked, both the male and female appear as their name indicates: scaly. Black margins of the gray chest and back feathers give them their scaly appearance. Because of the bushy, white crest on the plain, pale bluish-ash head, it has been locally named "cotton top" as well as "blue quail." This ground bird measures ten to twelve inches in length and has a dusky colored bill, brownish legs, and a dark iris.

The female's crest is slightly smaller and appears more buffy. The juvenile is mottled-looking, and the scaly effect begins to appear as it matures.

The Scaled Quail is most often seen on the ground and runs quickly on strong legs, only flying short distances when extreme threats of danger prevail. In fall this species forms large coveys, splitting into pairs the following spring. Its voice is a low, nasally *pay-cos, pay-cos* most often heard during mating season. Each sex calls to locate the other.

Habitat and Diet

Semi-deserts with grasslands, brush, and arroyos house this elegant bird. Because it must have water regularly, it is not found in extremely dry areas. It is often affiliated with sagebrush and is mostly affiliated with the Chihuahuan Desert.

The Scaled Quail is omnivorous, but the majority of its diet consists of grass and weed seeds, and approximately one-fourth includes insects. Even though it frequents cultivated, agricultural areas, we are seeing a decline in population of this species with the disappearance of grasslands.

Nesting and Mating Behaviors

The nest is a scraped-out depression usually well hidden under sagebrush, mesquite, catclaw, cactus, or creosote bushes. The female lays nine to twenty creamy, pear-shaped eggs marked with small brown dots. The shell is smooth with little gloss.

The female does the incubation alone, which takes twenty-one to twenty-three days. The young hatch in a synchronized fashion, then both adults share in rearing the immediately active youngsters. Two or three broods are reared each season.

GAMBEL'S QUAIL*
Callipepla gambelii

Description: Top-knot; chestnut flanks

The Gambel's Quail is predominately a ground bird measuring approximately ten inches long. It is gray with brown-and-white streaking,

*Plate 21

and has a top-knot consisting of several black, flexible feathers that curve forward from the crown. The male has a black patch on a light belly, and a russet crown. The female appears more sedate with her buff coloring.

Habitat and Diet

Coveys of Gambel's Quail can be found in desert thickets where mesquite trees and palos verdes are abundant, or in the midst of cacti forests. Although it is a prized game bird in the Southwest and many are killed each year, the greatest threat to its survival as a species is development and the continual loss of its natural environment.

Not only does the Gambel's Quail need to live in an area with ample food, but during breeding season in the arid desert, it is also extremely important for it to access a reliable water source because the eggs contain such a high percentage of moisture. In addition, when the chicks are hatched, it is essential that they can readily reach some type of water supply. Typical of resident, desert birds, however, the Gambel's Quail gains much of its liquid requirements through food choices; in non-breeding season, this species may survive in very arid conditions. Grass seeds, fruits, and occasional insects are the main diet.

The majority of quail seek the safety of desert shrubs for roosting purposes, but some choose to sleep together in a clump on the ground. This is an interesting protective measure and is very effective when a predator invades their privacy. They suddenly fly in unison, leaving in all directions, totally confusing the intruder. Because they are basically ground birds, they only fly a few yards, then light and quickly camouflage themselves in the brush. When the danger is past, these desert birds communicate in low clucking sounds and again seek each other out for warmth and the security of unity.

Nesting and Mating Behaviors

The Gambel's Quail usually scrapes out a shallow hole underneath a shrub, nesting where it has concealment. The breeding season is mid-May to mid-September when the female lays anywhere from ten to twenty creamy-white eggs with brown speckles. The numbers seem to vary according to the availability of food and the amount of winter moisture. The hen does all of the incubation, but once the eggs are hatched the male aids in the upbringing.

It is always very exciting to find the nests, which are so well camouflaged in the sandy hollows under mesquites and other desert shrubs lining sandy washes. The egg count changes almost on a daily basis, sometimes even decreasing, as snakes and roadrunners are constant predators. It is no wonder that large broods are necessary for this species to survive.

Supplemental Information

Baby Gambel's Quail can walk as soon as they are hatched, even though they are only slightly larger than a bumblebee. In fact, they not only walk, they dart, and are extremely difficult to follow. They freeze instantly at a parent's warning, and in their stillness blend immediately with their surroundings.

It is a natural phenomenon that the baby quail all hatch at approximately the same time, even though the first egg might be laid some twenty days prior to the last one. The female begins incubation with the first egg laid, and some ornithologists believe that the unhatched chicks control the synchronization of their own hatching. In some way, they are able to produce a clicking sound that is, evidently, audible to other unhatched chicks when the eggs are touching one another. Somehow, it communicates to the older eggs to slow the development process and tells the newer eggs to hurry up. Hence, at the end of the incubation process, they are all hatched within approximately twenty minutes of one another. I continue to be in awe of nature's magnificent developmental processes!

California Quail
Callipepla californica

Description: Male—grayish body; chestnut crown; black plume; black and white face patterns. Female—shorter topnotch; plain, olive-gray head; white streaked sides

This exquisitely patterned quail has scaled underparts and brown plumage on its sides, which differentiates it from the Gambel's Quail. The male's crown is chestnut, delineated with white, and sports a glossy, black plume curving forward. His light forehead contrasts with his black face and throat, which are bordered by a white line. Covered with gray to brown plumage, a creamy belly patch, and creamy streaking on the flanks, the plump California Quail measures nine to eleven inches.

The female has a plain olive-gray head, neck, and breast. Her lower parts are intricately scaled, and her sides are streaked with white. Her top-notch is shorter than the male's. The juvenile is similar to the female, but shows only a hint of the scaly pattern.

Predominately a ground bird, this gregarious quail occasionally resorts to short bursts of flight when endangered, or to roost in trees. Additionally, one "sentinel" in a covey may find a high perch from which to survey the surroundings and warn the others of approaching danger. When surprised, these quail fly explosively in different directions to confuse the predator, then scurry into the underbrush and out of sight.

As secretive and quiet as this species can be during the nesting season, it is very loquacious, especially in spring and again in fall when coveys have formed. Its single call, *woook,* sounds almost owl-like, while its longer rendition sounds like *coo-coo-coo* with the accent on the second syllable.

Habitat and Diet

The California Quail is found in arid regions with chaparral, coastal scrub, desert grasslands, and dry washes, usually near a permanent water source. The ranges of the California and Gambel's quails overlap on the western edge of the Mojave Desert and the eastern portion of the Sonoran Desert. Hybrids are known to occur in this zone.

The diet of the California Quail consists of weed and grass seeds and insects. Although it also feeds in grain fields, the loss of natural grasslands has contributed to the decrease in population of this species in the past twenty years. Hunting has also contributed to its decline.

Nesting and Mating Behaviors

Springtime is pleasantly filled with beautiful renditions of mating calls by the California Quail. Competing males chase each other and loudly vocalize their desires while the females gracefully watch the charade. When a couple have mated, however, the chorus subsides and the female begins to lay ten to fifteen creamy-colored eggs in a shallow hollow lined with grasses and dried leaves. The male then calls only to warn of danger or to run other males out of the nesting territory.

Small, brown dots and blotches cover the creamy, oval eggs which are incubated by the female for twenty-one to twenty-three days. The chicks can run almost as soon as they are hatched and can fly from danger in just ten days.

By fall, when the chicks have fully matured, California Quail gather in coveys consisting of up to 200 individuals who jointly display their gregarious nature.

WHITE-WINGED DOVE*
Zenaida asiatica

Description: Large body; white wing patches; white-tipped tail

With April comes the anticipation of the arrival of the largest desert dove, the White-winged Dove. It is easily distinguished from the Mourning Dove, both in size and in feather markings. The White-winged Dove is a larger bird and greatly resembles a pigeon. Both sexes appear the same and exhibit dark gray coloration with a rather short, rounded tail tipped in white. Although the white wing patches can be plainly seen while the bird is on the ground, they become even more obvious while in flight. Although this dove is large and rather clumsy on the ground, it is very graceful in the air.

The White-winged Dove is not only conspicuous because of its size and typical dove-like walk, but it is also very noisy. It makes a rich, heavy cooing sound that can be easily heard, especially in the early mornings and late evenings.

Habitat and Diet

Although the White-winged Dove is essentially a seed eater, its special delight is the juicy red fruit of the saguaro cactus. In season, the giant cactus first puts forth the beautiful white blooms that, as in any other fruit-bearing plants, precede the actual fruit. As it ripens, the "tuna" becomes bright red and is very juicy and sweet. Although many desert birds seek this delicacy, it is predominately the White-winged Dove that can be seen savoring it. The White-winged Dove is very beneficial to the desert, as it plays an extremely important part in the cross-pollination of the unique saguaro cactus.

*Plate 21

The seasonal fruit is one source of moisture for the White-winged Dove. It also apparently receives enough liquid through other food sources, such as berries, because it does not often seem to seek water. This is in contrast to the behavior of the Mourning Dove, which is often observed drinking large amounts of water.

Nesting and Mating Behavior

The favorite nesting site of the White-winged Dove is the dense mesquite, but it will also nest in cholla cacti and other desert shrubs. The nest is very loosely constructed of small twigs and is relatively small considering the size of the bird. There is no lining in the nest, and it appears that one puff of wind could send the twigs whirling through the air. It always amazes me that the casual structure actually stays together long enough to house the nestlings until they are sufficiently mature to take wing.

Supplemental Information

One summer, a smart White-winged Dove made its nest in the "boot" of a saguaro cactus near my house. Although the usual small twigs were still haphazardly placed in the bottom of the cavity, the stable structure of the saguaro itself made a very secure nest. I watched it every day, and approximately two and one-half weeks later I noticed two tiny heads peeking out from underneath the adult. It was in the middle of the monsoon season and other doves were totally exposed to the wrath of wind and rain; but the family in the saguaro appeared quite content because it was protected by the insulated walls of its unique home.

MOURNING DOVE*
Zenaida macroura

Description: Long, pointed tail with slight white edges; black
                 spots on upper wing

Auditorily, the Mourning Dove is easily recognized by its three *coos,* which truly do sound somewhat mournful, thus giving this species its name. It is the most widespread dove of the West and is easily distin-

*Plate 22

guishable from the White-winged Dove, as the former is smaller, has a very pointed tail, a more streamlined body, and white coloring restricted to the edges of its tail. A typical feather is gray toward the bottom, darker gray with black in the middle, and white on the outer tip. The Mourning Dove's general appearance is slate-gray, and it is approximately twelve inches long.

Habitat and Diet

The Mourning Dove can literally be found all over the United States, especially in open country. Because it eats mainly grain and other seeds, it is a ground feeder and a frequent visitor to feeding stations. While eating seeds, it also consumes small pieces of sand and gravel, which help with the digestive process. As it struts around looking for food, it jerks its head back and forth in a manner characteristic of all doves and pigeons.

Nesting and Mating Behaviors

The Mourning Dove is one of the most obvious nesters in early spring and therefore creates a new air of excitement about the desert's bird life. The beginning bird watcher will find this bird fun to observe, as its nest is one of the easiest to find. I most often find nests in cholla cacti, although it is very common to find them in mesquite and palos verdes as well as in the giant arms of saguaros—even occasionally in the "boot" or cavity.

The nest is very casually constructed of small twigs gathered by both sexes. The female does the actual construction of this crude, shallow abode, but both the male and the female take turns in the incubation of the eggs. The male generally incubates during the daylight hours, then the female takes over at dusk.

The nest very seldom contains any grass for lining, and therefore one can often see the eggs through the bottom of the loosely-constructed home. The obvious visibility of the eggs calls immediate attention to the nest.

Breeding can begin as early as December or January, therefore Mourning Doves will have several broods in a season. I have always found two smooth, white eggs, evenly rounded at both ends and without any markings. Although I know that three and perhaps even four eggs can occasionally be found, I, personally, am still searching for that phenomenon.

Supplemental Information

The Mourning Dove appears to need more liquids than some desert birds and is only found where it has reasonable access to water. Because the Mourning Dove is prized as a game bird in some states, it is not uncommon to see a hunter waiting for a limit of doves somewhere near a water source.

Diurnal birds are most active in the early morning hours and again in the late afternoon just before sunset. I have nostalgic memories from my early ranching days of watching Mourning Doves flock to water during these crucial hours. Although the Mourning Dove is most definitely not limited to the desert, it is certainly a welcome year-round resident in my desert yard.

INCA DOVE*
Columbina inca

Description: Slim tail with white edges; scaly upperparts; rufous primaries

The Inca Dove, most easily confused with the slightly smaller Common Ground Dove, is approximately eight inches long and has a long, slim tail that best distinguishes it from the latter. In addition, the Inca Dove has a scaly appearance instead of dark spots on the wings. Like all doves, the pink legs and feet contrast with the gray body. When Inca Doves become aggressive with each other, their change of mood is sharply indicated by pointing their long tails in an abrupt manner.

The most fascinating characteristic of the Inca Dove is its huddling behavior. When roosting, the adults are found side by side, appearing very warm and secure with one another. As the young mature, they will join the adults and form a lineup on the limb. I have also seen several together, on the ground under a bush, where they seemed to be looking for shade. Still, they huddled together as if they needed the warmth produced by their closely grouped bodies.

The Inca's song is a monotonous *coo-hoo,* that seems to be saying "no hope." I don't think that the Inca Dove knows about that translation of

*Plate 22

its two-note call, however, as it always continues moving about, appearing as if it were very hopeful indeed.

Habitat and Diet

This friendliest dove in the Southwest is much smaller than either the White-winged or Mourning dove, and chooses to live in areas that are heavily inhabited with people. It is very rarely seen in the undisturbed natural environment.

This city-dwelling dove can be found easily in parks and back yards, and often along the sidewalks. It is not afraid of people and, in fact, moves about almost underfoot with a great deal of confidence. Its friendly, trusting ways attract the attention of almost every passerby.

Nesting and Mating Behaviors

The breeding season of the Inca Dove is extremely long, beginning in February and extending into June. The nest is constructed by both sexes and is saucer-shaped, typical of other doves' nests. It is smaller, however, and relatively secure for its loose appearance. There is neither insulation nor lining in the nest, so the small dove must turn the two white eggs quite frequently to keep them warm enough to incubate.

Supplemental Information

When I was living in the city, the Inca Dove was one of my frequent visitors. I would sit in the living room by the large window through which I could easily watch the birds. I had several feeding areas as well as a small birdbath located on the ground. At almost any time of the day I could see Inca Doves scratching around in the yard and taking advantage of the water, which they visited quite often. In the spring they would appear in pairs, but in the winter they grouped together in small flocks. The Inca Dove is occasionally seen fussing and bickering with another dove, but usually it is quite sedate. The little dove's gentle disposition always seems to be a calming influence to my own state of being.

COMMON GROUND DOVE
Columbina passerina

Description: Rounded black tail; scaled head and breast; rufous primaries show in flight; spotted wings; orange base to bill

The smallest of the North American doves, the tiny Common Ground Dove measures six and one-half inches long. The male's underparts, sides of head, neck, and forehead are reddish-gray and scaled, while the crown shows bluish-gray. Shoulders, rump, and upper tail-coverts sport a purplish coloration, and the feet are yellow or pink. The iris is orange-red as is the bill, but the tip shows darker. Especially noticeable in flight are the stubby, black tail and rufous primaries. On the ground, the scaly breast and spotted wings are obvious.

Generally, the male appears pink, while the female is grayish-brown. This dainty little dove is very tame, refraining from flight until danger comes incredibly close; then with short, strong wing strokes, it flies surprisingly fast.

Aptly named, this species is most often seen on the ground calling repetitiously *woo-oo, woo-oo.*

Habitat and Diet

In the desert regions of the Southwest, the Common Ground Dove may be found in brushy rangeland or river bottoms lined with mesquite trees or tamarisk. This dove appears to be partly migratory, as larger numbers are apparent from mid-March to October. Seeds are the main source of food, supplemented by insects and seasonal fruit.

Nesting and Mating Behaviors

Courtship behaviors take place on the ground. The patient female watches as the male struts about on short legs, bobbing his head in the typical, quick, pigeon-like fashion while cooing his monotonous song. After coupling, they build the nest in a bush, small tree, or cactus, or occasionally on the ground.

The nest is a flat, skimpy affair made of small twigs and is unlined. Both sexes incubate two, white, unmarked eggs for twelve to fourteen days. Because the breeding season is so long, there are often three or more broods.

YELLOW-BILLED CUCKOO
Coccyzus americanus

Description: Brownish-gray above; rufous wings; black upper mandible; yellow lower mandible; long, dark tail with white spots; white below

This long, slender bird measures eleven to thirteen and one-half inches in length and has a stout, slightly de-curved bill. Its head, back, and tail are deep, grayish-brown, wings are rufous, and underparts are white. From below, the tail shows black with starkly contrasting white spots. The upper mandible is slate-black while the lower one is yellow. The brown eye is accentuated by an obvious yellow eye ring. Both sexes appear similar, but juveniles have less-defined white spots on the tail, a darker bill, and lack the eye ring.

This cuckoo is a cousin to the infamous Greater Roadrunner, but behaviors appear quite different. The roadrunner prefers being on the ground, but the arboreal Yellow-billed Cuckoo is almost never seen there. Hiding among branches and leaves of deciduous trees, this elusive bird is more often heard than seen. Its voice has been described as hollow and wooden with a rapid, throaty *kakakowop-kowlp*.

Habitat and Diet

The Yellow-billed Cuckoo is a common summer resident in dense, riparian growth along main rivers and in fruit groves across the Southwestern lowlands. It arrives in early June to breed in these areas. This cuckoo forages through leafy vegetation and consumes large quantities of hairy caterpillars, which feed heavily on leaves and often destroy the trees. Without a doubt, this species plays a critical role in the natural world. This shy exterminator also eats beetles, grasshoppers, and other insects, as well as berries and grapes.

Nesting and Mating Behaviors

The Yellow-billed Cuckoo arrives in its breeding territory in early June and builds a frail, platform-type nest of sticks occasionally sparsely lined with grasses and leaves. The male usually brings materials to the site, but the female arranges them to her own specifications. Two to four pale, greenish-blue, unmarked eggs can sometimes be seen through the bottom of the nest, and because the saucer is so shallow, some occasionally tumble to the ground.

The female does most of the incubation, and because she lays the eggs at intervals, some hatch before others. The male begins feeding the early arrivals while the female finishes brooding the remaining eggs.

Greater Roadrunner*
Geococcyx californianus

Description: Streaky appearance; crest; long legs; long tail

The most unusual and, therefore, the most easily recognized bird of the Southwest is the Greater Roadrunner. Its size—approximately twenty-two to twenty-four inches in length—makes it easily visible. It is a member of the cuckoo family and is basically a ground bird, flying only to flee to safety. The name is an appropriate indicator of its behavior, as the roadrunner has been clocked running up to fifteen miles per hour.

Although the Greater Roadrunner, New Mexico's State Bird, can be very conspicuous, it can also seem to disappear right in front of your eyes. Because it is agile and has sharp instincts and reflexes, this bird quickly maneuvers itself to a safe distance on the ground, and then camouflages itself in the shade of a bush; its streaky black, white, and gray coloring makes it almost impossible to see.

Both sexes appear identical in their decor. Along with a streaky appearance, the roadrunner's long tail is almost the same length as its body. Its tail feathers are dark and gradually widen toward the tips, which are highlighted with white. The roadrunner's long legs are extremely strong, and its feet have four toes each, two pointing forward and two backward. The track is a very distinct "X" left in the soft dirt.

*Plate 22

PIED-BILLED GREBE, *Podilymbus podiceps* (breeding plumage)

EARED GREBE, *Podiceps nigricollis* (breeding plumage)

WESTERN GREBE, *Aechmophorus occidentalis* (breeding plumage)

Unless denoted male or female, sexes are similar.

PLATE I

BROWN PELICAN, *Pelecanus occidentalis* (breeding plumage)

BROWN PELICAN,
Pelecanus occidentalis
(immature)

**DOUBLE-CRESTED
CORMORANT,**
Phalacrocorax auritus

PLATE 2

GREAT BLUE HERON, *Ardea herodias*

GREAT EGRET,
Casmerodius albus

SNOWY EGRET, *Egretta thula*

PLATE 3

CATTLE EGRET,
Bubulcus ibis

GREEN HERON,
Butorides striatus

**BLACK-CROWNED
NIGHT-HERON,**
Nycticorax nycticorax

**BLACK-CROWNED
NIGHT-HERON,**
Nycticorax nycticorax (immature)

PLATE 4

WHITE-FACED IBIS, *Plegadis chihi*

LESSER SNOW GOOSE, *Chen caerulescens*

PLATE 5

CANADA GOOSE, *Branta canadensis*

GREEN-WINGED TEAL, *Anas crecca* (male)

MALLARD, *Anas platyrhynchos* (male)

PLATE 6

NORTHERN PINTAIL, *Anas acuta* (male)

CINNAMON TEAL, *Anas cyanoptera* (male)

NORTHERN SHOVELER, *Anas clypeata* (male)

PLATE 7

AMERICAN WIGEON, *Anas americana* (male)

RING-NECKED DUCK, *Aythya collaris* (male)

RUDDY DUCK, *Oxyura jamaicensis*
(male, breeding plumage)

RUDDY DUCK,
Oxyura jamaicensis
(male, non-breeding plumage)

PLATE 8

AMERICAN COOT, *Fulica americana*

**GREATER
SANDHILL CRANE,**
Grus canadensis

PLATE 9

KILLDEER, *Charadrius vociferus*

BLACK-NECKED STILT, *Himantopus mexicanus*

AMERICAN AVOCET,
Recurvirostra americana
(breeding plumage)

PLATE 10

GREATER YELLOWLEGS, *Tringa melanoleuca* (breeding plumage)

SOLITARY SANDPIPER, *Tringa solitaria*

WILLET, *Catoptrophorus semipalmalus* (breeding plumage)

WILLET, *Catoptrophorus semipalmalus* (non-breeding plumage)

PLATE 11

LONG-BILLED CURLEW, *Numeius americanus*

LEAST SANDPIPER, *Calidris minutilla*

PLATE 12

HEERMANN'S GULL,
Larus heermanni

RING-BILLED GULL, *Larus delawarensis*

BLACK VULTURE,
Coragyps atratus

PLATE 13

TURKEY VULTURE,
Cathartes aura

OSPREY, *Pandion haliaetus*

OSPREY, *Pandion haliaetus*

PLATE 14

BALD EAGLE,
Haliaeetus leucocephalus

COOPER'S HAWK,
Accipiter cooperii

COOPER'S HAWK,
Accipiter cooperii (immature)

PLATE 15

HARRIS' HAWK, *Parabuteo unicinctus*

HARRIS' HAWK,
Parabuteo unicinctus
(immature)

SWAINSON'S HAWK, *Buteo swainsoni*

PLATE 16

RED-TAILED HAWK,
Buteo jamaicensis

RED-TAILED HAWK,
Buteo jamaicensis

CRESTED CARACARA, *Polyborus plancus*

PLATE 17

AMERICAN KESTREL,
Falco sparverius

PEREGRINE FALCON,
Falco peregrinus

WESTERN SCREECH-OWL,
Otus kennicotti

WESTERN SCREECH-OWLS,
Otus kennicotti (immature)

PLATE 18

GREAT HORNED OWL, *Bubo virginianus*

ELF OWL,
*Micrathene
whitneyi*

PLATE 19

BURROWING OWLS, *Athene cunicularia*

RING-NECKED PHEASANT, *Phasianus colchicus*

WILD TURKEY, *Meleagris gallopavo*

PLATE 20

GAMBEL'S QUAIL,
Callipepla gambelii (male)

GAMBEL'S QUAIL,
Callipepla gambelii (female)

**WHITE-WINGED
DOVE,**
Zenaida asiatica

PLATE 21

MOURNING DOVE, *Zenaida macroura*

INCA DOVE, *Columbina inca*

GREATER ROADRUNNER, *Geococcyx californianus*

PLATE 22

BELTED KINGFISHER,
Ceryle alcyon (male)

GREEN KINGFISHER, *Chloroceryle americana* (female)

ACORN WOODPECKER,
Melanerpes formicivorus

PLATE 23

GILA WOODPECKER,
Melanerpes uropygialis
(male)

GILA WOODPECKER, *Melanerpes uropygialis* (female)

RED-NAPED SAPSUCKER,
Sphrapicus nuchalis
(male)

PLATE 24

GILDED FLICKER, *Colaptes cheycoides* (male)

BLACK PHOEBE,
Sayornis nigricans

SAY'S PHOEBE, *Sayornis saya*

PLATE 25

VERMILION FLYCATCHER, *Pyrocephalus rubinus* (male)

ASH-THROATED FLYCATCHER, *Myiarchus cinerascens*

CASSIN'S KINGBIRD, *Tyrannus vociferans*

PLATE 26

WESTERN KINGBIRD, *Tyrannus verticalis*

HORNED LARK, *Eremophila alpestris*

PURPLE MARTIN, *Progne subis* (male)

PLATE 27

BARN SWALLOW,
Hirundo rustica

GRAY-BREASTED JAY, *Aphelocoma ultramarina*

CHIHUAHUAN RAVEN, *Corvus cryptoleucus*

PLATE 28

COMMON RAVEN,
Corvus corax

VERDIN, *Auriparus flaviceps*

CACTUS WREN, *Campylorhynchus brunneicapillus*

PLATE 29

WESTERN BLUEBIRD,
Sialia mexicana
(male)

WESTERN BLUEBIRD, *Sialia mexicana* (female)

MOUNTAIN BLUEBIRD,
Sialia currucoides
(male)

PLATE 30

NORTHERN MOCKINGBIRD, *Minus polygottos*

CURVE-BILLED THRASHER,
Toxostoma curvirostre

PHAINOPEPLA,
Phainopepla nitens (male)

PHAINOPEPLA,
Phainopepla nitens (female)

PLATE 31

LOGGERHEAD SHRIKE,
Lanius ludovicianus

EUROPEAN STARLING,
Sturnus vulgaris

YELLOW-RUMPED WARBLER, *Dendroica coronata* (male)

PLATE 32

WILSON'S WARBLER, *Wilsonia pusilla* (male)

WESTERN TANAGER, *Piranga ludoviciana* (male)

NORTHERN CARDINAL, *Cardinalis cardinalis* (male)

NORTHERN CARDINAL, *Cardinalis cardinalis* (female)

PLATE 33

PYRRHULOXIA,
Cardinalis sinuatus
(male)

PYRRHULOXIA,
Cardinalis sinuatus
(female)

BLACK-HEADED GROSBEAK, *Pheucticus melanocephalus* (male)

PLATE 34

LAZULI BUNTING, *Passerina amoena* (male)

GREEN-TAILED TOWHEE, *Pipilo chlorurus*

SPOTTED TOWHEE, *Pipilo maculatus* (male)

PLATE 35

CANYON TOWHEE, *Pipilo fucus*

ABERT'S TOWHEE, *Pipilo aberti*

LARK BUNTING,
Calamospiza melanocorys
(male, breeding plumage)

LARK BUNTING,
Calamospiza melanocorys
(female, non-breeding plumage)

PLATE 36

WHITE-CROWNED SPARROW, *Zonotrichia leucophrys*

RED-WINGED BLACKBIRD, *Agelaius phoeniceus*

PLATE 37

EASTERN MEADOWLARK,
Sturnella magna

WESTERN MEADOWLARK,
Sturnella neglecta

YELLOW-HEADED BLACKBIRD, *Xanthocephalus xanthocephalus*

PLATE 38

BREWER'S BLACKBIRD, *Euphagus cyanocephalus*

BRONZED COWBIRD, *Molothrus aeneus*

HOODED ORIOLE, *Icterus cucullatus* (male)

PLATE 39

BULLOCK'S ORIOLE, *Icterus bullockii* (male)

SCOTT'S ORIOLE, *Icterus parisorum* (male)

HOUSE FINCH,
Carpodacus mexicanus (male)

HOUSE SPARROW,
Passer domesticus (male)

PLATE 40

The appearance of the roadrunner's head is unique with its long, curved beak and a crest that moves up and down in congruence with other displayed "body language." Behind the eye is a bare patch of skin that, with proper lighting, flashes the near-iridescence of red, blue, and white.

Habitat and Diet

The Greater Roadrunner can be found in cactus deserts or in dry, open country with various types of brush for cover. Its diet consists mainly of lizards, grasshoppers and other insects . . . and snakes, even rattlesnakes. The roadrunner will also eat mice, small birds, and eggs, especially quail eggs.

Nesting and Mating Behavior

The nesting season begins in March or April. The nest is a large durable structure, fifteen to twenty inches in diameter, and is constructed of sticks from mesquite or palo verde trees. The nest is situated three to twelve feet off the ground and, considering its size, is relatively difficult to spot.

The female lays four to seven eggs and begins incubation as soon as the first is laid. Both parents aid in incubation, which takes seventeen to nineteen days. The eggs are often laid several days apart, and the young hatch at various intervals. It is common for one young roadrunner to be mature enough to leave its abode while a younger sibling is still being fed in the nest. The fledglings grow very quickly, and it isn't long before they look very similar to the adults in size and markings. They give themselves away, however, when they flutter their wings and stand with their mouths open waiting for the adult to bring them their dinner.

Supplemental Information

I always look forward to my encounters with the roadrunner because I almost invariably find myself smiling. This feathered creature truly seems to have a way of non-verbally communicating with a flick of its tail, which seems to portray confidence; the uplifting of its crest, which suggests the raising of an eyebrow; and the continual cocking of its head, which implies curiosity. One day I found myself talking to one aloud as I often do with my little dog, who usually just looks lovingly back at me. I was very surprised when the roadrunner actually began to respond to me with guttural noises.

I have discovered that the Greater Roadrunner has a variety of sounds, none of which resembles the "beep, beep" sound emitted by the heroic cartoon character. Sometimes it makes a soft growling sound, and other times a rapid loud noise caused by the drumming of its mandibles. Soft sounds can often be heard as this magnificent creature fluffs its feathers up to twice its normal size and relaxes with the warmth of the sun.

LESSER NIGHTHAWK
Chordeiles acutipennis

Description: Mottled gray-brown; white wingbar near tip

The Lesser Nighthawk measures eight to nine inches long—making it smaller than the Common Nighthawk—and has shorter and more rounded wings. Its overall appearance consists of intricate designs of mottled grays and browns with pale underparts. The male has a white tail band, throat patch, and wing bar. The tail band is absent on the female, and her throat patch and wing bar appear more buffy. Juveniles resemble the female but may lack a prominant wing bar. The adults' wing patches are closer to the tips of the wings than those of the Common Nighthawk. Lesser Nighthawks may be seen flying low, especially in crepuscular light. Although the voice of this night creature is low and soft, it resonates with a hypertrilling sound resembling a toad.

Habitat and Diet

The Lesser Nighthawk is a common summer resident of the arid Southwestern lowlands and prefers areas near dry washes, grasslands, or agricultural fields where insects abound. It is a migratory species and does not hibernate like its cousin, the Common Poorwill. Throughout the deserts, this species is fairly abundant from March to September.

Look around agricultural areas, ponds, or where night lights attract insects. Dusk and dawn are the best times to see this active feeder, but it often feeds well into the morning. It flies closer to the ground when hunting than does the Common Nighthawk. Watch its large mouth scoop in several insects at a time.

Nesting and Mating Behaviors

The male's courtship display takes place on the ground as he moves about on tiny feet, mostly fluttering his wings for mobility and balance. His soft, prolonged call is accompanied by motions displaying his bright, white throat patch. The female lays two glossy, slightly speckled, grayish eggs directly on the ground. No nest is apparent, but it is usually in a sandy area containing small pebbles and located near a bush. The female does the incubation, which takes eighteen to nineteen days. Semiprecocial young may move about and leave the nest soon after hatching.

Supplemental Information

While hiking down a dry wash near my house one morning in mid-May, I unknowingly flushed a Lesser Nighthawk right from her nest. It did not occur to me until that evening what I had done. The next morning I cautiously approached the same area and there she was perfectly still and completely camouflaged by the similarly patterned ground.

COMMON NIGHTHAWK
Chordeiles minor

Description: Patterned grayish-brown; white wing bar near joint

Intricately patterned with shades of blacks, browns, grays, and whites, the eight-and-one-half to ten-inch long Common Nighthawk is larger than the Lesser Nighthawk. Additionally, the Common Nighthawk usually flies higher than its cousin. The long wings are pointed and highlighted with a white band appearing closer to the joint than that of the Lesser Nighthawk. The former's tail is forked, and the male has a white band near the end. His throat is white while the female's is buff colored. Juveniles have no distinct throat patch.

This bird's cryptic coloration is very effective because while roosting on the ground or on low branches it is hard to spot. This species is most often seen high in the sky at dusk, but is more diurnal than other nighthawks so it may be seen flying in daylight. A distinctive, nasal sound described as *peert* or *spee-ik* is heard as it darts through the sky.

Habitat and Diet

A rare transient to the arid regions of the Southwest, the Common Nighthawk may overlap territories with the Lesser Nighthawk in elevated grasslands near mountain ranges. It winters exclusively in South America, most commonly in the pampas of Argentina, and will not be found anywhere in the Southwestern United States until the end of May.

An insect diet provides the fuel for this active bird. Flying high in the sky, this nighthawk rids the environment of many pests by scooping in a mouthful at a time.

Nesting and Mating Behaviors

The male's courtship display is largely performed in the air where he dives from great heights, continually swooping down in front of the female. Finally he ends the show by singing his vibrant tune with husky intonations.

There is no time wasted on a nest. Directly on the ground the female lays two creamy eggs speckled with grays and browns blending perfectly with the gravely surroundings. She incubates them for nineteen days, always keeping the sun at her back. Semiprecocial young may move about and are capable of leaving the nest soon after hatching. This enables them to escape the vulnerability of their ground nest.

Common Poorwill
Phalaenoptilus nuttallii

Description: Mottled gray-brown body; white-tipped, short, rounded tail; lacks white on wings; broad, white band on dark throat

Smallest of the nightjars, the Common Poorwill measures seven to eight and one-half inches and sports variegated plumage ranging from gray, brown, and buff to black. A white collar contrasts with the black throat and mottled breast, while the underparts blend into a lighter, brownish gray. The short, rounded tail is tipped with white, and is more noticeable in males. Large eyes, small beaks, short legs, wide mouth, and whiskers characterize this species.

Camouflaged attire is nature's protection for this nocturnal bird who seemingly vanishes into its surroundings while sleeping during the day. Roosting directly on the ground or perching horizontally on a low branch, the Common Poorwill is very difficult to spot. At night, however, the bird becomes active and can be identified by its loud, repetitious call, *poor-will, poor-will.*

Habitat and Diet

The Common Poorwill is more abundant during the summer, when it is found in barren, arid regions, in open brush; dry, rocky hillsides; and chaparral. At night it is often seen in the beams of car headlights along dirt roads. It winters in small numbers in the Southwestern lowlands and has even been found hibernating in the Southern California desert. Surviving mainly on insects, the Common Poorwill models the behaviors characteristic of flycatchers. From its ground perch, it flies up to catch a night-flying insect, then returns to the same location. Its wide mouth is tailor-made for scooping in flying insects.

Nesting and Mating Behaviors

The Common Poorwill does not even attempt to construct a nest. Instead, the female lays her eggs directly on the ground in a sandy or gravelly spot, usually close to a bush. The two, oval, white eggs sometimes appear to have a pinkish tint and are typically unmarked. Both sexes incubate the eggs and bring insects to the young until they mature enough to fend for themselves. Semiprecocial young often leave the nest soon after hatching, and the parents feed them on the ground until they mature enough to fly.

Supplemental Information

The term "goatsucker," a common family name, came about in ancient times because it was thought that these large-mouthed, nocturnal birds sucked the udders of goats, causing them to go blind. In addition, the term "nightjar," European in origin, became another common name because the seldom-seen bird "jarred the night" with its loud call.

BUFF-COLLARED NIGHTJAR
Caprimulgus ridgwai

Description: Mottled gray-brown body; tawny collar; bristled gape

Slightly larger than the Common Poorwill, the Buff-collared Nightjar measures eight and three-quarters of an inch long and has rounded wings. It has patterns of mottled gray-brown coloration similar to the Whip-poor-will, but additionally has a buff collar, which is the distinguishing feature. Tiny feet and long facial bristles are characteristic of all nightjars.

Also known as Ridgeway's Whip-poor-will, this nightjar is a nocturnal feeder, snatching insects on the wing with its wide mouth. During the daytime, this species is very difficult to spot because of its intricately patterned and camouflaged markings, which enable it to blend so perfectly with the surroundings while perching lengthwise on a branch, a rocky ledge, or simply on the ground. The best way to find it is by sound. Listen for a series of unbird-like notes accelerating in pitch, and ending with an explosive *cukacheea,* seemingly jarring the night.

Habitat and Diet

The Buff-collared Nightjar is a rare and local inhabitant of southwestern New Mexico and southeastern Arizona, where it was first noted in the 1960s in Guadalupe Canyon. Habitat includes arid desert regions with grasslands and chaparral. It favors canyons and dry washes near major mountain ranges.

Insectivorous, this nocturnal nightjar spends its waking hours literally scooping up insects. From a perch on the ground, this unusual bird darts upward after prey.

Nesting and Mating Behaviors

The Buff-collared Nightjar nests in rocky slopes along brushy, arid hillsides.

Vaux's Swift
Chaetura vauxi

Description: Dark overall; slightly lighter underneath; cigar-
shaped body

The Vaux's Swift is our smallest swift, measuring four to four and one-
half inches long. Typical of all swifts, its wings are extremely long and
pointed, contrasting with a shorter body and an especially short, stubby
tail. Plumage appears dark overall except the throat and upper breast,
which are lighter. The bill is extremely small, but like a swallow has a
large mouth.

This little species clings easily to the sides of vertical surfaces somewhat like a woodpecker, but never perches on branches. It spends hours
in the air alternating between gliding and rapid flapping. While hunting
insects on the wing, it may be heard twittering or chippering with long,
rapid notes; otherwise, it is fairly silent especially during migration. At
dusk it is often mistaken for a bat.

Habitat and Diet

The Vaux's Swift is an uncommon transient throughout the lowlands
and is often seen near or over water.

This species is extremely valuable in maintaining nature's balance
because it dines entirely on flying insects. With long wings it darts
through the sky, scooping in insects with its large mouth. This tiny exterminator may fly hundreds of miles in the process of devouring scores of
flying insects.

Nesting and Mating Behaviors

For breeding purposes, the Vaux's Swift moves to higher elevations and
nests in hollow trees, affixing a saucer-shaped platform made of twigs or
pine needles to the inner wall of a cavity. Mucilage secreted from the sali-
vary gland is used as a glue to form the nest and attach it to the cavity wall.

The female lays three to six unmarked, creamy-white eggs. When the
chicks first hatch they are naked and are fed in the nest for about two
weeks. When fledglings first venture out of the little abode, they cling to
the inner wall of the cavity for security. Within a few days the fledglings
are ready to go outside.

WHITE-THROATED SWIFT
Aeronautes saxatalis

Description: Orca-patterned body: white throat; black-and-white belly; long, narrow wings; deeply forked tail

Larger than the Vaux's Swift, the White-throated Swift measures six to seven inches long and appears similar to a swallow. Its upperparts are black while the underparts are a striking combination of black and white, distinguishing it from other swifts. The long, pointed wings assure aerodynamic excellence. They are often seen flying in groups darting one way then the other, with the forked tail acting as a rudder.

This agile acrobat of the sky does not perch on horizontal branches, but clings to vertical surfaces instead, and like a woodpecker uses its tail for support and stabilization. Its extremely short bill, large mouth, and relatively large eyes are typical of all swifts.

The song of the White-throated Swift, louder than the Vaux's Swift, is a shrill, repetitive *je je je je je*. It is commonly seen near the face of steep cliffs and darts through the sky while calling incessantly.

Habitat and Diet

The White-throated Swift is a common summer resident and transient as well as an uncommon winter resident in canyons of the Southwestern lowlands.

This speedy swift feeds exclusively on insects captured on the wing, often scooping several into its large mouth at once. Not only does it feed in this fashion, but also drinks water on the wing as well. Zooming downward from a high flight zone, it swoops above the water's surface and scoops in water without the slightest hesitation.

Nesting and Mating Behaviors

The White-throated Swift is truly a master aerial wizard, even mating on the wing. Darting back and forth in the dance of the heavens, a pair of swifts will suddenly seize each other and drop a hundred feet in a whirlwind fall, parting just above the earth's surface.

The nest is made of fine grasses and feathers molded into a basket shape. It is glued to a cliff or wall of a cave using the bird's saliva as the adhesive. The female lays three to six unmarked white eggs. When the nestlings hatch, both adults are continually at work catching insects for the ravenous youngsters.

HUMMINGBIRDS

Description: Black-chinned—black chin; purple collar; white breast.
Anna's—red crown and throat.
Costa's—violet gorget and helmet.
Rufous—rufous back; red-orange gorget

The Hummingbird is not only the smallest bird in the world, it is also one of the most intriguing. Depending on taxonomical classification, there are between three hundred and twenty and three hundred and forty species of hummingbirds. All of the sixteen regularly occurring species in the United States are found in the Southwest—southeastern Arizona, southwestern New Mexico, southern California, and the Big Bend region of Texas. In the lower deserts and grasslands, four species most often occur: the Black-chinned Hummingbird is seen only in spring and summer; the Costa's Hummingbird is seen year round, but primarily in winter; the Anna's Hummingbird is a permanent resident in towns; and the Rufous Hummingbird is a spring and fall migrant, seen primarily in the fall on its way southward from its breeding territories.

The **BLACK-CHINNED HUMMINGBIRD** (*Archilochus alexandri*) is approximately three-and-one-half inches long, and the male has an obvious black chin with a purple collar and obvious white breast. The female is green above with a whitish throat.

The **ANNA'S HUMMINGBIRD** (*Calypte anna*) is three-and-one-half to four inches. The male distinguishes himself by being the only hummingbird with a red crown as well as a red throat. The female has a spotted throat, which distinguishes her from the female Costa's.

The next to the smallest Hummingbird, measuring only three-and-one-half inches, is the **COSTA'S HUMMINGBIRD** (*Calypte costae*). The male is green above with a violet gorget and helmet. The female is gray-green above and white beneath, some showing a small light-red patch on the throat.

The three-and-one-half inch **RUFOUS HUMMINGBIRD** (*Selasphorus rufus*) is the only hummingbird with a rufous back. The throat is red-orange and underparts are reddish-brown. The female has a green back as do most other female Hummingbirds, but also has light rufous on her sides and the outside edges of her tail.

The smallest of all Hummingbirds is approximately two and one-quarter inches in length, and the largest is eight and one-half inches. Dazzling iridescent purple, red, and green adorn the males, while the females are usually greenish above and white underneath. The hummingbird has a long, needle-like bill for probing into flowers, and an incredibly long tongue, which protrudes beyond the bill in order to secure nectar.

The hummingbird's flight pattern is the most unique among birds because it is the only bird that can fly backward. It can also hover in the air like a helicopter, fly sideways, and fly in small circles. Wing movements are so fast that they simply appear to be a blur while the hummingbird feeds from flower to flower. This means of feeding plays an important role in nature by contributing to the intricate system of pollination.

When feeding, the hummingbird usually hovers above the blossom and very seldom perches. Tiny feet and legs are so weak that it lands only where it can grasp a small perch with its delicate toes—not on the ground.

The hummingbird's small size portrays a false image of vulnerability. Actually, these little creatures are extremely assertive and surprisingly hardy. They are very territorial and dive-bomb each other at feeding stations. The males attack one another with sharp, intricate claws, but very seldom create any serious injuries. It appears that the sharply protruding beak could be a weapon, but the real function is to extract nectar from the flowering plant.

Habitat and Diet

Although a few hummingbirds are year-round residents, the majority migrate to warmer territories in late September and early October. They return when warmer temperatures and moisture bring forth the spring blossoms and insects. Prior to migration flights, the hummingbird can be seen feeding almost continually. For long distance, non-stop flights, the amazing little bird can store fat as up to fifty percent of its body weight.

These long journeys are not uncommon, and some species even cross the Gulf of Mexico, which extends about five hundred miles. The hummingbird has an extremely high metabolism and must eat often. Studies have shown that it eats as frequently as three hundred times per day. Just before dusk, the hummingbird stores as much sucrose as possible in its little body in order to survive through the night. A trance-like state and a slower metabolism also reduce need for food during resting hours.

The hummingbird is very gentle and is often seen in close proximity to people. Its natural diet consists of flower nectar, pollen, and small insects, but is also easily attracted to feeders filled with sugar water.

Nesting and Mating Behaviors

Hummingbirds are especially fun to observe during the nesting season. From the beginning of the mating dance to the time the fledglings leave the nest, every movement is deliberate and meaningful. The male expends all his energies wooing the female with his exquisite courtship flight.

I witnessed this magnificent performance as an Anna's male darted back and forth in front of the female, who was easily visible on a tiny mesquite branch that had not yet leafed out. It appeared as if the excited male was playing with the sunlight in order to illuminate his splendid iridescent feathers. After his deliberate show of colors, he suddenly climbed fifty feet in the air, then nose-dived quickly downward, stopping in mid-air directly in front of the female.

After copulation, the male leaves, and the female devotes herself to the tasks of building the nest, incubating the eggs, and rearing the young by herself. The nest itself is an architectural wonder. Soft materials are intricately woven together by tiny thread-like substances. The inside of the nest is delicately lined with feathers, and the whole structure is attached to a fork in a tree. From below, it simply appears to be a knot on a branch.

Like the hummingbird, the egg is the smallest in the world. In proportion to the bird itself, however, it is one of the largest. There are always two white eggs, which take approximately fifteen days to hatch. The baby birds snuggle together in the nest, and on a windy day they appear to be aboard a tiny vessel in a rough sea.

As the young mature, the adult female brings them food and keeps close vigilance from a nearby branch. The young stay in the nest from two to three weeks, and when they fledge they never return. The dedicated female stays with them for a few days until they demonstrate the skills necessary to survive in the world on their own.

Supplemental Information

Once, a friend and I were able to closely examine a hummingbird's needle-shaped beak. We found the tiny bird stuck in a glass of sugarwater. At first we thought she was dead, but soon we could see her breathing and blinking her tiny black eyes. Very gently we removed the delicate little creature and discovered that she was so sticky she could not move her wings in order to fly.

With extreme care we washed the sticky substance from her feathers, then took her out on the deck and placed the fragile bird on the rim of a lantern where she perched on the edge in obvious fright. Soon, tiny wings began fluttering until she was dry; then she darted away and was quickly out of our sight. Besides being impressed with the bird's obvious delicate condition and size, I was overwhelmed at the flexibility of her beak. I had always imagined the needle-like structure was as rigid as a needle. Instead, it was extremely pliable and obviously not intended for self-defense.

BELTED KINGFISHER*
Ceryle alcyon

Description: Bluish-gray above, white below; bluish breast band; prominent shaggy crest. Female—additional rufous breast band

Our largest kingfisher, the Belted Kingfisher measures eleven to fourteen and one-half inches in length. Both sexes are bluish-gray above, including the head and shaggy crest. Both have a slate-blue breast band and white underparts, but the female has an additional rufous band on her belly. A white throat makes the large head even more noticeable. Juveniles have rusty spots instead of the breast band.

*Plate 23

This stocky, short-legged bird has a dark, straight, heavy bill, a dark eye, and a small white patch on the lore. Although rather conspicuous when perched on a branch over water, its loud, rattling call also helps in locating this species.

The Belted Kingfisher is usually solitary except in mating season, and it is quite territorial year round. At fishing holes, it aggressively drives away approaching competitors.

Habitat and Diet

The Belted Kingfisher is a common to uncommon transient and winter resident to lakes, ponds, and rivers where fishing is profitable. It even frequents temporary water holes on the desert.

As indicated by this bird's name, fish is the main diet and a skilled fisherbird it is! From a perch that may be fifty feet high, or from a hovering position twenty feet above the water, the keen-sighted kingfisher high-dives into the water and spears fish with its sharp bill or seizes one between its mandibles. Back on the original perch, the kingfisher kills and tenderizes its catch by repeatedly beating the victim against a branch. Then, with a gentle toss into the air, the fish is turned and swallowed head first. Crawfish, frogs, beetles, and locusts also serve as sustaining morsels.

Nesting and Mating Behaviors

With strong feet, the Belted Kingfisher digs a horizontal cave in a sandy bank. On the bare floor at the end of the tunnel, the female lays five to eight glossy, unmarked eggs, which both sexes incubate for twenty-three to twenty-four days. When one bird approaches the nesting site to take its turn brooding the eggs, it calls from a nearby perch. The one on the eggs leaves so that the mate can enter the hollow.

The young feed on a rotational basis. Each time a parent brings food, a different nestling appears at the entrance to take its turn.

GREEN KINGFISHER*
Chloroceryle americana

Description: Small body; very long bill in proportion to its body;
metallic green upperparts; slight crest; white
underparts; white collar. Male–rufous chest-band.
Female–green chest spots

The Green Kingfisher, measuring seven to eight and one-half inches
long, is the smallest kingfisher in the Southwestern lowlands. Deep,
metallic green plumage adorns the upperparts, and there are white spots
on the wings. The underparts are white; the male has a rufous chest-band
while the female sports dark green spots on her breast in the form of a
band. Both have dark green spots on their flanks and a conspicuous
white collar. (Notice that it is the male who has the rufous chest-band
while it is the female Belted Kingfisher who wears this adornment.) Look
for the white outer tailfeathers, which are visible in flight.

This sparrow-sized kingfisher has a large crested head with a stout,
long bill comparable in size to the bill of a flicker.

Habitat and Diet

Birders delight in viewing this species in the Southwestern lowlands
because it is a rare but increasingly common resident found in southern
Arizona. Abundant in Mexico, a few have wandered north of the border
to excite many birders.

It may be found along small streams where trees provide shade and
branches extend low over the water. This iridescent green jewel perches
with eyes fixed on the water, ready to plunge after prey. Fish are the primary target, but this kingfisher also eats crawfish, beetles, locusts, and
other insects.

Nesting and Mating Behaviors

The Green Kingfisher nests high in the banks of rivers in a burrow it
digs with strong feet. This tunnel may be up to three feet long and is usually about two inches in diameter. The female lays three to six glossy,

*Plate 23

white, unmarked eggs on the barren floor at the end of the burrow. Both sexes incubate the eggs, but the female tends to this task alone at night. Both adults bring food to the nestlings and teach them the artful task of spotting and catching their own prey.

ACORN WOODPECKER*
Melanerpes formicivorus

Description: Clownish black, white, and red head; male–red crown; white forecrown. Female–smaller red crown patch; black forehead

Black, white, and red adorn this noisy eight to nine-and-one-half-inch-long woodpecker. A clown-like face with black around its bill contrasting with the white face and throat, and a red crown with a black nape distinguish the Acorn Woodpecker from other woodpeckers. (The Red-headed Woodpecker has a completely red head.) The white iris around the black pupil calls attention to the eyes. Its back, wings, and tail are black, the breast is white, and underparts sport bold, black streaking. A white rump and outer wing patches are conspicuous in flight. The sexes are similar, but the female has a smaller bill, less red on the crown, and a black forecrown.

The Acorn Woodpecker is a sociable species often seen in small groups. A variety of musical calls include *wake-up, wake-up* or *Ja-cob, Ja-cob.* Also, typical of many woodpeckers, it makes drum-like sounds by hammering its bill against dead limbs.

Habitat and Diet

The Acorn Woodpecker's main habitat is among large oaks in mountains throughout the Southwest, but a few occasionally wander into the lowlands in such areas as Organ Pipe Cactus National Monument and the Colorado River Valley. Most mountain birds that wander into the desert come during winter months, but the Acorn Woodpecker may show up in May and stay several months.

Aptly named, the Acorn Woodpecker prefers acorns for food. It even stores them for winter by drilling individual and perfectly sized holes,

*Plate 23

usually in soft, dead pines, where it inserts one acorn per hole. (Fence poles or telephone poles are also used for storage units.) In the desert, however, sap is sought as are insects such as grasshoppers, beetles, and ants. It also eats nuts such as pecans, almonds, and walnuts when available. This variable diet allows it to wander away from the acorn habitat. We are sometimes surprised to see a species seemingly out of its normal range, but when birds migrate to wintering territories, they adapt to many changes, sometimes including a complete change of diet.

Nesting and Mating Behaviors

Acorn Woodpeckers are not known to nest in the desert areas. They return to pine-oak forests where they drill nesting holes, usually in dead oak branches or ponderosa pines. Nesting communally, all members participate in excavating the hole, then take turns feeding and caring for the young. The entrance hole is only about one and one-half inches in diameter, and no lining is used in the cavity. The female lays four to six pure white eggs, which are incubated by both sexes for fourteen days.

Supplemental Information

Dead trees are essential for the survival of the Acorn Woodpecker. (Many other species also depend on them.) I have a cabin in the White Mountains of Arizona and have had numerous offers from well-meaning neighbors to help me by cutting down the dead ponderosa pines that stand on my property. They are amazed when I politely refuse the offer, explaining that they are homes for many bird species.

GILA WOODPECKER*
Melanerpes uropygialis

Description: Black and white striped back; plain face and underparts; male—red cap

The most common desert bird that is very visible, extremely active, and definitely audible is the Gila Woodpecker. It always gets my attention because it is so verbal and is continually in motion. In addition to the high-pitched and often abrasive squawk, this resident woodpecker

*Plate 24

may be identified by its black-and-white zebra-striped back, brownish underparts, and striking red cap of the male. As is typical of a woodpecker, it flies in an undulating flight pattern, showing flashes of white on the wings and tail while in motion.

Habitat and Diet

This woodpecker is found in abundance in the saguaro cactus forest. Its main diet consists of insects, and is supplemented with fruit and pulp according to the season and availability. During July and August, their favorite treat is the fruit from the giant saguaro. How convenient to feed right outside one's doorway. They also eat oranges, peaches, and other fruit, and will come to hummingbird feeders, as they are fond of the sugar-water.

At my house, the Gila Woodpeckers also love raw hamburger treats that I originally began feeding the roadrunners. In fact, I often know when the roadrunners are on their way for a snack long before they utter a cry because one Gila keeps a vigilance from the top of a saguaro. When the roadrunner appears, the Gila swoops down, lands in a nearby tree and squawks his head off. When I put a bit of hamburger out for them, the competition begins. Usually, the roadrunner gets a bite first, but occasionally the Gila becomes aggressive enough to snatch the delicacy, just inches away from the roadrunner.

Nesting and Mating Behaviors

The Gila Woodpecker is an expert sculptor of homes in the giant saguaros. It pecks through the pulp, which it eats, then through the ribs of the massive cactus. In defense, the saguaro secretes a liquid which soon hardens and seals the "wound," thus forming a "boot" or cavity which the Gila furnishes for a home.

Gilas are extremely productive and drill far more holes than are needed for their own nests. The effort is not wasted, however, as other birds quickly move in and set up housekeeping for themselves. It is difficult to find a saguaro that does not contain a cavity made by the busy woodpecker.

Both the male and female aid in excavations of a cavity, and both bring twigs and grass to line the nest before the female lays the usual three to five glossy white eggs. Although the peak of the breeding season is mid-

May, two or three broods may be reared in a year. The female incubates the eggs and, when they are hatched, the male moves back in to assist with the feeding.

Supplemental Information

Some people consider the Gila a nuisance because sometimes it drills holes in the eaves of homes. Instead of going to extremes in ridding themselves of the bird, I suggest they first take a hard look at its motive: It might be trying to tell them that the eave is full of woodboring insects, which could be causing more damage to the home than is the bird itself.

RED-NAPED SAPSUCKER*
Sphrapicus nuchalis

Description: Red forehead, throat and nape; white wing patch; white rump; bared back; female–less red on throat; yellowish belly

The Red-naped Sapsucker measures eight to nine inches long and is beautifully decorated with contrasting red, black, white, and yellow plumage. The black-and-white head is adorned with a red chin, throat, and crown similar to the Yellow-bellied Sapsucker, but additionally has a red nape, which the Yellow-bellied lacks. A black breast band gives way to a yellowish belly with light streaking on the sides. There is a white patch on the black wing, and the upperparts are mottled with black and white. The female has a white chin and a smaller red throat patch. Juveniles are brown instead of black and do not display red and white plumage until the first fall or winter. The Red-naped Sapsucker's tongue is slightly different from most woodpeckers. Small "brushes" on the tip help sweep in the sap it extracts from trees.

Its muted call is described as *whee-ur* or *mew*. Additionally, the male produces a drumming noise by drilling into a hard, dead branch, which is another form of communicating with a potential mate.

*Plate 24

Habitat and Diet

The Red-naped Sapsucker is an uncommon transient and winter resident in areas of the desert that support various types of deciduous trees. This species and its yellow-bellied cousin are the most migratory of all woodpeckers, and diet is a big factor in habitat choice. As its name implies, sap is a favored food source and is obtained by drilling holes in deciduous trees in a horizontal fashion, then extracting sap with its long tongue. This industrious species seems to apprehend "favorite" trees, and one study indicates that trees already injured in some fashion become those chosen targets. It also feeds on a bounty of insects attracted to the sap wells. (Other birds such as hummingbirds, Ruby-crowned Kinglets, and Yellow-rumped Warblers take advantage of the Red-naped Sapsucker's efforts and also feed from the tiny openings.)

Although sapsuckers also eat large numbers of insects including wasps, beetles, ants, and many tree-boring insects—all of which harm trees—this is one woodpecker that actually eats more vegetable matter than animal matter.

Nesting and Mating Behaviors

Moving to higher elevations for breeding purposes, the Red-naped Sapsucker most often nests in deciduous trees, usually those that have been infected by fungus, thus making the center soft for excavation purposes, yet hard enough on the outside for protection. A new cavity is excavated each year, but often in the same tree. The female lays three to six pure white eggs on the barren floor of the cavity, then both sexes incubate the eggs for twelve to thirteen days, afterward sharing the task of feeding the ravenous, noisy youngsters.

LADDER-BACKED WOODPECKER
Picoides scalaris

Description: Black-and-white striped back and face; spotted sides; male—red crown; female—black crown

The Ladder-backed Woodpecker is the smallest of the desert woodpeckers, measuring six to seven and one-half inches in length. As the name indicates, the back is ladder-like, or zebra striped. Sides and underparts are spotted, and the face has a triangular-shaped black line extending from the eye back toward the crown, then forward ending at the cere. The sexes are similar, except the male shows a red crown.

As is typical of most woodpeckers, the Ladder-backed has two toes pointing forward and two backward, which enables it to climb vertically on the trunks of trees. Additionally, sharply pointed tail feathers are used for balance. The Ladder-backed was formerly called the Cactus Woodpecker.

This vocal species has a distinctive *pik* call. When defending territory, it also has a harsh, warning call, *jeee jeee jeee.*

Habitat and Diet

The Ladder-backed Woodpecker is a common year-round resident in desert regions inclusive of mesquite, agave, desert scrub, and deciduous woods along streams.

The bulk of its diet consists of the larvae of wood-boring beetles, ants, caterpillars, and moths. Supplementing these delicacies, it also eats cactus fruit and insects. During winter when food supplies seem less abundant, its special bill is particularly useful for probing into crevices and boring into dead wood to extract hidden insects. Around feeding stations, Ladder-backs are fond of fruit, especially oranges, and also compete with hummingbirds for sugar-water.

Nesting and Mating Behaviors

A cavity nester, the Ladder-back Woodpecker typically builds from four to twenty-five feet high in a century plant, yucca, or saguaro. Because of its small size, however, it may also choose a mesquite, palo verde, hackberry, or some other dead branch of desert scrub.

The nest cavity is seven to ten inches deep with an entrance opening of one and one-half inch in diameter. The female lays two to six oval, glossy white eggs, which are incubated about twelve to fourteen days by both sexes. When hatched, the young may be heard squeaking while the busy adults take turns flying in and out carrying food to the ravenous youngsters.

GILDED FLICKER[*]
Colaptes chrycoides

Description: Brown head; black ascot; black bars on upperparts;
white rump; male—red mustache; yellow
underwings; black spotted breast

The largest woodpecker of the Sonoran zone is the Gilded Flicker,
measuring from twelve to thirteen inches. Previously grouped with the
Yellow-shafted Flicker and the Red-shafted Flicker, all given the name
Northern Flicker, this salient species has been separated from the other
two and again is assigned its original name, Gilded Flicker.

Its head and wings are brown, with black bars decorating the back and
wings. The throat is gray and contrasts with a red mustache on the male.
The underparts are white with black dots, leading up to a completely
black ascot. The wings and tail linings are bright yellow, and there is a
white patch on the rump, which is especially noticeable in flight.

There are two hundred and ten species of woodpeckers scattered
throughout every corner of the world. They all have some similar behavioral actions, including the undulating flight pattern, of which the Gilded
Flicker is no exception. It is for this reason that woodpeckers are especially easy to identify in flight. The other year-round, desert-dwelling
woodpeckers are the Gila Woodpecker, and Ladder-back, which are
both smaller than the Gilded Flicker and not quite as colorful.

Woodpeckers do not walk on the ground, but instead move around in
a deliberate hopping manner. It is comical to watch the Gilded Flicker as
it bounces up and down in a seemingly effortless manner. By the same
token, it does not walk up the trunk of a tree or even a thorny saguaro,
but moves in a bouncing manner, clutching the surface with sharply-
hooked claws.

Habitat and Diet

The Gilded Flicker uses its sharp, chisel-like bill for drilling into various types of wood in search of insects and larvae, its main diet. Woodpeckers' skulls have built-in shock absorbers to protect them from the

*Plate 25

harsh hammering as they drill into wood. Ants are a big part of the Flicker's diet, and the big woodpecker is often seen hopping around on the ground while devouring many of the little insects. It also supplements its high-protein diet with seasonal fruits and berries.

Nesting and Mating Behaviors

The Gilded Flicker usually makes its nest in a tree cavity or in a saguaro cactus. In fact, it not only makes its own home there, but also drills many other holes, which become the nesting sites for several other species of birds. Although the Gila Woodpecker also drills holes in the same saguaros, the two species have definite territorial rights and respect each other's privacy.

The saguaro pulp is softer than most wood, so the drilling is easier and faster. The Gilded Flicker drills into the center of the saguaro, then begins tunneling downward for fifteen to twenty inches and makes the bottom of the nest somewhat larger. The cavity remains relatively undecorated except for a few twigs and wood chips strewn in the bottom for nesting purposes.

There are usually six to eight pure white eggs, which are hatched in only eleven or twelve days. The hole for the nest is drilled by both sexes, but the majority of the incubation is actually done by the male. He does most of the incubation at night, while the daytime hours are shared by both sexes. After the eggs are hatched, the male still takes the major responsibility for the feeding and rearing of the young.

Supplemental Information

For several years, I have had a Gilded Flicker who, occasionally, thinks he should be my natural alarm clock. In the early dawn of spring, he flies up to the metal chimney of my free-standing fireplace and pecks away, making a loud, metallic, vibrating sound. One would think that even though the flicker has built-in shock absorbers, the non-resistance of the metal would jar the poor bird into a state of frenzy. Apparently it is the frenzied state itself that perpetuates this behavior, as it is a means to communicate to a potential mate. Shortly after the *rat-tat-tat* on the chimney, an answering call can be heard in the distance.

Section 3

LANDBIRDS/PASSERINES

MORE than half of the birds in the world are considered to be perching birds and are scientifically classified as the order Passeriformes. Sixty-nine families make up this order and are called passerines. Songbirds are a part of this category, as are flycatchers, swallows, and shrikes, to name only a few. The key characteristic they all share is a foot with three toes pointing forward and one pointing backward, adapted for perching.

Western Wood-pewee
Pacific-slope
    Flycatcher
Black Phoebe*
Say's Phoebe*
Vermilion Flycatcher*
Ash-throated
    Flycatcher*
Cassin's Kingbird*
Western Kingbird*
Horned Lark*
Purple Martin*
Tree Swallow
Violet-green Swallow
Northern Rough-
    winged Swallow

Bank Swallow
Cliff Swallow
Barn Swallow*
Steller's Jay
Western Scrub Jay
Gray-breasted Jay*
Chihuahuan Raven*
Common Raven*
Verdin*
Cactus Wren*
Rock Wren
Canyon Wren
Bewick's Wren
House Wren
Marsh Wren
Ruby-crowned Kinglet

Blue-gray Gnatcatcher
Black-tailed
    Gnatcatcher
Western Bluebird*
Mountain Bluebird*
Swainson's Thrush
Hermit Thrush
Northern
    Mockingbird*
Sage Thrasher
Bendire's Thrasher
Curve-billed
    Thrasher*
Crissal Thrasher
Leconte's Thrasher
Phainopepla*

Loggerhead Shrike*
European Starling*
Solitary Vireo
Warbling Vireo
Orange-crowned
  Warbler
Nashville Warbler
Lucy's Warbler
Yellow Warbler
Black-throated Gray
  Warbler
Yellow-rumped
  Warbler*
Townsend's Warbler
MacGillivray's
  Warbler
Common Yellow-
  throat
Wilson's Warbler*
Yellow-breasted Chat

Western Tanager*
Northern Cardinal*
Pyrrhuloxia*
Black-headed
  Grosbeak*
Blue Grosbeak
Lazuli Bunting*
Green-tailed Towhee*
Spotted Towhee*
Canyon Towhee*
Abert's Towhee*
Chipping Sparrow
Brewer's Sparrow
Vesper Sparrow
Black-throated
  Sparrow
Sage Sparrow
Lark Bunting*
Savannah Sparrow
Song Sparrow

Lincoln's Sparrow
White-crowned
  Sparrow*
Red-winged
  Blackbird*
Eastern Meadowlark*
Western
  Meadowlark*
Yellow-headed
  Blackbird*
Brewer's Blackbird*
Bronzed Cowbird*
Brown-headed
  Cowbird
Hooded Oriole*
Bullock's Oriole*
Scott's Oriole*
House Finch*
Lesser Goldfinch
House Sparrow*

*See color section.

WESTERN WOOD-PEWEE
Contopus sordidulus

Description: Olive-gray plumage; two buffy wingbars; white eye ring

The Western Wood-pewee is a sparrow-sized tyrant flycatcher measuring six to six and one-half inches long. Drab, olive-gray upperparts with a slightly lighter chest band, and yellowish-white chin and belly make this bird almost indistinguishable from the Eastern Wood-pewee. Both also have two buffy-white wingbars, dark bills, and white eye ring. The range and voice are the best determinants for positive identification. The Western species is the only one found in the Southwestern deserts. Although dull in coloration, its upright posture on an open branch makes it easy to spot.

Early morning is the best time to hear this tyrant flycatcher calling out its own name loudly and clearly in two distinct syllables: *pee-wee.* Its territorial call is a harsh *pheer.*

Habitat and Diet

The Western Wood-pewee is a common summer resident of the Southwestern lowlands, breeding locally in mountain canyons with riparian environments. It migrates to South America for the winter.

As an industrious and skillful hunter, this vigilant flycatcher suddenly darts after an insect, seldom missing the targeted meal. It also hovers momentarily over a stand of grass, then plunges downward to snatch an unsuspecting victim.

Nesting and Mating Behaviors

The Western Wood-pewee is not discrete about the location of its nest like most bird species; it appears quite indifferent, and will fly directly to its nest even when an intruder is in the area. Perhaps it does not feel threatened because the nest is placed fifteen to forty feet above the ground, unavailable to most ground predators.

The nest is a shallow cup of fine grasses, moss, and plant fibers. The delicate abode is "saddled" to a horizontal branch. The exterior is covered with lichens fastened with cobwebs, thus appearing almost indistinguishable from a knot on the branch.

The female lays two to four creamy-white eggs with a wreath of brown spots, and incubates them for about twelve days. Both adults bring food to the nestlings.

PACIFIC-SLOPE FLYCATCHER
Empidonax difficilis

Description: Yellow throat; bright orange lower mandible

The Pacific-slope Flycatcher measures five and one-half to six inches long and belongs to the Empidonax family, a group of flycatchers that are extremely difficult to distinguish from each other. The Pacific-slope Flycatcher, formerly named Western Flycatcher, is the one most often seen in the Southwestern lowlands, and differs from the others mainly by its yellow throat. It is olive-brown above, with yellow underparts divided by a light olive breast band. Its obvious oblong white eye ring and two light wingbars are typical of this family. The eye ring comes to a point behind the dark eye. The tail is quite long as is the bill, which has a dark upper mandible and a bright orange lower mandible.

The sexes appear similar, but the juveniles have whiter underparts, lack the olive tone on the back, and have buff-colored wingbars. The call is a high-pitched *pseat-trip-se.*

Habitat and Diet

As its name suggests, ninety-nine percent of this flycatcher's food consists of insects: beetles, bees, wasps, ants, flies, and moths. Caterpillars are also a delicacy. The remaining one percent is of vegetable matter.

Nesting and Mating Behaviors

The Pacific-slope Flycatcher chooses an array of nesting sites, such as a hollow tree, a ledge, a spot among the roots of an upturned tree, the crotch of a tree, or a woodpecker's excavation. The female builds the nest with moss, leaves, and bark strips, and lines it with finer materials such as grasses and feathers. She lays three to five dull, creamy-white eggs with brown spots, and incubates them for fourteen or fifteen days.

BLACK PHOEBE*
Sayornis nigricans

Description: Black body; white belly; white undertail coverts

The Black Phoebe is easy to identify because it is the only black fly-catcher found in desert areas. White appears on the belly and undertail coverts of this six- to seven-inch delight. The adults appear similar. Juveniles have dark brown plumage with rufous coloration on the rump as well as on the two wingbars.

Perching over water waiting for dinner to fly by, this handsome flycatcher sometimes appears to be wagging its tail while uttering a repetitious, descending rendition of its name, *fi-bee, fi-bee.* Two loud calls include: *tseee* and *tsip.*

Habitat and Diet

The Black Phoebe is a year-round resident in the Southwestern lowlands, especially prevalent during winter. It is found near water where it patiently perches for long periods of time, darting out now and then for passing insects. Look for it where branches hang over water sources, or where rocks or cliffs afford perching areas with easy access to water. Lowland ponds and streams bordered by deciduous trees are ideal locations.

Largely insectivorous, this tyrant flycatcher snatches most prey on the wing just above the water's surface or low above the ground. This diet is often supplemented by surface-swimming minnows.

Nesting and Mating Behaviors

Common among phoebes, the Black Phoebe builds its nest of mud, much like the Barn Swallow, and affixes it to rock ledges, bridges, root overhangs, or even on old buildings and underpasses. The mud construction is fortified with grasses and moss, then well lined with hair and feathers. The outside diameter measures about five and one-half inches, and the height is approximately three and one-half inches.

*Plate 25

The female lays three to six oval, white eggs covered with minuscule, light brown specks, and incubates them for fifteen to seventeen days. The Black Phoebe is a solitary nester and may raise up to three broods per year, always returning to the same area for nesting the following season.

SAY'S PHOEBE*
Sayornis saya

Description: Grayish-brown upper body; rufous belly and undertail coverts; black tail

The Say's Phoebe, measuring seven to eight inches, is the largest phoebe of the Southwestern lowlands. It is more common than the Black Phoebe. Appearing somewhat similar to a female Robin in coloration, the Say's Phoebe displays a pale, peach-colored belly and undertail coverts. However, the underparts are gray, the head and wings are darker, and the tail is black. Both sexes appear similar.

The decrescendo call sounds like *pee-ur, pee-ur* while the song is faster and often sung while in midair. It sounds like *pit-tse-ar.*

Habitat and Diet

While the Black Phoebe prefers habitat near a water source, the Say's Phoebe chooses dry, open areas of canyons, ranchlands, and semi-desert borders, where it may be seen perching in bushes or on cliffs watching for insects. Continually alert, this species pumps its tail and spreads it widely, as if anxious to spring into action.

In addition to being a common desert resident, it is highly migratory, so larger numbers are present from September through March. Although primarily insectivorous, the Say's Phoebe will dine on available fruits, especially if insects are scarce.

Nesting and Mating Behaviors

The Say's Phoebe prefers a dry site for nesting, and most frequently chooses an old, abandoned building. Other protected sites include caves, bridges, large holes along the banks of dry washes, and abandoned mine shafts.

*Plate 25

The saucer-shaped nest is made of dry grasses, moss, and forbs with a soft lining of hair. Atypical of phoebes, the Say's does not usually use mud as construction material.

The female lays three to five oval, white eggs with only a couple of them showing small, brown specks. Alone, she incubates the eggs for two weeks, and typically raises two broods.

VERMILION FLYCATCHER*
Pyrocephalus rubinus

Description: Male—red head and underparts; brownish-black upperparts; female—grayish-brown above; pink wash and streaks underneath

As the word vermilion has been defined "brilliant scarlet red," so indeed is the Vermilion Flycatcher. It is the most spectacular flycatcher of the Southwest, both in decor and in behavior. The male possesses the flashy, brilliant exterior. At first glance it appears bright red all over, but upon closer observation it is apparent that his upperparts and tail are a brownish-black. He often displays a slight crest on the top of his head. The female is a brownish-gray color with a white streaked breast and touches of pink on her lower parts. Both sexes are five to six inches long, comparable to the size of a sparrow.

Habitat and Diet

The Vermilion Flycatcher resides only where water is available. In the Southwest, this little bird is commonly found in the summer months in areas with mesquites, willows, sycamores, or cottonwoods.

As the name implies, the Vermilion Flycatcher is an insect connoisseur. It is often seen sitting on a post or perched on a wire, waiting for prey to appear. It quickly darts from its perch, snatches the insect on the wing, and then usually returns to the same perch to consume its meal.

Nesting and Mating Behavior

The grandest display of behavior comes in the spring when the male begins his courtship. As if his flashy red attire were not enough to attract

*Plate 26

the opposite sex, the male assures himself that he will gain the attention he is seeking by engaging in a most spectacular air show.

Flashes of red can be seen as he quickly climbs fifty to one hundred feet in the air. He then slows his flight and gracefully hovers in a suspended display until he begins to swing seductively in an arch, back and forth, back and forth. The whole time he is in motion, he is also singing a most beautiful song. The grand finale comes at the height of song when he terminates this courtship behavior in a dive. What a show!

As if the male is not to be outdone by his aerial display, neither is the female outdone in her architectural design: she constructs the delicate nest completely by herself.

The nest is one of the most refined homes made by our feathered friends. Constructed of fine twigs and fibers, the small, shallow cup is delicately lined with down and other bits of feathers. An outside cover of lichen camouflages the nest so that it is extremely difficult to detect. In a mesquite tree, the nest could be ten to fifteen feet off the ground. In a cottonwood, it could be as high as sixty feet. This abode is usually situated in the outer branches, and because of the unique way the female has securely attached it to the fork of a limb, the nest appears to have a triangular shape.

The eggs themselves are an oddity among the Flycatchers. Almost always, the Vermilion Flycatcher lays three creamy eggs, which are beautifully marked at the larger ends with deep brown and slight lavender colors. The incubation is accomplished totally by the female, while the male brings food to her.

Supplemental Information

As a youngster on a ranch, I always looked forward to the spring and the return of the Vermilion Flycatchers. The male, whom we named "Buggy," was a splendid addition to the abundant bird life that thrived in our ranch surroundings. I loved to watch the couple raise their little families, and since they have two or more broods, there was plenty of action all summer long.

Although the female takes the total responsibility for building the nest and brooding the eggs, once the young are hatched, the male teaches them the fine art of catching bugs. He patiently demonstrates flying techniques, and then encourages the fledglings to follow his example. After many aerial displays, along with a few misses, the young are soon snatching their own dinner and returning to the perch just like Dad.

ASH-THROATED FLYCATCHER*
Myiarchus cinerascens

Description: Grayish-white chin and throat; rufous wings and tail; pale yellow bill

This seven and one-half to eight and one-half inch flycatcher is slightly smaller than a kingbird and noticeably more slender. Washed with pale yellow, the belly and undertail coverts merge with the distinctive, red-rufous coloration of the tail, which is most noticeable from underneath. This hardy flycatcher also has rufous primaries and indistinct white wing-bars. Dark, grayish-brown upperparts contrast with the light gray-white chin, throat, and pale lemon-yellow breast. (The Brown-crested Flycatcher is similar, but its belly is darker yellow, its bill is thicker, and it shows less rufous on the tail.)

In typical flycatcher style, the Ash-throated Flycatcher is most often seen perching erect on an outer tree branch, usually near an open area, waiting for the opportune moment to seize prey. Watch while it darts after a flying insect, then comes back to the same branch to dine while waiting for the next victim to appear. Also notice the wide bill used to seize the insect.

The call of the Ash-throated Flycatcher is heard year round and sounds like *prrrt.* Its song is a series of *quee-eerr* with the accent on the second syllable.

Habitat and Diet

The Ash-throated Flycatcher breeds in the Southwestern lowlands, and a few even stay throughout the winter. Migrants arrive early in the spring, so begin looking for it in February.

Because bird distribution is closely tied to food availability, flycatchers will generally be found in desert areas more closely associated with water. Desert washes lined with mesquites are a favorite location for this early bird, but canyons with various deciduous trees are another common breeding ground. Surveying from a perch, this skilled hunter darts into action to take most of its insectivorous diet on the wing.

*Plate 26

Nesting and Mating Behaviors

The male Ash-throated Flycatcher changes from his usual quiet, watchful composure to a gregarious suitor during mating season. His loquacious cries are accompanied by flirtatious postures accentuated by his bushy, erect crest. Once mated, a nest is constructed in an available cavity. Holes in mesquites, sycamores, cottonwood trees, or saguaro cacti are the more typical locations, but this tyrant flycatcher may also choose a more unusual site such as a tin can, a rain gutter, old abandoned pipes, or an abandoned Cactus Wren nest.

A foundation of grass, roots, and even manure supports the cup-shaped nest of hair and fur. For a unique decor, a piece of snake skin is almost always woven into the well-made abode.

The female lays four or five creamy-colored, oval eggs, which are covered with brown and purple blotches. She alone incubates the eggs for fifteen days, then the male assists her in rearing the nestlings.

CASSIN'S KINGBIRD[*]
Tyrannus vociferans

Description: Yellow belly; dark gray breast; white-tipped tail; white chin

The Cassin's Kingbird measures eight to nine inches and is similar to the more prevalent Western Kingbird, as well as to the less frequently occurring Tropical Kingbird. All three species have light yellow bellies and gray heads. The Cassin's Kingbird has a deeper gray breast, however, which makes the chin area appear smaller and whiter than that of its two relatives. In addition, the Cassin's black tail is tipped with white, but lacks the white sides apparent on the tail of the Western Kingbird. Occasionally, the small orangish-red crown patch which is usually concealed by surrounding feathers, is observable.

An obvious additional aid in identification of the Cassin's Kingbird is its song. Its utterances are noisy and are described as *ki-dear, ki-dear,* as well as *chi-beer, chi-beer-eer-beer-rr.* In areas where there are sufficient numbers, they gather in groups to roost.

[*]Plate 26

Habitat and Diet

The Cassin's Kingbird usually prefers higher elevations, but its territory overlaps that of the Western Kingbird. In the Southwestern lowlands, the Cassin's is found in the higher areas of the Lower Sonoran Zone. Here it may be found in the foothills among mesquite thickets or around hackberry bushes. It also frequents riparian areas with cottonwoods and sycamores.

Kingbirds are in the flycatcher family, and therefore can be seen perching upright on a branch or on a wire waiting to dart after flying insects. This astute bird takes almost any insect on the wing, including bees and wasps.

Nesting and Mating Behaviors

The Cassin's Kingbird breeds in the Southwestern lowlands in areas generally above 3,000 feet. It usually chooses a limb twenty to forty feet above the ground to support its nest, which is slightly larger than that of the Western Kingbird. This abode is a bulky structure made of twigs and lined with grasses or animal hair. Although it is approximately eight inches in diameter and three inches high, the nest is usually well hidden on a horizontal branch.

The female lays three to five creamy-white, oval eggs with brown spots that are especially obvious on the larger end. She incubates them twelve to fourteen days, then the male assists her in feeding and rearing the young.

Supplemental Information

Kingbirds are notorious for their aggressive behavior during nesting season. When birds of prey fly too close to the nest, the kingbird will attack the larger bird to protect its young. Once I watched while a kingbird dive-bombed a raven over and over again. There was no doubt about the kingbird's message!

WESTERN KINGBIRD*
Tyrannus verticalis

Description: White margins on blackish, outer tail feathers; light gray head with dark eye line; yellow belly; white chin

Commanding territory from a conspicuous perch, the eight- to nine-inch-long Western Kingbird is easy to spot. Its head, throat, and breast are light gray, enunciating the darker gray eye line that fades into the lighter whitish chin. If you are very lucky, you may see a patch of orange-red on the crown, but it is usually concealed. The belly is bright yellow, contrasting with blackish wings and tail, and the back is grayish olive-green.

Unlike other kingbirds, the Western Kingbird displays white outer feathers on the squarish tail. Its bill is slighter and shorter than the Tropical Kingbird's, and the gray head and breast are lighter than the Cassin's. The sexes appear similar, and the juveniles are paler yellow with a brownish breast.

Aggressive in nature, the Western Kingbird will attack its natural enemies: hawks, ravens, and owls. It is more successful in defending itself against these threats than the one who is actually challenging its very existence by usurping habitat: *Homo sapiens.*

Overt in behavior but subdued in voice, the Western Kingbird has a rather sharp but low *kip* or *whit* for a call.

Habitat and Diet

The Western Kingbird is the most abundant kingbird of the deserts, arriving in late March to summer in the lowlands. Some linger here until late October or early November when they migrate as far as Central America for winter.

Preferring open areas and perching conspicuously on limbs or fence posts, this kingbird surveys the area for insects, then darts out to snatch one, often on the wing. This is a great opportunity to clench an identity because the tail is spread and the outer, white feathers become more visible during aerial sorties. It supplements this insect diet with approximately ten percent vegetable matter, including seeds and fruit.

*Plate 27

Nesting and Mating Behaviors

Mesquites and cottonwoods are favorite nesting sites, but other broad-leaved, deciduous trees will suffice. Fence posts, telephone poles, windmills, or any supporting structure from five to fifty feet above the ground may also contain the nest of the Western Kingbird.

The abode is large and well made of twigs, leaves, string, and rootlets, then usually lined with animal hair. Both sexes participate in building; then the female lays three to five smooth, creamy-white eggs blotched with lavender or brown, and incubates them for twelve to fourteen days. When the young fledge, it is fun to watch the whole family perching on various branches of the same tree, darting after insects and flying back to perch in the same vicinity.

HORNED LARK*
Eremophila alpestris

Description: Black bib; yellow face; black whiskers and "horns"; brown upper body

The Horned Lark appears pale brown, but sports a black breast bib and two small black "horns." The throat and face are light yellow with black whiskers, and the tail is black with white on each side. The sexes are similar, measuring seven to eight inches long, but the female is slightly lighter in coloration. Immatures have silver specks on their backs and lack the black on the face. As is often common with birds that inhabit open areas, the Horned Lark is very strong in flight, folding its wings after each beat.

This grassland bird is very difficult to spot in the field because it blends so perfectly with the environment. It is usually on the ground, but is more conspicuous when singing either from a short perch or a mound of dirt, or when circling high in the air. To locate this elusive bird, listen for the song: a high-pitched, irregular, tinkling series of notes that are often long and sustained. The call has been described as a thin *tsee-eep* and a buzz.

*Plate 27

Habitat and Diet

The Horned Lark is a common resident of the Southwestern lowlands, especially in open grasslands and around agricultural areas. Other popular habitats include airports, golf courses, deserts, and shorelines. These terrestrial birds can be seen in flocks outside the breeding season. As might be suspected in a grassy terrain, this lark feeds both on grass seeds as well as ground insects. The Horned Lark walks rather than hops and is more easily spotted in large feeding flocks because one alone blends so well with its chosen habitat. For every Horned Lark that can be seen, five others are hidden among the grasses.

Nesting and Mating Behaviors

The nest is a simple, grass-lined depression on the ground, and is either partially scraped under a tuft of grass or possibly right next to it. On one side of the nest, a "doorstep" is made of tiny rocks or dirt clods placed on the outer rim. The nest's diameter is about four inches, and the depth is only about one and one-half inches.

The female is solely responsible for the construction of the nest, which takes her two to four days. Three to five eggs are pale gray, oval in shape, smooth, and heavily blotched with brown spots. There are generally two broods; each incubated about eleven days by the female.

The male brings food to her, then assists in rearing the young when they are hatched. Additionally, he may lure potential enemies away from the area by feigning a broken wing. The nest is so well camouflaged that it is almost impossible to find without observing the behavior of the bird itself and following it to the site.

Supplemental Information

The word philopatric, "faithful to its birthplace," describes the Horned Lark perfectly. After each migration, this bird returns to its hatching site every year and, interestingly enough, even adopts to the color of the ground. On light, sandy soil the Horned Lark has a very pale plumage; on darker sand it is likewise darker; and even on red dirt this lark adapts a reddish plumage. In the west, fifteen subspecies have been identified using the coloration criteria.

PURPLE MARTIN*
Progne subis

Description: Male—glossy blue-black overall; female—blue-black
above; light below

The Purple Martin belongs to the Swallow family, and in fact is the
largest one in North America, measuring seven and one-half to eight and
one-half inches. The adult male is glossy blue-black both above and
below. The head reflects violet coloration in full sunlight with the forked
tail and wings showing dull black. It is the only dark-bellied swallow. The
female is light bellied with a smoky-gray throat and breast, and often has
a very light collar.

This swallow glides in circles and, as it alternates with flapping, notice
that the tail is also quite frequently spread. In flight its wings are more triangular than other swallows. The Purple Martin sings with a deep gurgling sound, and its call has been described as *pew pew,* or *tchew-whew.*

Habitat and Diet

The Purple Martin is a fairly common summer resident in the Southwestern lowlands. It is found in open or semi-open country where it can
find nesting sites in saguaro cacti or hollow trees.

Its insect diet makes it very beneficial to humankind; mosquitoes and
house flies are its prime targets. It feeds on the wing and can be seen high
on a saguaro, wire, or mesquite top poised to dart after a meal. Once it
snatches the insect in its large mouth, it usually returns to the same perch.

Nesting and Mating Behaviors

In the desert, the Purple Martin prefers nesting in cavities in saguaros
made by Gila Woodpeckers or Gilded Flickers. In other areas, it finds
hollow trees, or cavities drilled by other woodpeckers.

The male arrives in the nesting habitat ahead of the female and establishes a territory. The female selects the actual nesting site, though, and
together they decorate their new abode. The selected cavity is lined with
grasses, leaves, feathers, and sometimes even mud. There are three to

*Plate 27

eight oval, white eggs with a slight gloss. The female does all of the incubation, which takes fifteen to sixteen days.

The nestlings of swallows stay on the nest for more than three weeks in many species. Young Purple Martins stay the longest, remaining sometimes up to thirty-five days. From a very early age they must begin learning to catch their own food on the wing, for once fledged they get no help from the parents.

Supplemental Information

Five years ago, I observed Purple Martins nesting in three different saguaros near my home. Two years later, European Starlings took over one nest site, and the next year another pair of Starlings moved into the second saguaro boot. I have discovered that the Purple Martin seems to be diminishing in my area of the desert, not only because of the continual loss of habitat, but also because of the increase in competition for nesting sites. As European Starlings are increasing and claiming nesting sites earlier in the season, there are obviously fewer cavities left for native birds. Also, the Purple Martins of the Southwest do not choose to set up house keeping in commercial Martin houses.

Tree Swallow
Tachycineta bicolor

Description: Metallic bluish-green upperparts; white below; absence of white above eye and on rump

The five- to six-inch-long Tree Swallow soars through the heavens with speed and grace, displaying long, pointed wings while circling above. From below, the pure white underparts are easily visible; the white that stops below the eye distinguishes it from the Violet-green Swallow, who shows white extending above the eye. The glossy upperparts are dark green in the fall, but appear bluish-green during mating season. The long wings extend beyond the deeply forked tail, and the large mouth is accentuated by a short, triangular-shaped bill. Juveniles display a light, grayish-brown breastband and may be dusky in color.

Tree Swallows flock together during winter and may be seen perching in rows on wires or small branches. Migrating swallows fly during the daytime, whereas most species of birds journey at night. They also fly around large bodies of water rather than directly over them.

The Tree Swallow has a variety of calls, which are all very fluid: *Weet, cheet,* and *trit* all may be heard while this tireless bundle of energy sweeps through the sky. It even chatters while feeding.

Habitat and Diet

A common winter resident and transient, the Tree Swallow is most often found along rivers, streams, lakes, or ponds. An excellent place to find them is along the Lower Colorado River. Migrating in January, they are among the first to leave the desert areas.

Fruit is consumed when available, but the vast majority of its diet consists of insects taken on the wing. With a large, open mouth, the Tree Swallow swoops through a mass of flying insects collecting several at a time, some protruding and wiggling out of its bill when it reaches the other side of the swarming group. Swallows are tremendously beneficial to maintaining nature's order.

Nesting and Mating Behaviors

This early migrating species moves northward to breed in wooded areas with open spaces, especially where dead trees are available for nesting sites and where water is nearby. As a cavity nester, it will accept birdhouses, fence posts, or holes in buildings, but its natural choice is in old woodpecker holes. The female takes up to two weeks to meticulously build the cup-shaped nest with dry grasses and then carefully line it with feathers. The three to eight pure white eggs hatch in about fifteen days.

VIOLET-GREEN SWALLOW
Tachycineta thalassina

Description: Iridescent green above; white below extending over eye; white flank patches

Aerialist is the word that best describes this five- to five-and-one-half inch swallow. Darting first one way then just as smoothly the other way, the Violet-green Swallow tirelessly and gracefully commands the skies.

The vibrant, dark green upperparts and iridescent violet rump and tail starkly contrast with the pure white underparts and the white patches on the sides of the rump. The white of the neck and chin extends up and over the eye, distinguishing it from the Tree Swallow. The female is less brilliant than the male, and her underparts are grayish. The juvenile is grayish-brown above.

As is typical of all swallows, the Violet-green Swallow has very tiny feet, thus perches only on small branches, or on wires. Gregarious in nature, large numbers of swallows are usually seen perching in rows. The beak appears small, but watch this amazing bird when it dashes out to catch insects. The mouth seems to open eyeball to eyeball!

Darting about in the heavens, it utters a high-pitched *dee-chip*. Between gulps of insects it may be heard calling *chit-chit chit wheet, wheet.*

Habitat and Diet

In the desert areas, this transient swallow is most often seen during spring migration, which starts in February and continues through May. During fall migration it does not linger as long, and may be seen for short periods during October. Although relatively consistent, migration is determined by food availability and weather conditions, not by human calendars as the "Capistrano myth" would have us believe. (This tale would have us believe that swallows arrive on the same date every year.)

Usually living and feeding in colonies, the Violet-green Swallow is often found around croplands, where it is of tremendous benefit to farmers. Flying through hoards of bugs, this insectivore scoops up a mouthful at a time, all on the wing.

Nesting and Mating Behaviors

The Violet-green Swallow continues its migration northward to breed in coniferous and deciduous forests where woodpecker holes abound. Natural cavities in tall, dead trees, birdhouses, or under eaves of buildings will also suffice.

The nest is constructed of fine grasses and is always generously lined with feathers. The three to five oval eggs are plain white and incubated by the female for about fourteen days. Both adults feed the young for approximately three weeks. Because the young feed on the wing from a very early age, they must mature sufficiently before taking that first fledgling departure from the nest.

NORTHERN ROUGH-WINGED SWALLOW
Stelgidopteryx serripennis

Description: Brown colored above; lighter underparts; dingy brown throat; no breast band

A light, buffy-brown chin, throat, and breast, and absence of breast collar distinguish the Northern Rough-winged Swallow from the similar Bank Swallow. The remaining underparts are whitish, contrasting beautifully with the dark brown upperparts. There are no apparent plumage distinctions between the sexes, but juveniles show more buffy brown on the chest and have rufous-colored wingbars. Similar in size to most sparrows, it measures five to five and three-quarters inches long.

Compared to the Bank Swallow, the Northern Rough-winged Swallow makes fewer twists and turns while commanding the sky on feeding frenzies. Instead, it flies with graceful glides and at a slightly slower pace.

In typical swallow fashion, the feet are small and weak, and the beak is triangular, minuscule, and flat. The wings extend slightly beyond the forked tail. Its call is more harsh than that of the Bank Swallow and is more extensive, resembling *br-r-rat.*

Habitat and Diet

This graceful species is an uncommon summer resident and common transient throughout the Southwestern lowlands where water prevails. During winter it is only seen casually.

Chiefly insectivorous, this beneficial bird spends a great deal of time in the air gliding and swooping up insects. Its large mouth is capable of catching and holding several at a time.

Nesting and Mating Behaviors

Nesting Northern Rough-winged Swallows may be mistaken for Bank Swallows because of their choice of nesting sites. The latter, however, depart the Southwestern lowlands during breeding season. This leaves plenty of nesting sites for the Rough-winged, who then is the only swallow in this area to nest in dirt cavities along streams or river banks. This species is generally a solitary nester.

The actual nest is built at the end of a tunnel or cavity by placing twigs, forbs, and roots directly on the ground. Finer grasses are used for a lining. Four to eight slightly glossy, pure white eggs are incubated by both sexes for sixteen days. Although some swallows have several broods, the Northern Rough-winged Swallow raises only one family per season.

BANK SWALLOW
Riparia riparia

Description: Brown above; dark chest band; white underparts; white of throat extends to ears

The Bank Swallow is the smallest swallow in North America, measuring four and one-half to five and one-half inches long. Unlike the Northern Rough-winged Swallow, the Bank Swallow wears a distinctive dark breast band, which matches the dark brown plumage of the head and upper body. White underparts including the belly, throat, and chin contrast starkly with dark upper-body coloration. The white of the throat sweeps around, almost meeting at the back of the head. Fluttering long, pointed wings in a butterfly fashion, the wingbeats of this little swallow are rapid and irregular.

Both sexes have similar plumage, and the juveniles have thin, buffy wingbars and lighter brown heads. The song is a short trill sounding like *tri-tri-tri* or *pret.*

Habitat and Diet

The Bank Swallow is an uncommon transient throughout the Southwestern lowlands in April and early May, then again in August and September. These small, insect-hunting birds dart after prey on the wing. Large mouths seem to flutter through the sky scooping in insects along the way. Found primarily around water sources such as lakes, ponds, and even irrigated fields, this species is very beneficial during its short stay by assuming the natural role of "bug exterminator."

Nesting and Mating Behaviors

Although true to its name, the Bank Swallow nests in banks and moves out of desert areas to do so. The only nesting swallows in river banks of the desert lowlands are the Northern Rough-winged Swallows.

There are only a few species of birds that excavate their own nesting holes in the ground, and the Bank Swallow is one of them. Using the short, triangular bill as well as tiny feet, both sexes take turns digging a burrow at the side of a river or other embankment.

At the end of the fifteen-inch-long tunnel, grasses and straw are placed on the level floor. Some feathers are used for lining, and more are added when incubation begins. The female lays four to six smooth, pure white eggs, then both sexes take turns incubating them for fifteen days. Highly gregarious, many birds nest closely together, giving the river bank a honeycomb appearance.

CLIFF SWALLOW
Hirundo pyrrhonota

Description: Whitish forehead; ochre rump; squarish tail; rusty throat

This master of the sky has a deep cinnamon-colored throat, buffy collar, and steel blue upperparts with a conspicuous white forehead, which distinguishes it from the Cave Swallow. Like the latter, it has an ochre rump and white underparts. The sexes are similar and measure five to six inches long. The juveniles are dull, lacking the glossy, blue wash as well as the deep chestnut throat.

The Cliff Swallow is a bird of large colonies, and where they exist there is always a flurry of activity. They fly back and forth to snatch up insects or inspect nesting areas. Seldom do they perch for any length of time. A true bird of the air, they have extraordinarily developed wings and display tremendous endurance.

Habitat and Diet

The Cliff Swallow is a common transient and summer resident throughout the desert lowlands. Arriving in late March or early April from wintering territories in South America, it remains in the lowlands until late September or early October. Look for this aerialist in open to semi-open country such as irrigated farmlands, river areas, lakes, or as its name suggests, around cliffs. This is the swallow of San Juan Capistrano fame.

Less than one percent of food intake is vegetable matter, and the vast majority consists of a smorgasbord of insects including ants, bees, wasps, assassin bugs, leaf bugs, squash bugs, stink bugs, gnats, and dragonflies to name a few. Arachnids complete the course.

Nesting and Mating Behaviors

Throughout the Southwestern lowlands, nesting colonies exist where water prevails. Aptly named, it nests on cliffs, but also claims space on dams, bridges, culverts, sides of buildings, and under eaves. In some colonies, nests appear by the hundreds. Both sexes gather mud and clay as a molding substance for the gourd-shaped tunnel five to six inches long, which is lightly lined with grasses, hair, and feathers. The whole masterpiece may take up to two weeks for completion.

The female and male take turns incubating two to six smooth, white eggs, which are dotted with brown. In fifteen days, there are suddenly many large mouths to feed. The young eat the same food as their parents, but soft-bodied insects are most often chosen in the beginning, as they are more easily digested by the tiny hatchlings.

BARN SWALLOW*
Hirundo rustica

Description: Bluish-black above; cinnamon below; deeply forked tail

The Barn Swallow, perhaps the most widely known swallow, is steel blue above, light cinnamon below, with a rich chestnut throat and forehead. It measures five and three-quarters inches to seven and three-quarters inches long, is the only swallow with a deeply forked tail, and has white spotting underneath the tail. The sexes are alike, but the juveniles have buff-colored bellies and chests, and rust-colored throats.

Swallows have extremely small feet and therefore do very little walking on the ground. They perch on wires and thin twigs rather than on larger branches of trees.

Most characteristic of all swallows is the large mouth, which is used to "scoop up" insects as this acrobatic species swoops through swarms of unsuspecting victims.

*Plate 28

Habitat and Diet

The Barn Swallow is a common summer resident in the Southwestern lowlands and is found in open or semi-wooded country, often near water, and usually near habitation. It seldom nests away from human-made structures. It is found around farms, ranches, bridges, culverts, golf courses, and even in back yards. It migrates to the tropics for the winter.

The Barn Swallow consumes large numbers of insects and is therefore extremely beneficial to humankind. Wonderfully graceful in flight, this acrobat snatches all food on the wing. With its large mouth wide open, it swoops down, nearly touching the ground, then effortlessly flies up to a small perch, sometimes with a mouth literally stuffed with insects.

Nesting and Mating Behaviors

Barn Swallows often nest in colonies where they have access to various kinds of structures such as barns, bridges, culverts, outbuildings, or eaves of houses, to which they attach their nests. Both sexes participate in the construction of their unique little abode made of mud and straw. They roll mud into little balls and carry them away by mouth. This is about the only reason they land on the ground, where they shuffle around on their tiny feet.

The male seems to gather most of the mud, but the female molds it into the form of the nest she desires. It is semi-circular in shape at the top and extends downward into a cone. The outside measures about five inches. Studies show that an average of one thousand trips are made to acquire enough mud for the construction of a single nest! When it is molded to the satisfaction of the female, feathers are used to line the architectural wonder.

Although both sexes sit on the eggs, it has been determined that the male actually lacks the functional brood patch and therefore does not project heat for the actual incubation process. The four to six white eggs speckled with brown spots incubate for about fifteen days. Both parents bring insects to the nestlings.

Supplemental Information

Swallows are noted for their migratory behaviors. Their annual arrivals and departures have stirred up popular misconceptions. Especially legendary is the concept of the Cliff Swallows returning to San Juan Capistrano on a certain day each year.

Birds choose habitat largely because of food choice and availability, which of course fluctuates with seasons of the year. No bird arrives because of a certain day on our calendar. Instead, its presence is influenced by weather and food supply. The Barn Swallow winters throughout the Southern Hemisphere and arrives back in the Southwest in March and April. It can travel up to nine thousand miles during migration.

STELLER'S JAY
Cyanocitta stelleri

Description: Crest; bright blue body; dark gray head

The Steller's Jay is the only crested jay to appear in the Southwestern deserts. The sexes appear similar, displaying a hood of blackish-gray that fades into the otherwise bright blue body. Intricate black designs adorn the wings and tail. White flecks appear over the eye and on the chin to contrast with the dark eyes and bill. The Steller's Jay is the largest jay, measuring twelve to thirteen and one-half inches long. Typical of all jays, it is very social and is often seen in small groups.

The Steller's Jay is more reticent than other jays, and usually observes human intrusion from the top of a nearby tree before approaching too closely. It soon gains confidence, however, and boldly comes within close range for available food. Campers often delight to be in close proximity with this gregarious bird.

The Steller's harsh voice takes on many variations described as *shookshook-shook; shack, shack, shack, shack;* or *kwesh, kwesh, kwesh.* It can even imitate the cry of the Red-tailed Hawk and the Golden Eagle. A flock may be persistently noisy to announce the presence of an intruder or predator.

Habitat and Diet

The most common habitat for the Steller's Jay is in higher elevations with conifer forests or pine and oak woodlands. It is a casual winter resident in the Southwestern deserts, usually arriving in flocks.

Acorns and pine nuts supply the Steller's Jay with the largest percentage of food intake, which is supplemented with insects, seeds, and even bird eggs. This varied diet allows it to wander into the desert away from its primary food choices. It is a hoarder and takes advantage when supplies are plentiful, stashing food for leaner times. Watch for it feeding both in the trees and on the ground.

Nesting and Mating Behaviors

Although the Steller's Jay can create quite a raucous when intruders approach too closely, an opposite disposition emerges around nesting territories. Here, this large bird appears very quiet and elusive, being careful not to call attention to the site. If the nest is approached, however, both sexes burst into action to drive the intruder out of the area.

Both sexes build the nest, which may be from eight to forty feet from ground level. The nest is usually well concealed in a conifer, but occasionally placed in a lower bush.

The large nest, approximately fifteen inches in diameter, is a bowl-shaped structure made of sticks, leaves, moss, and even trash. It is banded together with mud, then carefully lined with roots, fibers, or pine needles. The female lays three to five bluish-green, spotted eggs which she alone incubates for seventeen to eighteen days. Both sexes attend to the young.

WESTERN SCRUB JAY
Aphelocoma californica

Description: Blue upperparts with gray back patch; gray underneath; white throat with blue band; white line over eye

This eleven- to thirteen-inch-long jay is crestless. The sexes appear similar with a blue head, tail, and wings. The white throat contrasts with the blue band, or necklace, distinguishing it from the Gray-breasted Jay. The back is dull brown, and the underparts are grayish white. Notice the white above the eye, gray patch on the blue back, and the long, stout bill. Juveniles are gray with blue showing on their wings and tail.

The Western Scrub Jay is aggressive and bold, readily coming into picnic areas or campsites looking for scraps of food. It appears in small groups and flies from tree to tree with an undulating flight pattern, often calling out in flight. Its voice is a loud rasping series of squawks including *jayy, kewsh . . . kwesh, check-check-check-check,* and *zhreek, shreek.*

Habitat and Diet

The Western Scrub Jay is most commonly seen in the conifer forests, but occasionally comes to the lower elevations to winter in the desert scrub where mesquites, canyons, and streambeds exist.

A varied diet helps sustain this jay in the dramatic changes of habitat. Feeding mostly on the ground, it eats acorns, seeds, insects, arachnids, eggs, and sometimes even young nestlings. It has even been known to land on the backs of deer to consume ticks. Survival skills include hoarding food by burying stashes in the ground. Forgotten acorns thus become planted seeds, making the Western Scrub Jay a vital link in maintaining oak forests.

Nesting and Mating Behaviors

This jay does not breed in the low deserts, but moves to higher elevations where both sexes take part in the nest construction. As raucous as they can become away from the nest, they are quiet and reclusive in their nesting territory. One bird brings nesting material while the other keeps guard, trading jobs until the nest is completed.

The neatly constructed abode is a platform of twigs, moss, and grasses neatly lined with hair and finer materials, and well hidden in trees or shrubs from three to thirty feet above the ground. The female lays four to six reddish or greenish speckled eggs. She incubates them for sixteen days, then both sexes share the task of rearing them.

GRAY-BREASTED JAY*
Aphelocoma ultramarina

Description: Muted powder-blue body; gray breast; no distinct white markings

Both sexes appear blue with gray breasts and underparts. Slightly larger than the similarly colored Western Scrub Jay, the Gray-breasted Jay measures eleven and one-half to thirteen inches long. It lacks the blue necklace, the white marks on the throat, and the white line above the eye

*Plate 28

that distinguish it from its cousin. Like the Western Scrub Jay, the Gray-breasted Jay has no crest. Its feet and stout bill are black, but Arizona juveniles often have a yellow bill.

The Gray-breasted Jay was formerly called the Mexican Jay. This bird is very gregarious and is almost always seen in flocks—as many as twenty birds may share the same territory. They are fun to watch when they move around on the ground, hopping in typical jay fashion with bursts of energy, even appearing comical at times. Its flight is more direct than the undulating glide of the Western Scrub Jay.

Bold and noisy, the Gray-breasted Jay calls with a loud, high-pitched *week,* repeated several times.

Habitat and Diet

Although it prefers oak and pine woodlands, the Gray-breasted Jay sometimes wanders into the deserts. Its main diet consists largely of acorns, but is supplemented with insects, arachnids, and seeds.

Like other jays, the Gray-breasted Jay hides acorns by making holes in the ground with its bill, then pushing dirt over them. Many more are "planted" than are later eaten, thus this species contributes greatly to the abundance of its own food source.

Nesting and Mating Behaviors

The Gray-breasted Jay often nests in loose colonies of up to twenty birds. Pairs build separate nests while non-breeders help with the construction, then later help by feeding the young. The nest is a bulky, loose structure of sticks most often placed in a live oak from six to fifty feet above the ground, then lined with grasses, animal hair, and small rootlets.

The Arizona race female lays three to five glossy, unmarked, greenish eggs; other races have brown spots. Both sexes incubate the eggs for sixteen days. When the eggs hatch, the parents receive help in feeding them from the "extended family." If an intruder approaches the nest, all the adults in the colony join forces to drive it out of the territory by scolding loudly.

CHIHUAHUAN RAVEN*
Corvus cryptoleucus

Description: Heavy bill; wedge-shaped tail; white neck feathers, usually concealed

Ravens are the largest of passeriform birds, and the Chihuahuan Raven is somewhat smaller than the Common Raven. The former measures nineteen to twenty-one inches and is closer to the size of an American Crow. Both sexes appear similar.

The Chihuahuan Raven is all black, and has a somewhat wedge-shaped tail; long, pointed throat feathers; and white upper neck feathers which can only be seen if the wind ruffles the overlying black plumage. This characteristic gave it the former name, White-necked Raven. Its scientific name, *cyptoleucus,* actually means "hidden white."

Along with the white neck and the smaller size, it can also be distinguished from the Common Raven by its higher-pitched call: It has a hoarse, prolonged *caaaa* that is higher and flatter than the call of the Common Raven.

The Chihuahuan Raven flies with the flat-wing glide typical of other ravens. It not only soars high in groups, but also roosts communally. This common resident is very gregarious.

Habitat and Diet

The Chihuahuan Raven is common in the arid Southwestern lowlands, preferring mesquite groves, yucca desert, semidesert grasslands, and desert scrub for its habitat. They are also found around irrigated farmlands and in towns. The Common Raven is more widespread, thus additionally inhabiting mountains and canyons.

The diet of the Chihuahuan Raven is extremely varied, including small rodents, bird eggs, and even young nestlings, lizards, insects, fruits, and

*Plate 28

seeds. It is often seen competing with vultures for carrion, including those animals hit by vehicles.

During the winter, these ravens can be found feeding in large flocks. They retreat at the end of the day to communal roosting trees.

Nesting and Mating Behaviors

Sometimes the Chihuahuan raven nests in colonies where there is a convergence of trees or shrubs to provide enough space for several nest sites. More often, it is found nesting in solitary trees, utility poles, yuccas, or even windmills. This Raven nests later than the Common Raven. It is thought that its timing coincides with the rainy season, thus assuring the young an abundance of food, which might otherwise be scarce in the desert areas.

The female builds the nest entirely by herself and often simply refurbishes an old nest, making it bigger and bigger each year. The bowl-shaped nest is loosely constructed of twigs, thorns, and even barbed wire. Depending on the proximity to humans, it may be thatched with trash such as rags, newspapers, and other paper products. The outside diameter is approximately twenty inches, and the inside depth measures five inches and may be lined with animal hair, fur, grass, or even more trash.

There are three to eight greenish-gray eggs, which are oval and blotched all over with lavender coloration. Incubation takes eighteen or nineteen days and is done by both sexes.

Supplemental Information

Monogamy among birds means that a pair stays together during any one nesting period. Many birds fit into this category, but fewer birds actually stay together for life. The Chihuahuan Raven is one that is thought to form lifelong pair bonds.

COMMON RAVEN*
Corvus corax

Description: Black body; thick bill; wedge-shaped tail; shaggy
throat feathers

The Common Raven is the most abundant of the large birds in the
Southwest. Though it has been mistaken for the Common Crow, it is
actually almost double the crow's size and has a wedge-shaped tail
instead of the square tail of the crow. Also, very few crows visit the Southwestern region.

More than half of all birds are classified as passerine, or perching
birds. Of this group, the Common Raven is the largest, measuring twenty-two to twenty-seven inches. The smaller Chihuahuan Raven measures
nineteen to twenty inches. When perched, the Common Raven often displays its shaggy throat feathers.

In flight, the Common Raven appears almost hawk-like while gracefully riding the thermals and soaring with the currents, alternating between
this smooth gliding action and the more deliberate flapping of its wings.
Notice the wings are stretched straight out horizontally from its body
while soaring. Because the rising air thermals are best around mountains,
it is here that the Common Raven especially loves to spend hours floating effortlessly in the ever-reaching sky.

The Common Raven's voice is an aid in identification. It utters a variety of sounds, including deep guttural croaks and a hoarse cry resembling
a metallic sound. It is not unusual to hear the Common Raven calling out
while soaring with the air currents.

Habitat and Diet

This species adapts extremely well to many environments and can be
found in the mountains, valleys, canyons, and deserts, as well as on the
coast. It seems to prefer to nest on a cliff, but it is also easily found nesting in trees and sometimes even on telephone or power line poles. Even
though numerous ravens may be seen perching together in a tree or soaring on the same air currents, they almost always nest in privacy. Nests
may be several miles apart.

*Plate 29

A bird's anatomy is specifically designed for its individual requirements, especially those involved with obtaining food. The heavy bill of the Common Raven is its special "tool" for gathering a wide variety of foods. While feeding on carrion, the beak is used for tearing meat. The bird is also a seed eater, and the bill is used to crack various kinds of seeds. Ultimately this tool is used for probing, digging, and scraping while searching for insect larva and small bugs. Its feet are also adapted for many uses such as perching, scratching, holding, and walking. The Common Raven can live almost anywhere because of its ability to abscond many available food sources.

Nesting and Mating Behaviors

Both sexes gather the material for the nest, but the female does the actual construction. The nest is a large, bulky structure measuring two feet to four feet on the outside. It is approximately six inches deep with an inside opening about one foot in diameter. It is constructed of medium-sized twigs and sticks, then heavily lined with finer material such as hair and grasses. Sometimes the Common Raven uses the same nest over again the next nesting season, merely renovating it.

There are four to seven eggs, which are pale green with splotches of brown and olive. The shell is fairly rough and exhibits no gloss. The female begins laying eggs the last part of April and does the majority of the incubation, which takes approximately three weeks. The male may take a turn for a short period of time.

Supplemental Information

It has been suggested that the Common Raven exhibits a type of intelligence not apparent in most other birds. Obvious examples are adaptability to different environments and the ability to readily substitute food sources. In addition, the Common Raven will sometimes carry a closed, hard shellfish high above the ground, then drop it in order to crack it open. This does not appear to be instinctive behavior, but rather a learned behavior using some sort of reasoning process. It has been stated that the Common Raven has an intelligence comparable to that of a dog, and some authorities have likened the Common Raven's intellectual abilities to that of a four-year-old human!

Verdin*
Auriparus flaviceps

Description: Yellow head and throat; rust colored shoulder patch; gray above; light underparts

The Verdin is one of the smallest of the desert birds and always appears quite hyperactive. Even though it is a relatively shy bird, it seldom sits motionless and, therefore, can be easily detected in the thick brush where, paradoxically, it appears to be trying to hide.

The Verdin is four to four and one-half inches long. It can be identified most easily by its yellow head and throat, and rust-colored shoulder patches on an otherwise gray body. The dark eyes appear somewhat large for its small head, and the bill is straight and sharply pointed. The adults look identical, while the juveniles are gray until maturity. The Bushtit resembles the immature Verdin, but has a longer tail and is usually not found in the desert shrubs.

Habitat and Diet

At home in the lower elevations, the Verdin lives comfortably in the thorny brush. In some areas where the mesquites have increased, so have the numbers of Verdins in the vicinity. The Verdin is perfect for the desert, as it exists even in areas that seem extremely dry.

The Verdin's diet consists of seeds, insects, and berries. If a small bird is seen flitting around in a creosote bush, it will almost assuredly be a Verdin because there are few other birds who will choose to feed there.

I have discovered that, along with its natural food, the Verdin loves the sugar-water that I feed to several other species. It is also very fond of the suet treats I occasionally add to the variety of bird hors d'oeuvres. During these feeding times, I have my best opportunities to observe the little creatures without the natural protection of thorny brush.

Nesting and Mating Behaviors

The Verdin's nest, a relatively large, elliptical structure made of thorny twigs with a hole in one side, is easily detected. It can be found in the

*Plate 29

thorniest branches of a cholla, the arms of a palo verde, or attached to the crotch of a mesquite tree. The three to five greenish, dotted eggs are well protected, as are the young by the well-constructed, roofed domicile.

Supplemental Information

The Verdin's small size makes it vulnerable to predators including small hawks, owls, and even roadrunners. Its main protection is its ability to dart quickly into the thick brush. For such a small bird, the Verdin has a very audible song with abrupt, detached notes. Often, its loud call serves a very beneficial purpose for all the bird world.

One evening I was watching the usual large number of birds feeding in my yard. Especially in abundance were Gambel's Quail. They were all over the ground, as well as stacked three deep on my feeders. Many other birds were perched in the palos verdes, anxiously waiting their turn, and among them was a Verdin flitting from branch to branch. All of a sudden the Verdin gave out a loud, sharp call, audible even above the continuous chattering of the quail. Instantly, all birds flew to safety just as a hawk came diving toward the feeder in anticipation of a quail for its own dinner. Three evenings later the incident repeated itself, and once again because of the perception and warning call of the Verdin, the hawk flew away empty-taloned.

CACTUS WREN*
Campylorhynchus brunneicapillus

Description: Dark brown crown; black-and-white streaked back; black spotted breast; barred tail; white superciliary

The Cactus Wren, Arizona's State Bird, is very typically a year-round desert resident. The sexes are identical in size and in field markings. Approximately eight inches in length, the Cactus Wren is the largest of the wrens in the United States. Its upperparts and head are light brown with much variegation, while the underparts are white with black speckles. Larger spots appear on the breast, and the outer wing feathers show splashes of white. The bill is unusually long and narrow in proportion to the head.

*Plate 29

Habitat and Diet

The Cactus Wren is found throughout the Southwestern lowlands, but, as the name suggests, it is especially abundant in the cactus forests. Its diet consists of all kinds of insects and spiders as well as berries and seeds.

Nesting and Mating Behaviors

The nest is uniquely constructed and is extremely conspicuous. This large, bulky pouch approximately twelve inches long is neatly constructed of various types of grasses. In the center of the cylindrical structure is the opening, which is one and one-half to two inches in diameter and extends down into the cavity that opens up three inches to four inches. Wrens are continual nest builders and, in fact, construct both breeding and roosting nests.

Both sexes aid in the design and construction of the first seasonal home, but it is the female who does the incubation. The male usually starts on a second nest, which will be ready for the next brood. Also, the female may use it for a roosting nest for herself when the original nest gets a bit crowded with the maturing young.

When the nest is finished, the female lays three to six cream-colored eggs with little brown spots. They hatch within approximately fifteen days. Sometimes, if a second brood is started right away, the male will completely take over the feeding of the first one, while the female incubates the second set of eggs.

The adult wren is very territorial, especially during the nesting season, and continues so until the fledglings become independent. Its protective nature is especially displayed by a very loud, grating song.

Supplemental Information

In becoming a mature adult, the Cactus Wren goes through four stages during the first year. The parents stay with the young longer than many other species, often up to fifty days, and work with them through most of these stages.

As soon as the egg is hatched, the tiny bird becomes a nestling and is immediately fed little fresh insects. This stage lasts approximately twenty days until the chick first departs the nest, at which time it becomes a fledgling. From this moment on, most of the feeding is done on the ground. In the evening, the parents also begin guiding it to a roosting nest of its own. When the fledgling becomes independent, it is labeled a juvenile. When it finally goes through its first molting season in the fall, it becomes a mature adult.

Although I have never seen a Cactus Wren bathing in my birdbath, I surmise that, "desert style," they are extremely clean birds. They are always taking dust baths and are especially fond of the areas where I feed quail. Apparently they like the sand where the quail have scratched away all the larger pebbles, leaving the ground soft and silty. It has been said that adult Cactus Wrens take a dust bath every night before going to roost.

ROCK WREN
Salpinctes obsoletus

Description: Pale gray body; rufous rump; buffy tail corners;
faintly streaked breast

The Rock Wren is the lightest in coloration of the desert-dwelling wrens and measures five to six inches long. The sexes appear similar in plumage; underparts show buffy-white with light gray streaking on the breast. The mottled gray head and back give way to the rufous rump and tail. A light eye stripe calls attention to the slender, slightly decurved bill.

In typical wren fashion, the Rock Wren flicks its tail momentarily, cocking it in an upright fashion. Mocking the Canyon Wren, it bobs up and down while perching vigilant on a rock, or when alarmed.

A series of trilling notes described both as mockingbird-like and cricket-like announce this bird's presence. Its call sounds like *tick-ear*.

Habitat and Diet

The Rock Wren is a common resident on rocky slopes, dry washes, and cliffs in both arid and semi-arid regions.

Insectivorous, this wren comes equipped with a slender, decurved bill to poke into crevices to abscond insects for dinner. Few can hide from this skilled and agile hunter.

Nesting and Mating Behaviors

The nesting behavior of the Rock Wren is very unique and not completely understood. The nest itself, placed under an overhanging rock or hidden in a crevice, is made of grasses, hair, and bark, then lined with even finer materials. The interesting twist is that they pave a path to the "doorstep" with small, smooth rocks which ironically announce its presence after going to so much trouble to conceal it.

The four to eight white eggs are speckled with tiny reddish-brown spots. There may be two or more broods per season.

CANYON WREN
Catherpes mexicanus

Description: Pepper and salt head; white throat and breast; rufous rump, tail, and belly with dark spots

A companion for hikers through the rocky canyons, this exuberant wren is a favorite to many. Its uplifting song always makes me smile. With short, clear, descending notes, the *tee-tee-tee-tee-tee tee-teer teer teer* resounds from the canyon walls. Then suddenly and silently, a curious wren appears, flicking its tail then holding it upright while pausing. A conspicuous white bib contrasts with its mottled brown and rusty body. The deep chestnut belly has dark streaking while mottled, rufous designs cover the rump and banded tail. Pepper and salt coloration on the back extends over the flattened crown down to its slender, long, and slightly decurved bill. The sexes appear similar, measuring five and three-quarters inches long. Along with its infamous song, listen for its sharp call which is a simple *jeet.*

Habitat and Diet

The Canyon Wren is a common resident in the deserts where rocky canyons, cliffs, and rocky hillsides exist. This insectivorous wren comes equipped with a slender body, flattened head, and long, decurved bill, all of which enable it to reach into rock crevices and probe for prey.

Although common, Canyon Wrens are not especially numerous because they hold large territories and therefore are more widely spaced than other wren species.

Nesting and Mating Behaviors

Rock crevices and hollows in remote canyons beckon to this wren in the breeding season. The nest placed in a rock crevice is made of sticks, grasses, and wood chips, then lined with plant down, fur, feathers, and spider silk. The female lays four to six white eggs marked with reddish dots and incubates them by herself. Both parents share the tasks of feeding and rearing the young.

BEWICK'S WREN
Thryomanes bewickii

Description: Plain grayish-brown above, white below; white spots on outer edges of tail; white eyebrow

A long tail with white spotted edgings and a distinct, white superciliary are the two main characteristics that identify the Bewick's Wren (pronounced Buick). This fussy, five- to five-and-one-half-inch-long wren is slightly larger than a House Wren. Both sexes appear the same, wearing a plain, unpatterned, brown plumage above and pure white on the underparts.

Typical of all wrens, it flicks its tail about, momentarily holding it in an upright vertical position. In flight when the tail is spread, a surprising amount of black is displayed along with the conspicuous white tip. The slightly de-curved bill is slender and shorter than its head, and the iris is brown.

The song of this energetic little bird is varied and loud. Clear trilling notes follow a rather soft, buzzing sound resembling that of the Song Sparrow. Also, typical of wrens, it has a scolding call sounding like *vit vit vit*.

Habitat and Diet

The Bewick's Wren is a permanent resident in much of the Southwestern lowlands, and is found in brushy areas, brush piles, and edges of streambeds. Look for it on the ground or low down in bushes where it forages for food. When singing, it may be perched high on a branch.

Feeding mainly on insects or arachnids, the wren's downward-curving, pointed bill is extremely efficient for reaching into small, tight areas for food sources seemingly hidden from sight.

Nesting and Mating Behaviors

The nesting behaviors of the Bewick's Wren are much like those of the House Wren. Some nests are made in natural sites such as woodpecker holes or other cavities in rotted limbs and rock piles, but sometimes the nest is made in some human-made orifices: tin cans, fence posts, mailboxes, flowerpots, pipes, or birdhouses, indicating that this species is one that has adapted well to the ever-increasing encroachment of *homo sapiens*.

The nest is supported by a foundation of haphazardly placed sticks, leaves, and other available material, upon which the actual nest is situated. The refined, cup-shaped style of nest is made of hair, feathers, fine grasses, and moss. The female lays four to eleven oval, white eggs, which have purple and brown spots concentrated on the larger end. She incubates them for approximately fourteen days. Both sexes feed the young numerous insects.

HOUSE WREN
Troglodytes aedon

Description: Grayish-brown body; slight, buff eyebrow; short tail

This rather plain-looking wren is four and one-half to five inches long with brown upperparts, and underparts showing grayish-brown. The back, shoulders, and tail are faintly barred with black, and the buff-colored superciliary is very slight. Tapering gradually, the pointed bill is only slightly decurved. Both sexes appear similar as they strut about, cocking their short tails in expressive and seemingly communicative fashions.

Less melodious than the Bewick's Wren, the House Wren is none the less an avid songster, especially during spring and summer. It bursts forth with a trill that rises with exuberance, then falls away at the end. In typical wren style, it also has a scolding call sounding like *trrrr*.

Habitat and Diet

The House Wren is a migratory species to the Southwestern deserts, wintering in the more vegetated areas, usually near water. It is a welcomed species because it feeds largely on insects and arachnids. One study showed that a House Wren was insectivorous 98% of the time, with the remaining 2% of its food content consisting of vegetable matter.

Watch the House Wren forage for food either on the ground or low in bushes. It snatches small insects on the wing, or pokes its long, decurved bill into cracks and crevices while cocking its tail in expressive positions.

Around houses, this species frequently hops along window sills, darting forward suddenly in pusuit of potential dining delicacies.

Nesting and Mating Behaviors

By April, most House Wrens leave the lower desert areas to nest in higher, cooler locations. The male arrives first, establishes territory, and even begins construction of a nest. The whole housing arrangement is really up to the female, however, and when she arrives, she may accept the male's choices, or she may start anew, with both location and nest construction.

As a cavity nester, the House Wren competes with other species for available sites. Aggressive and occasionally even destructive, the House Wren has been known to oust other birds, either the same or a different species, right from a nest, throwing eggs and even young nestlings out the door! The House Wren will choose almost any kind of cavity including woodpecker holes, bluebird houses, flowerpots, and even boots.

Twigs are first carried to the cavity and used as a foundation for the feathered, grassy, cup-shaped home. The female lays five to eight slightly glossy white eggs, which she incubates for twelve to fifteen days. When the young hatch, the male assists the female in feeding and rearing them.

Marsh Wren
Cistothorus palustris

Description: Heavy white eye stripe; plain brown cap; bold black and white stripes on back

Secretive but curious, the Marsh Wren will come to inspect you if you stand quietly in its territory and wait. Both sexes have similar plumage: mottled rufous wings, rump, and tail that give way to conspicuous black and white stripes on the shoulders and back. The plain, brown crown and heavy eye line also help set it apart from other wrens. The chin and throat are white, while the belly and undertail coverts are buff. This small bundle of energy measures four to five and one-half inches long.

During breeding season, this avid songster sings both during the day and at night. The song is a loud, bubbling, buzzy repertoire sounding like *cut-cut-turrrrr-ur*. Its call resembles *tick-ear*.

Habitat and Diet

Marshes in the desert? Well, how about weedy irrigation ditches, ponds, and man-made reservoirs? According to the Marsh Wren, they will suffice. In fact, in these locations in the lowlands it is a common transient and winter resident, and a few remain year round.

Look among the weeds and reeds for this hyperactive bird that feeds by hanging on stems and gleaning insects from foliage, as well as snatching insects from the water's surface. Flicking its tail, moving from one stem to another, it is seemingly in perpetual motion.

Nesting and Mating Behaviors

By April, the majority of Marsh Wrens have left the desert terrain to migrate northward to breed in marshy areas. The male arrives first in the territory and compulsively builds several "dummy" nests. When the female arrives, she builds the actual brooding nest in her typical, secretive fashion, finding a secure space among the reeds. She attaches an oblong structure woven of reeds, grasses, and cattails, then lines it with feathers, fine grasses, and rootlets. The "dummy" nests may be used for roosting.

She lays three to six cinnamon-colored eggs covered with dark brown spots, then incubates them for thirteen days. When they have hatched, the male assists the female with the tedious task of feeding the hungry youngsters. There are usually two broods per season.

RUBY-CROWNED KINGLET
Regulus calendula

Description: Interrupted eye ring; two white wingbars; very slender, dark bill; male—red crown patch, usually concealed

This tiny, active bird is extremely difficult to distinguish from the Hutton's Vireo. The Ruby-crowned Kinglet has a smaller, darker, and more slender bill, a slightly forked tail, and the male has a scarlet crown patch, which is not always visible unless he is excited. The red is also flashed during mating season to communicate with other males.

Olive-gray coloration covers the upper portion of the Ruby-crowned Kinglet, while darker wings display two conspicuous white wingbars.

The chin and throat are buffy-white leading down to the light yellow belly. Appearing nervous, the Ruby-crowned Kinglet seems to always be in motion. When calling, it even flicks its wings in a rapid, nervous fashion, displaying its four-and-one-half-inch-long body.

Its song is a joyous surprise coming from such a tiny creature. A full, rich, loud rendition consisting of several high notes is followed by a series of low notes. The call is a sharp *ji-dit*. In the lowlands, look for this minuscule bird feeding on the outer branches of deciduous trees.

Habitat and Diet

The Ruby-crowned Kinglet is a common winter resident and transient in the Southwestern lowlands. In this winter range, it is mostly seen singly, whereas in summer it appears in flocks. Look for this insectivorous species gleaning aphids and other insects from dainty, outer branches, and hovering above larger branches searching for caterpillars.

Nesting and Mating Behaviors

By the middle of April, most of the Ruby-crowned Kinglets have left the desert lowlands to return to coniferous forests to breed. Both sexes share in the task of nest construction. For a small species, they build a rather bulky, pensile nest in the dense foliage of a conifer, spruce, or fir. Materials include moss, lichens, twigs, grasses, and bark on the outside; feathers and fur line the inside. This neatly constructed, well-camouflaged nest is very difficult to spot.

The female lays five to eleven buffy-white eggs covered with reddish-brown spots, and incubates them by herself. She and all the eggs are totally concealed during this period. When all the eggs have hatched, this delicate-looking species is kept very busy feeding its sizable family.

BLUE-GRAY GNATCATCHER
Polioptila caerulea

Description: Blue-gray with white underparts; black tail with outer white feathers, conspicuous white eye ring

This active little bird measures only four and one-half inches in length and is very slender. Its long, black-and-white tail is often held vertically upright, showing the extensive white, outermost tail feathers that distinguish it from the female and the non-breeding male Black-tailed Gnatcatcher (white outer corners on latter). From below, the Blue-gray Gnatcatcher's tail appears mostly white.

Appropriate to its name, the upperparts are mainly bluish-gray with underparts displaying white. The male's forehead and crown are outlined with a black line forming a "U." The female lacks this demarcation and is more gray. Both sexes have a white eye ring and white wing edgings. The Blue-gray Gnatcatcher's overall appearance is reminiscent of a minuscule Northern Mockingbird.

The song is delightfully melodious, but somewhat of a wheezy imitation of a warbler. Although many birds are quiet when nesting, this little songster bursts forth with vocal gusto only a few feet from the nest and sometimes even while brooding the eggs.

Habitat and Diet

Wintering in the Southwestern lowlands, the Blue-gray Gnatcatcher may be found in desert washes and arid brushlands. As its name implies, it is insectivorous. It gleans insects from foliage while flitting about in a bush, cocking its tail upright when feeding. This species is absent from the desert in summer.

Nesting and Mating Behaviors

The Blue-gray Gnatcatcher does not nest in the lower desert areas; it migrates instead to higher, cooler regions of the Southwest to nest in deciduous woods, usually in oak or juniper trees. Both sexes contribute to the exquisitely constructed, lichen-covered nest, which takes one to two weeks to complete. Situated on a horizontal branch or fork of the chosen tree, the abode is often conspicuous early in spring until leaves burst forth to surround the two inch, cup-shaped work of art. It is built of fine, fibrous materials, and generously lined with plant down, feathers, and strips of inner bark.

The female lays four or five pale blue eggs speckled with reddish-brown dots. For thirteen days both sexes take turns incubating the eggs, then they also share the duties of feeding and rearing the young.

Black-tailed Gnatcatcher
Polioptila melanura

Description: Black tail with white outer corners on undersurface; inconspicuous white eye ring; male—black cap in summer

The Black-tailed Gnatcatcher is a small, slender bird measuring only four and one-half inches long. The pointed, black bill is shorter than that of the very rare Black-capped Gnatcatcher, and the eye ring is less distinct. Its upperparts are blue-gray with underparts showing a lighter grayish-white.

In summer, the male sports a black cap that comes down to his dark eyes. From February to August, he closely resembles the primarily Mexican Black-capped Gnatcatcher. In winter, without his cap, he is very difficult to distinguish from the Blue-gray Gnatcatcher; but look closely at his tail because it truly has more black than either of the other two species, especially when seen from below. Only a narrow band of white appears, showing most noticeably on the outer corners of the tail.

Watch for this rather tame but active little bird as it hops through the branches, barely pausing to snatch tiny insects. The voice of the Black-tailed Gnatcatcher is raspy sounding like *chee chee chee.*

Habitat and Diet

Black-tailed Gnatcatchers are found throughout the year in arid areas, especially along washes bordered by creosote bushes. They also exist where mesquite and sage abound. (The Blue-gray Gnatcatcher is absent from the lower, arid areas in the summer.)

Feeding strictly on insects, this hyperactive bird flits from branch to branch, gleaning minuscule insects from foliage. It also takes insects on the wing. The Black-tailed Gnatcatcher and the Verdin are the only two birds commonly found in creosote bushes.

Nesting and Mating Behaviors

The nest is a well-constructed woven cup approximately two and one-half inches in diameter and three and one-half inches in height. It is inevitably placed low in a creosote, mesquite, sagebrush, cactus, or other desert bush and is carefully lined with plant down, fiber, feathers, and leaves.

Three or four pale blue eggs adorned with reddish specks are incubated by both sexes for fourteen days. Both adults rear the young.

Western Bluebird*
Sialia mexicana

Description: Male—blue hood; chestnut breast and sides.
Female—bluish-gray upperparts and throat; light chestnut breast

Slightly smaller than the Mountain Bluebird, the Western Bluebird measures six to seven inches long, and like all bluebirds is a member of the thrush family. The male has a deep blue hood as well as a blue back, tail, and wings. Rich chestnut coloration adorns his breast, and he sports a crescent shape on his back. His belly is very light blue, or may show white. The blue hood distinguishes him from the similarly plumaged Eastern Bluebird, which has an ochre chin.

The Female Western Bluebird is bluish-gray with a subtle chestnut-colored breast and light blue wings and tail. The juveniles are gray with spotted underparts.

Perched in a hunched-type posture on low branches, fence posts, wires, or even sturdy weed stalks, the Western Bluebird watches for insects moving among the grasses. Displaying flycatcher-type behaviors, it darts after prey and often returns to the same perch with a wiggling victim.

The Western Bluebird's song is a short series of notes sounding like *cheer, cheer-lee, churr.* Its call includes a soft *few* or *mew.*

Habitat and Diet

The Western Bluebird breeds in higher, cooler elevations. It winters in the lower, more arid regions of the Southwest, where it congregates in flocks and may be seen in grasslands, farmlands, and areas supporting mesquite mistletoe, the berries of which are among its favorite plant food.

Along with other seasonal berries, the Western Bluebird's diet consists largely of insects including grasshoppers (its most frequent meal), crick-

*Plate 30

ets, beetles, and ants. It is also fond of cutworms, earthworms, maggots, millipedes, centipedes, and caterpillars, and has been known to eat snails. The Western Bluebird is only partly migratory, so some species stay in the same territory year round.

Nesting and Mating Behaviors

Natural tree cavities or those excavated by woodpeckers provide nesting sites for the Western Bluebird. As deforestation continues, however, fewer cavities are available for nesting sites. Nesting boxes have certainly helped perpetuate this species.

The Western Bluebird leaves its wintering ground in early spring in order to be first in line for available nesting cavities. The male searches for several possibilities, but the female gives final approval by choosing one, thus also showing acceptance of the male.

His courtship behavior is quite spectacular. He spreads his tail, stretches his wings, and sings sweet medleys. He also flashes the chestnut-colored crescent shape on in his back to warn other males to stay out of his territory and away from the female he is pursuing. Finally, the female chooses one of the nesting cavities, signaling that she accepts his proposal.

The female does the actual construction of the nest, but the male often helps by bringing materials. The female broods the four to six pale blue eggs for fourteen days, then both sexes stay extremely busy hunting for insects, worms, and grubs in order to feed the ravenous youngsters. If something happens to one parent, the other continues to raise the young alone. There are often two broods per season.

Supplemental Information

Bluebirds are among the most loved birds in North America, and providing them with nesting boxes has increased populations of all three species (Western, Mountain, and Eastern). If you live in bluebird breeding territory, you could have a lot of fun by participating in this movement. Remember, however, that nesting boxes alone do not resolve the whole problem. Continued deforestation includes the loss of food sources as well as shelter.

MOUNTAIN BLUEBIRD*
Sialia currucoides

Description: Male—completely sky blue; lighter breast. Female—
gray-brown; blue highlights

The Mountain Bluebird is the only completely blue bird found in the Southwestern deserts. The male displays dazzling, sky blue plumage on his upperparts and lighter blue coloration, sometimes appearing almost white, on his breast and underparts. The female is gray-brown, with striking blue highlights on her wings, rump, and tail. Juveniles are brown with traces of pale blue on the wings and tail, and under parts delicately spotted. Larger than the Western Bluebird, the adult Mountain Bluebird measures six and one-half to eight inches from beak to tail.

Bluebirds often appear hunched when perching, and although the Mountain Bluebird is no exception, it appears more erect than the Western Bluebird. It may be easily spotted, perching on low branches, fence posts, or wires, flying after insects and returning to the same perch, which imitates the behavior of a flycatcher. Hovering in midair, the Mountain Bluebird waits for the opportune moment to pounce on an unsuspecting insect.

Although not as melodious as the Western Bluebird, the Mountain Bluebird has a beautiful song heard mostly in the early dawn hours. Various calls include a quiet *phew, trrrr,* or *eor.*

Habitat and Diet

True to its name, the Mountain Bluebird breeds in higher mountainous regions. By fall, they begin flocking together to migrate to the Southwestern regions where they are found in open farmlands, grasslands, and among berry-bearing bushes. This species is highly migratory.

The Mountain Bluebird has a diverse diet consisting largely of insects: grasshoppers, crickets, beetles, flies, butterflies, dragonflies, alfalfa beetles, and moths. It also consumes many cutworms, earthworms, maggots, millipedes, centipedes, and caterpillars. To add variation, this opportunist also eats seasonal berries. Some favorites include blackberries, chokecherries, wild grapes, and especially in the desert, mistletoe.

*Plate 30

If your birding experiences include backyard birding, remember that the Mountain Bluebird is not a seed eater. To attract this beauty, you will need to offer fruit, insects, earthworms, or mealworms. Don't be surprised when this bird forms a friendly bond with you.

Nesting and Mating Behaviors

The Mountain Bluebird leaves the desert areas in early spring to arrive in breeding territory as early as March. Because it is a "secondary" cavity nester, it must arrive early to compete for the available natural cavities or woodpecker excavations. The male appraises several possibilities, but it is the female who makes the final choice. Mating behaviors are really quite touching. The male spreads his tail and stretches his wings as if to intensify his brilliant blue plumage. He perches beside the female, sings to her, and brings her gifts of food. The female finally chooses one of the nesting sites, which indicates acceptance of the male. Copulation usually begins before nest building.

Both sexes defend territory conspecifically, but only toward their own sex: Males drive away males, females drive away females. Both sexes participate in the construction of the nest, which may be of grasses, pine needles, or small twigs, with finer grasses and feathers forming the cup-shaped portion upon which the eggs are laid. No matter the depth of the cavity, the female builds up the nest so that it is within three inches of the cavity opening.

The female lays three to seven pale-blue eggs and does the brooding entirely by herself. Occasionally the male relieves her for a short period, but he does not have the brood patch to truly incubate. The eggs hatch in fourteen days, then both sexes share the task of feeding and rearing the nestlings. There are generally two broods per season.

Supplemental Information

Mountain Bluebirds have increased in population in areas where nesting boxes have been introduced. Previously, their numbers were on the decline due to habitat destruction and the loss of available nesting sites. If you live in this species' breeding territory, you might find it fun to offer it a "home," and you will be giving the bluebirds and the rest of the world a beautiful gift.

SWAINSON'S THRUSH
Catharus ustulatus

Description: Brown above; dark spots on light underparts; buffy
eye ring and lores

The Swainson's Thrush is distinguished from other thrushes by a bold,
buffy eye ring and buffy lores. Its tail, back, and head are deep brown
(*swainsoni* form) or reddish-brown (*ustulatus* form), and its light underparts are decorated with heavy spotting on the breast. The dusky-brown
bill shows flesh coloration on the basal portion of the lower mandible.
This thrush measures six and one-half to seven and one-half inches from
beak to tail.

Thrushes are avid songsters, and the Swainson's is no exception. A
flute-like series of notes begins low, then gracefully slides up the scale
and becomes softer with the higher notes eventually fading away. The
call sounds like *whit,* or sometimes *foot.*

Habitat and Diet

The Swainson's Thrush is a spring and fall transient in brushy areas of
the Southwestern lowlands, most often showing up in riparian areas.

Thrushes are chiefly insectivorous, finding most prey on the ground by
probing the soil, turning over leaves, and searching in other forms of
decayed vegetation. Worms, snails, insects, and arachnids are the targeted victims, especially ants, wasps, ground-beetles and spiders. Fruit is
also savored, however, and when wild supplies are available, the Swainson's will eat large quantities.

Nesting and Mating Behaviors

By June, the Swainson's Thrush has vacated the lowlands to relocate in
higher elevations where it chooses mixed and coniferous forests for
breeding territory.

It chooses small trees or bushes for a nesting site, where the female
constructs a well-made but bulky affair of twigs, bark, grasses, and
rootlets; then she lines it with finer fibers such as hair and lichens. She
lays three to five smooth, pale blue eggs blotched with brown, and incubates them for fourteen days.

HERMIT THRUSH
Catharus guttatus

Description: Olive-brown upperparts; reddish tail; white eye ring;
spotted chest

The Hermit Thrush measures six and one-half to eight inches from bill
to toe and sports a rufous tail. Upperparts show olive-brown, while dark-
brown spots appear on the white throat, chest, and belly. Both sexes
appear similar in coloration and markings.

This aptly named thrush retires quickly into brushy cover, then ner-
vously cocks its short, reddish tail up and down, paradoxically advertis-
ing its location. Even though this shy bird seems to elude attention, one
cannot miss the eloquence of its song. Beginning with a long, mellow
note, it proceeds with a clear series of flute-like notes that ascend and
descend the scale. These phrases are repeated, each time beginning with
a different pitch. What a treat to hear this medley! It is no wonder the
Hermit Thrush has been honored by many with the title of "best songster." The call note is a soft *chup-chup.*

Habitat and Diet

The Hermit Thrush is a winter resident in the higher desert elevations,
especially in riparian areas, and is a spring and fall transient in the more
arid regions.

This omnivorous species feeds largely on insects including ants,
wasps, and beetles. Worms and arachnids are targeted victims as well. It
habitually feeds in trees, but also searches for prey among decaying vegetation on the ground. When fruit is available, the Hermit Thrush does
not hesitate to partake.

Nesting and Mating Behaviors

For breeding purposes, the Hermit Thrush relocates at higher elevations where mountains support aspen or coniferous forests. The western
form, unlike the eastern, chooses a nesting site in a bush or low tree
instead of the ground.

The female tackles the nest construction without assistance from the
male. She uses moss, grass, bark, and stems for the base structure, then

lines the large, well-made abode with finer materials such as hair and grasses. When finished, she lays three to five smooth, slightly glossy, pale blue, unmarked eggs and incubates them for twelve days.

NORTHERN MOCKINGBIRD*
Mimus polygottos

Description: Gray body; white wingbars; white outer tail feathers

The Northern Mockingbird is best known because, as its name suggests, it copies a repertoire of songs from other birds in its territory. Visually, this beautiful songster is rather plain, with a nine- to eleven-inch slender, gray body. While this agile bird is in flight, however, more striking markings are visible. It conspicuously displays flashes of white on the wings, and black and white patches on the tail feathers. Both sexes appear the same and are comparable in size to a robin.

Both the male and the female seem to delight in the expression of song. Experiencing its melody is an auditory as well as visual delight. One can actually see and feel the vitality of this vivacious bird as it throws its whole body into the performance. From a high perch with wings slightly spread and tail moving in perfect rhythm, this vocalist sings to the world, repeating each act several times before going on to a new series.

Habitat and Diet

The Northern Mockingbird is a common resident throughout the Southwest; however, due to the mild climate, their numbers are augmented in winter by birds from the north. Come spring, the majority begin preparing for a new family, beginning in April.

Although they prefer to nest in thick, thorny shrubs, they also like to be near grassy areas where they feed on grasshoppers, beetles, and small lizards. They supplement their diet with prickly pear cactus fruit, mesquite mistletoe berries, as well as fruits and berries of domestic gardens.

Nesting and Mating Behaviors

The Mockingbird's nest is approximately eight inches in width as well as in height, with the inside depth measuring about four inches. It is con-

*Plate 31

structed of grasses and sticks, and is sometimes lined with hair or leaves. The female chooses the construction site, usually low in a bush, then both sexes diligently build the nest. Generally there are three to five bluish-green eggs, which are slightly glossy and completely covered with olive-brown spots. The female does most of the incubation, but both sexes aid in caring for the young.

The domineering and parenting behavior of the Northern Mockingbird is to be admired. Both the male and the female will go to extremes to defend their young from possible predators. I once witnessed such behavior while a Northern Mockingbird defended its territory from an intrusive cat that had apparently moved too close to the nest. Every time the cat tried to come out from under the car, he was immediately dive-bombed by the aggressive mockingbird. The frustrated feline got the point and finally reluctantly left the persistent bird in peace.

Supplemental Information

The Mockingbird sings not only in the early morning or late evening, but can be heard any time during the day. One of its most special performances occurs during the night when the full moon is in its magnificence.

My love for the full moon stems back as early as I can remember. As I was raised in the country and without street lamps, I was always excited when the moon bathed the glorious outdoors with its soft light. I think our resident mockingbird must have shared my sentiment, because it would sometimes sing throughout the entire night whether the moon was full or almost full. Several nights in a row, the mockingbird would sing its medley of tunes. I would usually catch a few songs and then drift peacefully into sleep.

SAGE THRASHER
Oreoscoptes montanus

Description: Small body; bold streaking underneath; short, slender bill; yellow eye; white eye ring; white tail corners in flight

The eight- to nine-inch-long Sage Thrasher is the smallest of the desert thrashers. It is grayish-brown above, and the buffy-white underparts are decorated with bold streaking from chin to undertail coverts. Two white wingbars and white-tipped outer tailfeathers highlight the drab coloration. The slender bill is shorter than the head, and appears much straighter than the de-curved bill of most thrashers. The iris is lemon-yellow. The sexes appear similar, and juveniles show streaking on the head and back.

Most often, this species is seen running around on the ground hunting for insects. Although less numerous than other thrashers, it often appears more conspicuous because it loves to perch in the open while singing a rendition of mockingbird-like notes. Calls includes *chuck* and *churr*.

Habitat and Diet

A year-round resident in parts of the Mojave and Chihuahuan deserts, it is an uncommon-to-rare winter resident in select and sparsely vegetated areas of the Sonoran Desert. True to its name, sagebrush as well as other sparse desertscrub define its habitat. Not only is it at home in uninhabited desert regions, it is also comfortable around human habitation. Insectivorous, the Sage Thrasher is an asset to farming areas adjacent to its desert habitat. In payment for this service, the farmer contributes small portions of fruits and vegetables, which supplement the protein diet.

Nesting and Mating Behaviors

The nest is concealed in a low bush only one to three feet above the ground, or placed on the ground hidden under a bush. Although inconspicuous, it is a bulky affair made of twigs and lined with grasses, roots, and horsehair.

The female lays four or five glossy, bluish-green eggs with brown splotching. Both adults incubate the eggs for fifteen days, then share the task of feeding the young and ultimately teaching them to fend for themselves.

BENDIRE'S THRASHER
Toxostoma bendirei

Description: Grayish-brown body; short, decurved bill, triangular-shaped streaking; yellow eye

This light, grayish-brown thrasher is distinguished from other desert thrashers by its shorter and less decurved bill. The lower mandible is straighter and lighter in coloration than that of the Curve-billed Thrasher. Although the latter has light streaking on the breast, the streaking of the Bendire's is distinct and triangular. Both sexes appear similar, measuring nine to eleven inches in length. The eyes are yellow, but are not as obvious as the orange-yellow of the Curve-billed Thrasher. Be sure to look closely at these three characteristics: bill, type of streaking, and eye. Otherwise you may confuse the Bendire's with the more common Curve-billed Thrasher.

The distinctive song of the Bendire's Thrasher is beautiful, continuous, and melodious with various repetitions. The call is a low *chuck* sound.

The Bendire's Thrasher is more likely to be seen flying than other thrashers who characteristically prefer to run on the ground from bush to bush.

Habitat and Diet

The Bendire's Thrasher is a common summer resident of the more open areas of the desert. A few winter among the mesquite or creosote bushes, and they are also seen around farmlands and grasslands. Although many migrate further south after breeding, they return to the Southwestern desert areas by late January or early February. Their diet consists mainly of insects, but is supplemented with available fruits and seeds.

Nesting and Mating Behaviors

During breeding season, the musical, warbling call of the Bendire's Thrasher commands attention. While auditioning for the female, the male also entertains all who care to listen.

The nest may be found in mesquite, palo verde, catclaw, or cholla cactus, and is somewhat smaller and more compact than the nest of other thrashers. Made of sticks and lined with horsehair, fine grasses, string, and even cloth, the nest is situated three to ten feet above the ground. The female lays three or four eggs, which are usually pale green, but are sometimes grayish or even pinkish. Regardless of hue, they are blotched with darker coloration.

Curve-billed Thrasher[*]
Toxostoma curvirostre

Description: Brownish-gray body; light chest streaks; long, decurved bill; yellow eye

The Curve-billed Thrasher is one of the most abundant, permanent desert birds. Blending very smoothly with the surroundings, both sexes are a brownish-gray with only faint, rounded chest spots and paler brown underparts. The most distinct characteristics are the bright yellowish-orange eyes and the obvious, decurved bill. It is approximately ten to eleven inches in length, has a long slender tail and can vanish with incredible speed. Although there are other desert thrashers, the Curve-billed Thrasher is by far the most common.

Habitat and Diet

The Curve-billed Thrasher inhabits the low desert areas and is primarily found among chollas, mesquites, palos verdes, and creosote bushes. It mainly forages on the ground for food, which consists largely of insects. It supplements this diet with some fruits, seeds, and berries.

Thrashers are extremely aggressive and become very competitive around feeding stations. One evening a very comical scene occurred between a Round-tailed Ground-Squirrel and a Curve-billed Thrasher. Every critter had been eating quite peacefully until there was only one piece of fruit left on the ground. The squirrel zipped up to it, picked it up in its paws, and began to eat. A thrasher flew down from a nearby creosote bush, deciding he wanted the fruit for himself, and the comedy began. The thrasher tried to snatch the fruit away from the squirrel who immediately became infuriated and escaped a few feet away. When he again tried to consume his delicacy, the thrasher very domineeringly approached him and began pecking him on the head. The squirrel hunkered down on the ground until he could take no more of this bird's obnoxious treatment. He quickly fled, leaving the Curve-billed Thrasher to the snack he had left behind.

* Plate 31

Nesting and Mating Behaviors

The breeding season of the Curve-billed Thrasher is longer than many of the typical desert birds, extending from mid-January to mid-July. The nest itself is a large, prominent structure made of twigs, and is often found amid the arms of a cholla. The outside of the nest is approximately twelve inches deep, and the inside cavity is half that depth. Its width is about ten inches, and the cavity is often lined with grass. Extremely well protected in the middle of a thorny shrub, this bulky stick nest will eventually contain two to four greenish, speckled eggs, which are incubated by both sexes.

Supplemental Information

The song of the Curve-billed Thrasher is somewhat similar to the Northern Mockingbird, but the notes are not ended quite as abruptly and there is a softer quality in the tone. The Curve-billed Thrasher has a large variety of very pleasing medleys, which prompted the Mexicans to name it *Cuitiacoache,* meaning "songbird." Its loudest and most abrupt call is a two-note whistle.

I once witnessed a thrilling mating dance displayed by Curve-billed Thrashers. It began with two males aggressively attacking each other as they ran back and forth on top of a brick wall. Eventually both retreated with neither appearing to be the victor, and then began a series of growling and purring sounds. I watched to see what would happen next, as did a female who was perched in a palo verde next to the wall. Much to my surprise, both males suddenly puffed up twice their normal sizes and began strutting up and down in front of the female. Finally, after many little dance steps and many purring sounds, the males returned to their previous aggressive behavior and one ultimately emerged as the winner. He immediately flew into the palo verde; then the newly formed pair glided down to the desert floor a short distance away.

Birds sing basically for two purposes: to establish their territories—which was probably the reason for the growling types of sounds exhibited by the males, and to stimulate a mate. The soft, melodious sounds that prefaced copulation were simply beautiful. When the two birds finished, they flew to the top of a cholla where they began another repertoire of expressive medleys.

CRISSAL THRASHER
Toxostoma crissale

Description: Long, decurved bill; dark malar marks; plain breast; chestnut undertail patch; dark eye

The Crissal Thrasher is the largest and most slender thrasher of the Southwestern lowlands, measuring ten and one-half to twelve and one-half inches long. Dark upperparts fade into lighter, grayish-brown underparts with a light breast void of streaking. The distinctive undertail patch is chestnut and most obvious in flight. This patch is called the crissum, thus the name Crissal Thrasher.

On the whitish throat, a dark, narrow line appears as a mustache running up to the deeply decurved bill. The tail is dark, slim, and long, and the eyes are dull yellow or brownish. Both sexes appear similar. The Crissal Thrasher is the most secretive of the thrashers foraging inconspicuously in the dense underbrush.

Its song is varied and very smooth compared to other thrashers. Loud repetitions including *chorelee, pichoory,* or *toit-toit* aid in spotting this reclusive bird, especially in the early mornings when it is most vocal.

Habitat and Diet

Although a permanent resident in the hot, low deserts, the Crissal Thrasher is very hard to locate because it is shy and prefers habitat along streams or dry washes where dense groves of mesquite, palo verde, or other desertscrub abound. It may also be found in riparian woodlands.

Eating mainly insects, this bird uses its decurved bill as a tool for probing into the ground for seemingly hidden prey.

Nesting and Mating Behaviors

This elusive thrasher builds a nest two to eight feet above the ground in dense brush along washes or hillsides, often directly under a heavy branch to protect the entrance. The bowl-shaped structure is made of thorny twigs, and lined with grasses and feathers.

The female lays two to four slightly glossy blue-green eggs; they are unmarked and therefore unique for thrasher eggs. Both sexes take turns incubating the eggs, then also in feeding and rearing the young when they hatch. There are usually two broods per season.

LeConte's Thrasher
Toxostoma lecontei

Description: Pale gray body; plain breast; dark eye; long decurved
bill; white chin

The LeConte's Thrasher is palest of the desert thrashers and measures
ten to eleven inches long. Upperparts are light grayish-brown while underparts are grayish-white with no streaking. The tail, decurved bill, and eyes
are dark, as is the eyeline. Both sexes appear the same with tawny undertail coverts becoming deeper, buffy-brown during breeding season.

The LeConte's Thrasher may be seen running on the ground where its
sandy coloration serves as excellent camouflage. Dodging quickly, this
crafty bird can hide in the slightest bit of cover. Using remarkable speed
to retreat from danger, it will fly when surprised or overtaken.

Highly vocal at dusk and dawn, it may also be heard breaking forth
from the stillness of the night with a beautiful and somewhat repetitious
medley. What a treat! Calls include *tweep* and *whit*. Because this thrasher
chooses the hottest, driest, and most barren parts of the desert, a noon
reprieve during the hottest part of the day is necessary. During this time it
is seldom seen or heard.

Habitat and Diet

In the lowest portions of the Mojave and Sonoran deserts, the Le-
Conte's Thrasher may be found in sparsely vegetated areas of cholla cactus, creosote bushes, and small mesquite trees. An uncommon but permanent resident, this elusive species feeds on insects in the early
morning and evening when it is cooler and when more insects abound.
Like other thrashers, it uses its decurved bill to probe into arid, sandy soil
for prey.

Nesting and Mating Behaviors

An early nester—beginning in January—the LeConte's Thrasher builds
a bulky, bowl-shaped structure of thorny sticks lined with leaves, rootlets,
and feathers placed four to eight feet above the ground. Most often it is
situated in the middle of a cholla cactus or a mesquite tree where it is easily seen from a distance. Both sexes cooperate in building the nest and in
incubating the three to four glossy, pale, greenish-blue eggs, which are

slightly spotted, especially at the larger end. Incubation takes fourteen days, then the adults jointly feed and rear the young. They usually raise two to three broods per season.

PHAINOPEPLA*
Phainopepla nitens

Description: Red eye; crest; male–black body; white underwing patches. Female–gray body

The name, Phainopepla (pronounced fay-no-pepla), is a Latin word meaning "shiny cloak," an appropriate title for the male, who, indeed, has a flashy black appearance. Under the wings there are conspicuous white patches that can only be seen in flight. The Phainopepla has bright red eyes, an expressive crest, and a long slender tail, which adds to its elegant appearance. The female is dark gray, and both sexes are approximately seven to seven and one-half inches from the crest to the tip of the tail. The Phainopepla has been called the Black Cardinal because its silhouette appears very similar to that of the Northern Cardinal's.

This active bird is fun to watch while it exhibits flycatcher-type behaviors. The Phainopepla perches in the top of mesquites or palos verdes and flies down to snatch insects in midair. Phainopeplas dart quickly, but with much grace and grandeur, and the male displays the white wing patches that contrast so starkly with his shiny black cloak.

Seldom still, the phainopepla continually flicks its tail and raises its crest, even while perching; but the real action begins when clouds of insects appear to lure this bird into a perpetual feeding frenzy.

Habitat and Diet

This slender bird is found in areas of the Southwest that are populated with shrubs densely infiltrated with mistletoe; the berries are its favorite food. Because mistletoe is seasonal, however, the Phainopepla supplements his diet with insects and other available fruits.

The Phainopepla inhabits the hot deserts only during the cooler months of the year. It raises a first brood in this environment, then leaves in late May or early June when the weather becomes too hot. In a cooler,

* Plate 31

wetter location, usually riparian woodlands in northern California or northern Arizona, this versatile species raises a second brood, then returns to the deserts in October.

Nesting and Mating Behaviors

Mistletoe is not only beneficial as a food source for the Phainopepla, but also serves as a perfect camouflage for this elusive bird. The Phainopepla is well hidden while peacefully consuming this gourmet food, and usually chooses to build its nest near a clump of mistletoe for protection. The nest is so well concealed that it is often passed by unnoticed. Most of the nests are constructed high enough in a tree to afford protection from ground predators, but occasionally a nest is found hanging from the mistletoe in the lower branches of its parent tree.

The Phainopepla's nest is extremely well made of the finest of twigs, which are bonded together with spider silk. The twigs are fastened together so that they appear to be woven as one piece around the outside of the nest. Soft feathers and down-like substances line the securely woven, cup-shaped interior. The whole structure is skillfully fastened to the low hanging branches of the mistletoe; from a distance it appears to be simply an extension of the plant itself.

In some species, the male and female together choose a nesting site. In species that do not stay together during the entire nesting season, and in which the male leaves even before incubation begins, the female alone chooses the nesting site. In the case of the Phainopepla, it is the male who independently selects the spot for the new nest and takes the main responsibility for its construction. The eggs are a beautiful, light blue-green and are generously splashed with black specks.

Supplemental Information

Some of the literature suggests that the Phainopepla is usually silent. Other authorities claim that it sings when large numbers inhabit essentially the same territory. My experiences with this species have been mainly in areas densely populated with mesquite and palo verde mistletoe, affording much food and protection for large numbers of them. In this environment, the Phainopepla truly adds to the melodious sounds of the desert. Its song is casual and short, with a soft, sweet tone that always leaves me smiling.

LOGGERHEAD SHRIKE*
Lanius ludovicianus

Description: Gray upperparts; white below; black face mask; hooked bill

The Loggerhead Shrike–between eight and ten inches long–not only appears about the size of a Mockingbird, but also has the gray and white coloration, and even repeats its notes and phrases in a Mockingbird style. The Loggerhead Shrike has a gray back, white underparts, and a conspicuous black eye mask that continues across the forehead over the beak. The head is relatively large in proportion to its body, and it has a very distinctive, strong hooked bill. There is a small white patch on its rump and also on the back close to each black wing. In addition, it has short legs and a slender tail.

It is similar to the Northern Shrike, but has a solid black bill and a continuous line over the eye. Also, the Northern Shrike is very rarely seen in the arid Southwestern lowlands.

The Loggerhead Shrike flies with rapid wing beats in a direct manner, usually dipping close to the ground then sweeping upward to land on a chosen perch.

The notes and phrases of this bird are sometimes repeated up to twenty times, which is similar to the Northern Mockingbird, but the shrike sounds more harsh, has long pauses, and does not have the same repertoire. Although it is a songbird, its behaviors resemble that of a hawk, sitting on a perch surveying the surroundings for possible prey. Also, the Loggerhead Shrike hovers in midair, much like the American Kestrel, before pouncing on its victim.

Habitat and Diet

The Loggerhead Shrike can be found in the desert among thickets, or in semi-open country where there are appropriate perches from which to hunt. This raptor-like songbird mainly consumes large insects, as is typical of many other song birds, but also eats reptiles, small mammals, and even other small birds. It often impales prey on barbed wire or on thorns, which is why it was formerly named Butcher Bird.

* Plate 32

This shrike swoops down on prey, landing on top of it with heavy feet used for gripping, then stuns its victim with its large hooked beak. The Loggerhead Shrike immediately carries the victim to a thorny branch and either begins dismembering it into bite size pieces to eat, or may simply hang the squirming prey there to die. The Loggerhead Shrike may leave prey without even a nibble and go back for more if the hunting is good.

Nesting and Mating Behaviors

It is almost certain that the Loggerhead Shrike will nest in thorny brush or in close proximity to it. Both sexes bring material to the nesting site, which is chosen by the male. There is much controversy about which sex actually builds the structure.

In any case, it is made of sticks, grasses, twigs, and bark fibers carefully woven into a cup-shaped nest, meticulously lined with feathers, cattle hair, rootlets, and bark fibers. Nests are very substantial and may be used year after year. The structure measures about four and one-half inches high and the outside diameter is about ten inches.

The female lays four to eight eggs, which are an off-white color and are oval to long-oval with a smooth shell. She does the majority of the incubation, but the male stays close by and feeds her. In approximately sixteen days, the young hatch, and both parents take turns hunting for food and feeding the young.

Supplemental Information

Because its feet are not strong enough to kill prey in the same manner as raptors, the Loggerhead Shrike carries its dazed victim to a thorny bush or a barbed wire fence, using this sharp "instrument" to assist in killing and dismembering its victim into edible pieces. Barbarious as it may seem, this action really indicates intelligence and is an example of the use of a tool to assist in the feeding process.

There seem to be a number of theories for the practice of leaving an uneaten victim hanging on a thorny branch. Some think it is a rapacious habit with no particular purpose; others think that it may serve as a lure to draw in other insects and birds; and further speculation indicates a means of storing food so that when game is scarce, the Loggerhead Shrike can resort back to its own personal supply.

EUROPEAN STARLING*
Sturnus vulgaris

Description: Black body; purplish-green sheen

The European Starling is seven to eight inches long, about the size of a meadowlark, and has a short, stubby tail. Both sexes look the same, and in summer are generally black. They change color with the seasons, however, showing iridescent highlights of green and purple during the spring. The bill, usually dark, turns yellow during the breeding season. In winter, contrasting white speckles are added to its black feathers. Immature starlings are ashy gray in coloration. They are very swift in the air and navigate in a very straight flight directly to their destination.

Habitat and Diet

The European Starling is very common all over the Southwest, and has even been said to outnumber the House Sparrow; however, neither is indigenous to America. This starling was brought from Europe and was introduced into New York's Central Park in the late 1800s. Since then it has spread very rapidly throughout the country, and was first recorded in Arizona in 1946. This species is now abundant throughout the entire Southwest.

This aggressive intruder propagates in large numbers and apparently has few natural enemies. Hordes of starlings have invaded cities, creating many problems due to excreta from such an overwhelming number of birds congregating together. Because of the fear of disease from this species, there have been many attempts, in various cities, to get rid of them. Still, starlings abound.

The starlings' diet consists largely of insects and fruits. Farmers have always dreaded the onslaught of starlings, for they can utterly consume the fruits of a harvest. Also, various feedlot owners hate the intrusion of the starling because their excreta contaminates the commercial food for the livestock. In the agricultural industry, the damage apparently far outweighs the benefits gained by the consumption of insects.

* Plate 32

Nesting and Mating Behaviors

The European Starling prefers to nest in natural cavities of trees, saguaro cacti, and occasionally in rocky cliffs. Damage to native birds occurs from starlings moving into available nesting sites early in the spring, thus displacing birds indigenous to the area. It is especially damaging to the birds that winter further south and return in the spring, only to find their homes already occupied by this gregarious species. Sometimes the starling even intrudes into a nest already occupied by a bird who is nesting. The starling will occasionally kill the occupant with its sharply pointed beak in its attempts to appropriate the site.

In the desert, the European Starling often chooses a cavity high in a giant saguaro. Sometimes it has a single nest, but often it joins a group nesting in a colony.

Both sexes share in the task of building a nest, or more accurately, in lining an existing cavity with haphazard piles of material consisting of various combinations of twigs, grasses, leaves, and feathers. The male and female share equally in the incubation process as well as in the feeding and rearing of the young birds. It is a full-time job for the parents to nutritionally satisfy the young, as they seem to demand food every fifteen to twenty minutes.

The female lays four to six slightly glossy eggs, which are a pale turquoise color and are without the slightest markings. The incubation period is approximately twelve days, a relatively short time in comparison with some native species. The adults usually have two broods per season.

Supplemental Information

There have been many attempts to rid the country of the European Starling. In 1957, an experiment was conducted to discourage the starling from congregating in certain areas of cities. Even though the starling is accused of creating a messy environment, it can be quite finicky when it comes to its own feet. A sticky material, which was called "Roost-No-More," was placed where starlings were accumulating enmass. The starlings would have no part of the mess on their feet, and quickly avoided the area. I question if the sticky goo that prevailed was worth the trade-off.

SOLITARY VIREO
Vireo solitarius

Description: White spectacles; two bold, white wingbars

The two races occurring most frequently in the Southwestern low-lands are the Rockies form and the West Coast form. A third form, East-ern, is an accidental in this region.

The Rockies breeding form is gray and white, while the West Coast race has an olive back with yellow sides and flanks. Both have white throats and underparts, and conspicuous white spectacles. Broad, white wingbars adorn the dark wings. The rather thick bill has a small hook on the tip, and the forehead is partially covered with bristle-like feathers.

An avid songster, it is not uncommon to hear this little bird singing from high in a tree even in winter. Deep, rich notes with deliberate pauses sound like *chuwee, cheereo, bzurrp, chuweer.* Its call is *chv chv chv chv.*

Habitat and Diet

The Solitary Vireo is an uncommon migrant and occasional winter res-ident in riparian areas of the desert lowlands.

The majority of food consists of insects and their larvae, which are gleaned from leaves and bark. When available, fruits and berries are eaten in small portions.

Nesting and Mating Behaviors

The Solitary Vireo breeds in higher elevations where it chooses to be among evergreen and deciduous woodlands. The male brings materials such as grasses, bark strips, rootlets, and hair to the female, which she uses in the design and construction of the nest. The loose, bulky affair takes the form of a semipensile basket suspended from a horizontal fork of a branch.

The female lays three to five smooth, creamy-white eggs dotted with brown and black. Both sexes take responsibility in incubating the eggs for thirteen to fourteen days. A hearty songster, the male cannot contain himself, even when incubating.

WARBLING VIREO
Vireo gilvus

Description: Plain olive-gray plumage; no black edgings on white eyebrow; no wingbars

This small bird measures four and one-half to five and one-half inches long and is dressed in very plain plumage. The sexes are similar with olive-gray coloration above, white breast, and yellowish sides and undertail coverts. White eyebrows lack the dark borders sometimes apparent in other vireos, and the plain wings are a distinguishing feature in themselves.

The eye is dark and the short bill is heavier than that of a warbler. Also, notice the slight hook at the tip. Most vireos have a touch of green plumage—in fact, the Latin word *vireo* means "I am green."

While its call note is a soft, wheezy *vit*, a melodious song pours fourth with long warbling notes resembling those of the Purple Finch.

Habitat and Diet

The Warbling Vireo is an uncommon migrant throughout the Southwestern lowlands. Only the Western form is seen in desert areas where deciduous vegetation affords appropriate food and protection.

Mainly insectivorous, it gleans insects from foliage, and any invading insects are readily devoured by this tiny bird. Seasonal fruits and berries also supplement the protein diet.

Nesting and Mating Behaviors

The Warbling Vireo breeds at higher elevations in deciduous woodlands. The nest is meticulously built by both sexes with leaves, grasses, and stems, then lined with horsehair. The cup-shaped structure is woven together with spider webs and attached to a horizontal fork of a branch, usually no higher than twelve feet from the ground.

The female lays three to five smooth, white eggs with brown spots. Both adults share the task of incubation, which takes about two weeks. This melodious songster even sings while incubating the eggs.

ORANGE-CROWNED WARBLER
Vermivora celata

Description: Yellow undertail coverts; slight streaking on breast; usually concealed orange crown patch; thin decurved bill

The Orange-crowned Warbler is four and one-half to five and one-half inches long and is extremely plain looking. This fact alone makes it identifiable. The olive-green upperparts and the greenish-yellow underparts are adorned only by the orange crown, which is seldom visible; a narrow, dark eye stripe; faint streaking on the breast; and yellow undertail coverts. No decorative eye ring or wingbars exist. The crown patch is displayed only when threatened or during courtship.

This little species is usually seen flitting about the branches, singing its rather plain song consisting of trills going either up or down the scale. Try standing still and making *pish* sounds. It is not shy and will come closer to check you out.

Habitat and Diet

The Orange-crowned Warbler is a common transient and winter resident in areas of the Southwestern lowlands containing dense brush, especially along rivers or streams that support cottonwoods. It may also be seen in towns where it can find sufficient bushes for privacy.

Foliage is not only necessary for protection of the warbler, but also hosts this dainty little species' food supply. Flitting along limbs and trunks, the Orange-crowned Warbler finds insects and their larvae, which it consumes in great numbers.

Nesting and Mating Behaviors

By late April, the majority of wintering birds leave for higher elevations to breed. They usually choose territories with trees and shrubs near open areas such as pastures, burns, or meadows.

The nest is placed on the ground among clumps of bushes, or low in a shrub up to three feet high. The nest appears large for this small bird and is made of strips of bark interwoven with dried grasses, and generously lined with hair, feathers, and animal fur. The three to six creamy-white eggs are finely speckled with chestnut.

NASHVILLE WARBLER
Vermivora ruficapilla

Description: Bold, white eye ring; yellow throat and undertail coverts; white patch at base of legs

This four- to five-inch-long songster has olive-green plumage on its back and tail, and a bright yellow throat, belly, and undertail covert. Look for the white patch at the base of its legs, and the distinct white eye ring on the gray head. The male occasionally displays a chestnut crown patch, but don't count on seeing it for identification purposes. The female and immatures are very similar, but not quite as brightly colored as the male. Watch closely because this slender bird appears to wag its tail!

Its sweet melody is comprised of two series: *see-pit see-pit see-pit see-pit* and *titititi*. The call is a sharp *chink*.

Habitat and Diet

The Nashville Warbler is an uncommon transient in the Southwestern lowlands, and is found among brush, weeds, and deciduous trees. Flitting incessantly among the leaves and branches, this little creature devours insects, thus contributing to the delicate natural balance necessary for vegetation to survive. Hunting in the crevices, in blossoms, and on leaves, few insects escape this warbler's scrutinizing surveillance.

Nesting and Mating Behaviors

After wintering further south, the Nashville Warbler migrates through the desert lowlands lingering to feed, then follows high ground to its breeding territory where forest edges provide nesting sites. Directly on the ground, or in a small depression near the base of a bush, the tiny female makes a tidy cup of bark, leaves, and grasses, or sometimes just pine needles; then lines it with feathers, fur, and moss. She lays four to five smooth, creamy-white eggs with brown spots. Alone, she incubates them for eleven to twelve days.

Lucy's Warbler
Vermivora luciae

Description: Gray body; rufous rump; reddish crown patch

The only warbler that nests in the desert is Lucy's Warbler. Gray upper plumage is simply decorated with a rufous rump and a chestnut crown patch. The lighter gray head practically fades into the white eye ring, making the ring nearly non-discernable. Underparts are whitish. Immatures have a buff-colored rump similar to the female.

Look for this species in mesquites or cottonwoods. When you find a Lucy's Warbler, it will most assuredly be flitting about continually in motion, flicking its tail with each pause. Beginning in late March, the males perch high on a branch and sing incessantly, announcing to the world that they have established territory. The call is a soft metallic *plenk* that is often repeated, and the song is *chit chit chit chit sweeta che-che-che.*

Habitat and Diet

The Lucy's Warbler is the only true warbler of the Southwestern deserts, meaning that it nests in this habitat. It usually chooses areas where streams or washes support mesquites or cottonwoods.

Like other warblers, it is insectivorous and feeds by gleaning insects from foliage. Additionally, the bill confiscates unsuspecting victims from crevices of bark.

Nesting and Mating Behaviors

Lucy's Warbler is a cavity nester, choosing abandoned woodpecker holes, natural cavities, or even slips behind loose pieces of bark to set up housekeeping. The nest is made of fine grasses, leaves, and stems; then lined with horsehair and feathers. The female lays three to seven creamy-white eggs sprinkled with brown spots. She is very secretive about the location of her nest.

YELLOW WARBLER
Dendroica petechia

Description: Yellow overall; male—brighter with rusty breast
streaks, yellow tail flashes

Extensive yellow plumage easily identifies this four and one-half to five
and one-quarter-inch-long delight. Both sexes are yellow, but the male
appears brighter and sports rust-colored streaks on his breast and flanks.
The female may have faint streaking, and her plumage sometimes
appears more olive-green, especially in fall. Watch closely for the yellow
tail flashes.

An energetic bird, the Yellow Warbler flits among the foliage and sings
with similar vigor. Its upbeat, cheerful song sounds like *wee-chee, wee-
chee, chee, chee* or even seems to be exclaiming words of its own disposition: *sweet, sweet, sweet, sweeter, sweeter.* The call is a loud *cheep.*

Habitat and Diet

The Yellow Warbler is a common transient in the lowlands and a common summer resident in riparian habitat where water is permanent.
Look for it in willows, cottonwoods, and sycamores. It is virtually absent
from the deserts in winter. Typical of all warblers, this dainty little
species is insectivorous and feeds by gleaning insects from foliage.
Although short, its bill suffices for picking small creatures from the
cracks in bark.

Nesting and Mating Behaviors

Cottonwoods and willows are the main hosts for the well-constructed,
cup-shaped nest. Grasses, plant fibers, hair, and milkweed fibers are carefully interwoven, then lined with finer fibers; this is all done by the female
in about four days. After she completes the nest, she begins laying three
to six smooth, slightly glossy, bluish-white eggs, which are decorated
with light scrawling. She incubates them for eleven to twelve days, then
begins the on-going task of finding food for her young.

Supplemental Information

The Yellow Warbler is one species frequently parasitized by the Brown-headed Cowbird. Whereas some victimized species seem to tolerate the intrusion, the Yellow Warbler is not only aware of the potential danger imposed on her own young, but takes strides to terminate the intrusive act. When an outside egg is found in her nest, she simply builds an additional "floor" over it and continues with her own brood. Why other bird species do not protect in the same way is just one more of nature's mysteries.

BLACK-THROATED GRAY WARBLER
Dendroica nigrescens

Description: Male–black and white head; plain black crown; yellow spot on lore; black bib. Female–lacks black bib

Blacks, whites, and grays adorn this four and one-half to five inch warbler. The male has a black head and bib with a white streak above the eye and another extending from the base of the bill down the side of its neck. A yellow spot appears between the black, slender bill and the dark brown iris. His underparts are white with black streaking on the sides. Upperparts are various degrees of dark gray with two white wingbars matching the outer white tail feathers.

The female resembles the male, but is slightly lighter and lacks the black bib. Instead, she sports black streaks on her chin accompanied by a dark patch on each side of the lower throat. The non-breeding male and the immature birds resemble the female in this respect.

Warblers are some of our most skilled songsters, and the Black-throated Gray Warbler is no exception. It has various repertoires, but perhaps the most frequent rendition is a buzzy sound described as *weezy weezy weezy weezy-weet*. The call is an abrupt flat *tup*.

Habitat and Diet

The Black-throated Gray Warbler is a transient and winter resident in the deserts of the Southwest. It inhabits brushy areas along washes, chaparral, and riparian areas that support cottonwoods, sycamores, willows, and mesquites.

This insectivorous bird plays a big role in controlling populations of pesky insects. It gleans them from foliage high in tree tops and takes them on the wing as well.

Nesting and Mating Behaviors

The Black-throated Gray Warbler leaves the lower desert areas by early March to nest in the higher elevations, choosing coniferous and other mixed woods including manzanita trees for nesting sites. It may build a nest as low as seven feet off the ground, or as high as thirty-five feet up in a tree. In larger trees the nest may be placed as far out as ten feet from the trunk, but in smaller shrubs, it is often constructed near the center. The style is cup-shaped and is an eclectic combination of leaves, plant fibers, and bark all attached to the tree with spider-like silk.

The female lays three to five pinkish-white eggs with reddish-brown spots, which are more concentrated on the large end, and incubates them by herself. Then, both sexes participate in feeding and rearing the nestlings.

YELLOW-RUMPED WARBLER*
Dendroica coronata

Description: Yellow rump, crown, side patch, and throat;
    otherwise gray with black markings

Not only does the Yellow-rumped Warbler have a bright yellow rump as denoted by its name, but it also has a yellow cap, yellow throat (Audubon's race), and yellow patches on its sides. Dark gray plumage variegated with black streaks dominate the upperparts, while white and dark streaking appear on the underparts. A white tail patch and two white wingbars are obvious. The female has grayish-brown upperparts, and lighter yellow showing on her throat, rump, and cap. Immature birds and non-breeding males resemble the female.

This species was formerly two distinct species: Audubon's Warbler and Myrtle Warbler. Because of interbreeding, the two forms are now considered conspecific.

*Plate 32

The song is loud and is described as *seet-seet-seet-seet, trrrrr*. From a high perch, the male sings his trilling melody that first rises, then falls in pitch. The call of the Yellow-rumped Warbler is a crisp *cheep*.

Habitat and Diet

The Audubon's form is a common winter resident in desert oases where brush, thickets, and riparian growth abound. When fall transients arrive, it is truly abundant. The Myrtle form is a rare transient and winter resident. During the non-breeding season, Yellow-rumped Warblers are seen in loose flocks where they may be heard making soft calls to keep track of each other.

This active, insectivorous warbler gleans multitudes of tiny insects from foliage and is also skilled in taking insects on the wing. Drawn to orchards when fruit is ripe, this little bird takes many insects that are drawn to the fruit itself.

Nesting and Mating Behaviors

The majority of Yellow-rumped Warblers leave the desert areas in early April to breed in higher elevations containing coniferous and mixed forests. The nest is placed on a conifer branch usually near the trunk, and can be as low as four feet off the ground or as high as fifty feet up in the tree. The nest is a well-made, cup-shaped affair constructed of twigs, bark strips, and fibers, then heavily lined with hair, grasses, and feathers.

The female lays three to five greenish eggs with brown blotches, and incubates them for twelve to thirteen days. Both sexes feed and rear the young.

TOWNSEND'S WARBLER
Dendroica townsendi

Description: Black crown and eye patch on yellow face; yellow breast with dark streaking; male—black bib, olive back, white wingbars

This intricately decorated warbler is perhaps the most striking of those seen in the lowland areas. Intense black, yellow, and white adorn both sexes. A black crown, nape, and eye patch are accentuated by lemon-yellow plumage on the head. In summer, the male has a black throat and bib that changes to resemble the female in winter. In this plumage, both sexes show a yellow throat and breast highlighted with black streaking on the breast and flanks. The belly and undertail coverts are white. Grayish-black wings sport two conspicuous white wingbars, and the back and rump are olive-green with light streaking. Females and juveniles are less intensely colored and have more white on the belly. This little delight measures four and one-fourth to five inches long.

Seemingly restless, the Townsend's Warbler is found flitting among the foliage of trees, perpetually searching for food. In warbler-like fashion, it is an avid songster with a rendition consisting of two phrases, each repeated several times resembling *weazy weazy weazy twea* or *dee dee dee-de de*. In contrast, the call is a short, soft *chip*.

Habitat and Diet

Wintering as far south as Central America, the Townsend's Warbler is a transient throughout the Southwest, and is uncommonly seen in the desert lowlands during this journey. It is most often seen in brushy areas adjacent to higher elevations, especially where the desert runs into the "sky island" mountains, which rise abruptly from the desert floor.

Warblers are insectivores, scanning every inch of foliage or bark for possible victims. Watch them as they peer underneath leaves and in every crevice of a branch. They consume even the tiniest of insects and especially delight in the delicacy of insect larvae.

Nesting and Mating Behaviors

The Townsend's Warbler journeys to the Pacific Northwest for breeding purposes, preferring coniferous forests for nesting sites. The meticulously constructed, cup-shaped nest is usually placed near the trunk of the tree. Made of twigs, bark strips, and fibers, the abode is ultimately heavily lined with feathers as well as hair and finer grasses.

The female lays three to five slightly glossy, creamy-white eggs spotted and blotched with brown. She alone incubates them for twelve to thirteen days.

MacGillivray's Warbler
Oporornis tolmiei

Description: Broken, white eye ring; gray hood; blackish-gray bib;
                  yellow belly and undertail coverts; olive upperparts;
                  no wingbars

Although brightly colored, this warbler is often inconspicuous among heavy growth because it keeps to the understory of dense tangles. MacGillivray's Warbler displays a distinguishing white eye ring that is actually two white crescents—one above the eye and one below—easily seen on the otherwise slate-gray head. This dark mantle extends onto the breast, where it appears blackish. Upperparts are olive-green and underparts are lemon-yellow.

The female is similar, but has a lighter gray hood with a whitish-gray throat. This beautiful warbler measures four and three-quarters to five inches long and moves around on the ground by hopping. The MacGillivray's Warbler is most similar to the Eastern Mourning Warbler, but the latter does not frequent the Southwestern lowlands.

The song of this brightly colored warbler is delivered while its head and bill are held outward almost vertically. In a chanting fashion, it sings *tree tree tree tree sweet sweet*. The call is a harsh, sharp *tsik*.

Habitat and Diet

MacGillivray's Warbler breeds north and winters south of the Southwestern deserts, therefore it is seen through the lowlands during spring and fall migration. It is fairly common in April and again during August and September where dense brush and undergrowth abound. Preferring the lower limbs of vegetation, this tiny bird is often difficult to spot because it skulks and is so well camouflaged in dense foliage.

Largely insectivorous, the MacGillivray's Warbler finds most victims on foliage or in the crevices of bark. Dense undergrowth offers both protection as well as food, and when fruit or berries are available, it can't resist small portions.

Nesting and Mating Behaviors

In higher elevations, the MacGillivray's Warbler nests in low, dense undergrowth usually two to three feet above the ground. Supported by heavy plant stalks, the nest is constructed of coarse grasses, pieces of bark, and weed stems, then lined with finer grasses and hair. The female lays three to five creamy-white eggs spotted with brown and incubates them about thirteen days.

COMMON YELLOW-THROAT
Geothlypis trichas

Description: Black mask; white forehead; yellow throat; plain olive wings and upperparts

The male Common Yellow-throat is easily identified by his distinctive black mask bordered on the forehead with white. His throat and breast are bright yellow fading to light yellow on the belly, and the upperparts and tail are olive-green. The female lacks the black mask, instead showing an olive face and crown with a whitish eye ring. Her throat, breast, and belly are light yellow. The immature male shows slight darkening on the face as the mask begins to appear.

This warbler's movements are more deliberate than typical warbler behavior, even pausing to cock its tail, which appears somewhat similar to a wren's posturing. The Common Yellow-throat measures four and one-half to five and three-quarters of an inch from beak to tail.

Its song is very distinct, described as *wichity-wichity-wichity* often repeated and sometimes ending with an additional *wich*. Its low call sounds like *dip*.

Habitat and Diet

The Common Yellow-throat is a transient and common summer resident in arid desert sections where dense riparian growth exist. Also look for it around ponds and lakes that support dense stands of cattails and tules. Males commonly winter in this habitat, but it is rare to see a female at this time. Feeding among the dense vegetation, Common Yellow-throats glean insects from foliage. They usually skulk low to the ground under cover of dense vegetation, but can easily be *pished* into view.

Nesting and Mating Behaviors

Male Common Yellow-throats winter in the desert and are joined by the females in mid-February. By the end of March, most pairs are on their way north for breeding. Fresh- or saltwater marshes or wetlands are the choices for breeding territory. The female builds a bulky nest woven of reeds, grasses, leaves, and moss; then lines it with hair and finer grasses. She lays three to five creamy-white eggs spotted with brown and black. Alone she broods them for eleven to thirteen days.

Common Yellow-throats are very secretive during nesting season and cautiously approach the nest from tall growth to feed the young. When ready to leave, they depart in another direction. Males may be observed singing on the top of a stalk, but never near the nest.

Wilson's Warbler*
Wilsonia pusilla

Description: Black cap; yellow head and underparts; green upperparts

This very small warbler measures four and one-half inches long and is brightly decorated with green and yellow plumage. The male displays a distinctive black cap contrasting with the bright yellow superciliary, forehead, chin, and underparts. Also bright are the olive-green upperparts. The female's cap is less pronounced than the male's, and is sometimes even absent. While perching, it is common to see the tail cocked upward in a wren-like fashion.

Look for the Wilson's Warbler in shrubs or lower branches of trees. It is not shy and will easily come into plain view as it feeds on the outside branches.

Its song consists of a rapid series of *chip chip chip chip chip chip chip.* The call is a sharp *chimp.*

Habitat and Diet

The Wilson's Warbler is a common transient throughout the Southwestern lowlands, preferring mesquites and low shrubs of open country. In riparian areas it may be casually seen in winter.

* Plate 33

This tiny species searches tirelessly through the vegetation for its main food source: insects. Scrutinizing every leaf, bud, or blossom, it maneuvers through the low growth and consumes multitudes of tiny insects. Also, watch for this warbler catching part of its meal on the wing. Larvae are cherished, and fruit is also consumed as a very small percentage of its diet.

Nesting and Mating Behaviors

Northward bound, this little migrating warbler is essentially absent from the desert lowlands by early May. It chooses thickets along woodland streams for nesting territory, and builds a nest either directly on the ground or low in the dense undergrowth. Built of grasses, stems, and bark fibers, the nest is then lined with finer grasses and hair.

The female lays three to six creamy-white eggs heavily dotted at the large end with brown; then without the help of the male, she incubates them for eleven to thirteen days.

Yellow-breasted Chat
Icteria virens

Description: White spectacles; yellow throat and breast; large body; thick bill; long tail

Substantially larger than other warblers, the Yellow-breasted Chat measures six and one-half to seven and one-half inches from beak to tail. Distinctive white spectacles and black lores with a white line underneath adorn the face. Brilliant yellow plumage on the chin and breast contrast with the white belly and undertail coverts while the upperparts, including the relatively long tail, sport olive-green plumage. The shape of the dark, stout bill appears more like that of a tanager than a warbler.

The sexes appear similar, but the female may have lighter gray lores, and the male's breast may appear more orange for a brief period during breeding season.

This unique warbler's song is very unwarbler-like with clucks, rattles, and whistles, and the male even sings while in flight. The best time to view this atypical warbler is when it is singing from the top of a branch. Otherwise, the chat is usually concealed among the tangles of branches searching for food.

Habitat and Diet

The Yellow-breasted Chat is a very common summer resident in the Southwestern lowlands, especially where dense mesquites accompany rivers and ponds. It is a rare transient in the more arid parts of the desert and is absent in winter.

An expert flycatcher, the Yellow-breasted Chat is essential in nature's balance. It consumes numerous insects, protecting the trees and plants upon which it depends for cover and protection.

Nesting and Mating Behaviors

During mating season, the male displays and sings for the female. With rapid, fluttering flight, this curious warbler dangles his legs, raises his head, and ascends above the trees to hover and sing. As the song dies away, he drops back down to perch, usually on the same branch from which he began. He may also be seen perching on a branch leaning far over to one side then the other, the whole time keeping his mouth wide open.

The Yellow-breasted Chat nests in thick shrubs two to eight feet above the ground. The bulky, cup-shaped structure is comprised of vines, leaves, and grasses, then lined with finer grasses. The female lays three to six white eggs speckled with brown, and alone incubates them for eleven days.

WESTERN TANAGER*
Piranga ludoviciana

Description: Male—yellow body; red head; black back, wings and tail; two wingbars. Female—greenish yellow body; olive head; gray back, wings and tail; two wingbars

Startling contrasts of red, black, and yellow adorn the dazzling Western Tanager. Primarily bright yellow, the male is adorned with a red head and black back, wings, and tail. Additionally, it is the only tanager in the United States with two wing bars: the upper showing yellow, the lower one white. The red coloration vanishes in the fall, eventually appearing yellow-green with some darker streaking. The following spring before

---

* Plate 33

this six- to seven-and-one-half-inch bird begins mating activities, the brilliant red re-appears.

The female wears camouflaged plumage, which protects survival of the species. She is greenish-yellow with an olive head, and a grayish back and tail. Her two wingbars are similar to the male's and distinguish her from other female tanagers. The bill is heavy with curved edges, which is different from female orioles, whose beaks are more pointed and whose bodies are slimmer with longer tails.

The Western Tanager has a soft call sounding like *prit-it*. The song, however, is easily heard and resembles that of the Robin's, but differs with hoarser and shorter stanzas.

Habitat and Diet

The eye-catching Western Tanager is a common summer resident of the coniferous and pine-oak forests of the Southwest. But because it primarily winters in central Mexico and Central America, it is also a common, sometimes abundant transient through many areas of the Southwestern lowlands.

Tanagers are strictly arboreal birds, so they frequent areas in the deserts and adjoining riparian habitats where they have protection in denser shrubs and can feed on insects, arachnids, nectar, and fruit.

Nesting and Mating Behaviors

While transitioning northward from their winter habitat in the tropics, some Western Tanagers may loiter in desert areas late into the spring and early summer. They do not nest in these areas, however, instead choosing higher, mountainous regions, usually in the southern part of the ranges.

The nest is constructed fifteen to sixty-five feet high in the fork of a horizontal branch, usually a Douglas fir, pine, or spruce. Occasionally the pair will choose oak or aspen. The shallow, saucer-type nest is woven with weeds, rootlets, and twigs, with smaller pieces of roots, strips of bark, and hair carefully positioned as lining.

The female lays three to five greenish-blue eggs, which are heavily and evenly spotted. She does all the incubation, which takes approximately thirteen days. The hatchlings are fed by both parents, who take turns bringing them nourishment. At first, the food is regurgitated for the young, but as they mature, the parents bring them whole insects and pieces of fruit.

NORTHERN CARDINAL*
Cardinalis cardinalis

Description: Orange-red beak; crest. Male—red; black face and
throat. Female—buff-brown; red highlights

The most widely recognized bird all over the United States is the daz-zling Northern Cardinal. The brilliant red male makes himself easily visible, for he seldom wears natural camouflage.

The name is fitting in two respects: Cardinal means "of prime importance," and that is definitely how this beautiful bird displays itself. It also means "deep rich red," which describes the brilliant coloration of the male. His thick, seed-eating beak is emphasized by black feathers forming a "V" at the throat and ending at each eye. The prominent red crest and the long tail add to the streamlined appearance of this seven-and-one-half to nine-inch bird. The female has the same slender elegance, but is definitely more subtle with her buff-brown color, only slightly highlighted with a touch of red in her crest and wings. Because her coloring is more toned down than that of her male counterpart, the orange-red beak is more apparent. This feature is also one distinction between the female Northern Cardinal and the Pyrrhuloxia, which has a yellow beak.

Habitat and Diet

In the desert, the Northern Cardinal is found in mesquite thickets, but also frequents gardens, shade trees, forests, and riverbeds. As a resident, this beauty will come to feeders year round. It is a seed eater, as indicated by the cone-shaped bill, but also eats insects—the only food given to the young in their earliest stages.

Nesting and Mating Behaviors

The coloration of birds reaches a brilliant peak in early spring, and the Northern Cardinal is a splendid example of this phenomenon. In his finest attire, the male begins courtship in April, and even though desert temperatures allow for a longer possible breeding season, it is in this environment that the Northern Cardinal has only one brood each year.

*Plate 33

The female lays three or four light greenish-blue eggs with tiny spots in a cup-shaped nest that is loosely constructed. The inside of the nest appears more tightly woven of grasses, roots, small sticks, and sometimes assorted pieces of leaves. The female does the twelve- or thirteen-day incubation by herself.

The young birds remain a drab buff color until maturation. It is after the molting season that the male gains his full coloration, and the following spring he is ready to dazzle a mate.

Supplemental Information

The cardinals in the Southwest tend to be much brighter in coloration than cardinals in the Eastern parts of the United States. In the Southwest, the Northern Cardinal's song is more harsh, but is still very lovely, and can be heard year round, which is not true of many other birds. Also in many other species the male does the majority of the singing, but the Northern Cardinal is one species where both sexes enjoy this lively means of communication.

PYRRHULOXIA*
Cardinalis sinuatus

Description: Gray with rosy highlights; yellowish, parrot-like beak; crest

The Pyrrhuloxia is a common, year-round resident in the brushy desert, and is most often seen hiding in the midst of thorny protection. Its name is quite unusual, stemming from both Greek and Latin, meaning "bullfinch with a crooked bill." The dictionary defines Pyrrhuloxia as a "cardinal-like grosbeak."

It definitely is cardinal-like, and the male Pyrrhuloxia is sometimes confused with the female Northern Cardinal. The Pyrrhuloxia is a slightly smaller bird, however, being shorter and noticeably more slender. As an even more obvious means of identification, the bill has a definite yellow hue and appears stubbier and slightly more hooked than the orange-red bill of the cardinal.

The male Pyrrhuloxia is essentially grayish-brown, highlighted with splashes of magenta on the wings and throat. His breast is a rosy color,

*Plate 34

and his tail displays touches of pale pink. The expressive crest shows varying degrees of reds depending upon its position. The female is gray with obvious brown tones on her breast and slight hints of red on her wings and crest. Both sexes measure from seven and one-half to eight and one-half inches in length.

Pyrrhuloxias can be found in groups of ten or more during the winter months. In the spring, they pair off and stay mainly with a mate until the breeding season is over. By late fall they begin appearing in groups again.

Habitat and Diet

In the Southwestern lowlands, the Pyrrhuloxia is especially fond of ironwood trees. Where these trees are absent, the bird is also perfectly content in the thorny branches of a mesquite tree. Mainly a seed eater, this bird can be seen feeding on the ground in open areas. When disturbed, however, it will quickly return to the security of the thorny protection offered by desert shrubs.

Nesting and Mating Behaviors

The Pyrrhuloxia begins nesting in late May and continues through June. The nest is constructed in a cup shape and is extremely tidy and compact. It is built mainly of small twigs and coarse grasses, with the inside neatly lined with fibrous material such as hair, cobwebs, and sometimes bark fiber. The nest is approximately four inches by four inches with an inside diameter of about three inches. The Pyrrhuloxia is well adapted to the arid desert—June is often the driest month. The brood consists of two to four antique-white eggs with a speckling of dark spots to add a very distinguishing touch.

Supplemental Information

Although the Pyrrhuloxia is an unobtrusive bird that lives throughout the brushy desert, it can be easily found around various camping areas in the Southwestern deserts. Especially in the late fall and early spring, these campgrounds abound with people, many of whom are birders. Campers often provide a constant supply of food, which attracts a great variety of birds. In these areas, the usually timid Pyrrhuloxia eventually acclimates to the constant flow of human activity.

BLACK-HEADED GROSBEAK*
Pheucticus melanocephalus

Description: Male—black head; black and white wings and tail;
rufous breast, collar. Female—yellowish brown
breast; gray back; dark ear patch and head stripes

Aptly named, the Black-headed Grosbeak displays a black head that
emphasizes a prominent, pale, triangular bill. The male's collar, breast,
sides, and rump are rusty orange. His contrasting wing patterns of white
and black are especially salient in flight. Also notice his lemon-yellow
belly and wing linings.

The female has grayish-black streaking on her crown and a pronounced black-and-white face pattern emphasizing the darker eye patch.
Her rump is light rust-colored as is her breast, which has fine streaking
down each side, and her belly is pale yellow or white. Immatures are similar to the female. This large finch measures six and one-half inches to
eight inches long, and displays a dark brown iris.

The Black-headed Grosbeak has a strong, melodious song consisting
of rising and falling notes interspersed with *whirring* sounds. It is similar
to the Robin's song but is more audible and flowing. It readily performs
early in the morning, late in the evening, and even at high noon when
most other songsters are silent. Both sexes sing this warbling song even
while incubating the eggs! After mating season, however, this musical
wizard becomes quiet and rather secretive for the rest of the summer. Its
call is a sharp *ik.*

Habitat and Diet

This finch-like bird is a common transient in the desert areas of the
Southwest. It prefers riparian woodlands, but is also seen in mesquite
forests or any type of scrubby thickets. It is chiefly a seed eater, but in the
spring can often be seen moving from branch to branch picking fresh
buds from the trees. The Black-headed Grosbeak is aggressive at seed
feeders, but will also eat fruit, and is a connoisseur of insects, which actually constitute one fourth of its diet.

* Plate 34

Nesting and Mating Behaviors

The female takes three to four days to construct the frail-looking nest in a bush or small tree, preferring deciduous woods and shrubbery. She places the nest five to fifteen feet off the ground. The frail, cup-shaped structure is made of weeds, grasses, fine twigs, and often contains a snakeskin. It can be exceedingly flimsy, often even showing the eggs from below. The two to five eggs are greenish-blue and speckled with chestnut and purple. The female does the incubation at night, but the male alternates with her during the daytime.

BLUE GROSBEAK
Guiraca caerulea

Description: Male—dark blue body; cinnamon wingbars; heavy conical bill. Female—brown

Dark blue plumage highlighted with two cinnamon wingbars distinguish this species from the similar Blue Bunting and Indigo Bunting. Also as its name indicates, the Blue Grosbeak has a short, conical bill, especially swollen at the base and encompassed by black plumage.

The female is warm brown instead of blue and lacks the black around the base of her heavy bill. She has two chestnut wingbars with light blue plumage above the top bar and on the rump as well, but these marks are difficult to view from afar. Juveniles are similar to females but by the first spring young males show a combination of brown and blue. This oversized bunting measures six to seven and one-half inches, and when perched on a branch has the habit of spreading its tail and flipping it around.

Its song is very warbler-like, resembling that of the House Finch, with phrases that rise and fall. Its clear call is a sharp *pink*.

Habitat and Diet

The Blue Grosbeak is a common summer resident in the less arid regions of the desert where lush stands of mesquite and other desert scrub thrive. Riparian areas along rivers and washes adjacent to grasslands as well as the more humid farmlands are also excellent habitat for this omnivorous species. It is rare or absent in winter.

Mainly a seed eater, its short, stout bill easily cracks the hulls and separates the meat from the husk with great precision. However, a large portion of its diet consists of insects, including grasshoppers, locusts, and weevils, and in early spring this melodious songster picks buds from the tree tops.

Nesting and Mating Behaviors

During breeding season from June to September the beautiful male can be seen perching high on a branch singing his sweet song which communicates his desires to a female and announces his territory to other males.

In a low tree or bush, the well-built, compact nest is constructed of dried grasses, leaves, and plant fibers; it is often intertwined with a snakeskin. It is delicately lined with finer grasses, rootlets, and horsehair.

The female lays three to five unmarked, pale-blue eggs and incubates them for eleven to twelve days. Insects are the main diet for the young nestlings, and there are usually two broods per season.

LAZULI BUNTING*
Passerina amoena

Description: Male—turquoise; rufous breast; two white wingbars.
Female—brownish; light turquoise rump

The male is a real eyecatcher with his bright turquoise head, throat, and rump contrasting with his rufous breast and sides. This small finch has a white belly and measures five to five and one-half inches long. The tail and wings are adorned with two white wingbars, the top one showing wider. (There is a slight resemblance to the Western Bluebird, but the Lazuli Bunting is smaller, and has wingbars and a conical bill.) The female has a light brown head and back, buffy-yellow throat and breast, white belly, dark wings and tail, and a light turquoise rump.

Finches are generally exceptional songsters, and the Lazuli Bunting is one great example. During breeding season, the striking male sits on an obvious perch and announces his territorial boundaries by singing. The melody described as *sweet-sweet-chew-chew-seet chew* begins on a high note and gently descends down the scale.

*Plate 35

Habitat and Diet

The Lazuli Bunting is a common transient throughout the Southwestern deserts, gravitating especially to the dry slopes of foothills. Look for it in flocks amid clumps of bushes, weedy thickets, or in recently burned areas. Typical of most birds, the Lazuli eats some insects, but its main diet consists of seeds that are easily cracked open with its conical bill.

Nesting and Mating Behaviors

The nest is a cup-shaped structure intricately woven with coarse grasses, then lined with horsehair and finer grasses, and securely affixed to a fork in a low bush usually only two to four feet off the ground. The outside diameter is four inches, and the structure is approximately three inches high. The female lays three to five plain, pale-blue eggs and incubates them for twelve days.

GREEN-TAILED TOWHEE[*]
Pipilo chlorurus

Description: Green body with rufous cap; white throat; dark, thin mustache

There are no apparent plumage differences between the sexes. Both are adorned with a rufous crown, gray face and breast, and white throat, lores, and belly. A dark moustache extends through the white bib. The back, wings, and tail are olive-green, while the rump and wing linings are yellow. Juveniles appear streaked overall with buff underparts, olive-brown upperparts, and two light-olive wingbars. This six-and-one-half to seven-inch-long bird is the smallest of the towhees.

The Green-tailed Towhee is rather shy, preferring to stay concealed under low brush. Watch for movement, and listen for scratching sounds as this bird vigorously searches for food among the leaves. Hopping backward, flicking its tail then stopping momentarily with its rufous crest erect, this towhee puts on quite a show, and all so unpretentiously. This species will most often choose to run along the ground when approached, but will fly as a last resort.

Its call is a short, cat-like *mew*. The song varies, but sounds loud and sweet with its *weet-churr-cheeeee-churr*.

[*] Plate 35

Habitat and Diet

The Green-tailed Towhee is a transient and winter resident in the desert areas of the Southwest, and winters east of California. It prefers dry, brushy foothills, manzanita, and sagebrush.

It forages for food mostly on the ground, consuming hidden seeds and numerous insects as well as their larvae. During the appropriate season, however, the Green-tailed Towhee eagerly supplements this mainstay diet with fruits.

Nesting and Mating Behaviors

The Green-tailed Towhee not only forages for food on the ground, but also often nests there. If it chooses a bush, the site is no more that two feet from the ground. The loosely constructed, cup-shaped structure is interwoven with grasses, twigs, and bark, then lined with finer grasses and hair.

The female lays two to five greenish-white, oval eggs generously covered with brown and gray dots on the large end. Both adults participate in feeding and brooding.

Spotted Towhee*
Pipilo maculatus

Description: Male—black hood, back and tail; rufous sides; two white wingbars. Female—brown body instead of black; both have red eye

The Spotted Towhee of the West was previously lumped together with its Eastern cousin—the Rufous-sided Towhee. Now split into two distinct species (actually back to their original names), the Rufous-sided is the Eastern bird and the Western bird is the Spotted.

The beautiful plumage worn by this species should be displayed openly for the world to see. Instead, this shy bird often hides in the shrubs, scratching around in the leaves. The male has a black hood, back, and tail that shows white, outer feathers. The belly is white, and rufous patches appear on the sides. The wings have two white wingbars and much spot-

* Plate 35

ting, which spills over onto the back, hence the name. Look for the bright red eyes that adorn this species. The female is similar, except she has deep, chocolate-brown coloration instead of black.

This active towhee is often heard long before it is seen. Listen for scratching sounds made as it vigorously kicks leaves backward, out of its way, with both feet. At first, you may suspect a much larger animal because of all the ruckus. The call of this colorful towhee is a raspy *meewww,* and the song is deliberate and buzzy-sounding, described as *chweeeee* or *chip chip chip zeeeeeee.*

Habitat and Diet

The Spotted Towhee is found year round in the brushy canyons and river valleys of the Southwestern lowlands. It frequents thickets, chaparral, and open, brushy fields, and is also attracted to riparian woodlands and desertscrub. It doesn't overlook suburban gardens for suitable habitat, either. This ground bird forages for insects in dead leaves where steady scratching sounds announce its presence. A varied diet includes weevils, ants, wasps, bees, tree-boring beetles, seasonal fruit, as well as weed seeds, which actually comprise about one-third of its food intake.

Nesting and Mating Behaviors

The bulky nest is usually placed in a depression in the ground, but occasionally is located low in a bush five feet or less above the ground. The sturdy structure is made of leaves, grasses, and bark, and is lined with finer grasses and sometimes hair. The three to five eggs are creamy-white, smooth, slightly glossy, and are covered with chestnut specks. The female incubates the eggs for twelve to thirteen days.

The nest's location places the eggs and young in jeopardy of ground predators. A bigger threat, however, comes not from this earthly proximity, but from the avian world itself. The Brown-headed Cowbird frequently parasitizes the nest of the Spotted Towhee. There are reports indicating that as many as five or six eggs of the Brown-headed Cowbird have been found in one single nest!

CANYON TOWHEE*
Pipilo fucus

Description: Brown body; rufous cap; dark chest spot

I have a non-birding friend who jokingly said, "I notice that there are brown birds, and birds that are not brown. I also notice that they seem to have different shapes." Well, what can I say? She has a beginning. A bird that could essentially be described as brown, however, is the Canyon Towhee, and was even formerly called Brown Towhee.

At close range, a rufous cap, a dark spot on the chest, a faintly streaked throat, and traces of reddish-brown under the tail are apparent on this eight- to ten-inch-long bird. It is paler and grayer than the California Towhee. Both sexes appear the same year round, and immature birds are like the adults. This species mates for life, so it is often seen in pairs.

The Canyon Towhee's song is as unobtrusive as its coloration. A series of squeaky, one-note chips accelerate into a soft, pleasant trill. Its call sounds like a hoarse hiccup.

Habitat and Diet

The Canyon Towhee is an abundant resident of the Southwestern lowlands, existing in desertscrub, open brush in riparian woodlands, dry washes, and even in suburban gardens.

It feeds mainly on the ground, with various seeds supplying the main stay of its diet. As with almost all birds, however, the Canyon Towhee supplements this diet with some insects.

Nesting and Mating Behaviors

The nesting season for the Canyon Towhee is rather lengthy, extending from March to September. Lifemates construct a rather bulky, cup-shaped nest of twigs and grasses, and line it with horsehair, fine grasses, and rootlets. Although placed low in a bush or tree, this nest of five to seven inches in diameter is amazingly well hidden.

The female lays three or four light, bluish-green eggs with reddish-brown markings consisting of spots, scrawls, and blotches. She incubates the eggs while the male sits on a nearby perch singing his territorial song.

* Plate 36

Supplemental Information

The Canyon Towhee is a regular visitor around my feeding stations. As a ground feeder, it has plenty of competition from the Gambel's Quail, Mourning Doves, as well as White-winged Doves during summer. Although I notice that it appears quite timid at times, it always seems to get its share of seeds. It forages quietly among the shrubs, and scratches through the leaves, often bouncing backward while overturning small debris to find seed treasures underneath. I like to watch while it vigorously hops from one feeding area to another.

Abert's Towhee*
Pipilo aberti

Description: Brown body; plumage at base of bill

The Abert's Towhee is eight to nine inches long. It is dull brown above, and the underparts appear a lighter buffy color. The relatively long tail is lighter underneath, sometimes appearing quite pink. The main feature distinguishing the Abert's Towhee from the Canyon Towhee is the black patch that circles the light-colored bill of the former. Also, both sexes of the Abert's Towhee are paler all over than the Canyon Towhee.

The Abert's Towhee is one of the most elusive birds of the Southwestern lowlands. It has been called friendly and well-mannered, as well as timid. It does not display the more aggressive types of behaviors exhibited by many other bird species, and therefore appears more shy. This introverted behavior, along with its rather drab appearance, supports its nickname: Recluse of the Lowlands.

Habitat and Diet

The Abert's Towhee is a common, permanent resident of the Southwestern lowlands and is the bird most often seen scratching in the soft soil underneath desert shrubs. Although it appears quite timid, it can easily be attracted to feeding areas simply by placing seeds on the ground. I love to watch them as they virtually bounce back and forth in their efforts to scratch for tiny hidden seeds.

* Plate 36

The Abert's Towhee loves mesquite country, and although it will nest in other desert shrubs and low trees, it most frequently nests in the lower, protective branches of thorny mesquite tree. It is always fun to follow the winding arroyos through areas densely populated with desert shrubs—mesquites tend to grow larger than usual along the banks of these washes, and it is in this area that the nesting site of the Abert's Towhee is found.

Nesting and Mating Behaviors

The nest is fairly bulky and is designed in a cup shape. The female does the actual construction, utilizing a variety of coarse materials. The outside does not appear very secure or refined, but the inside is finished with hair and other delicate materials to make a soft, insulated home for the young nestlings. The female lays three or four greenish-blue eggs, which are heavily dotted with brown variations. The female does all of the incubation while the male perches nearby uttering the single note that must, in this instance, be some sort of territorial announcement.

Because most birds have life spans of only a few years, an annual nesting cycle is critical to assure the continuation of a species. Although some birds are monogamous, meaning that they stay together throughout an entire breeding season, the Abert's Towhee is monogamous in the true sense of the word. It mates for life, and remains within a definite territory where it continually perpetuates its own existence. So even though it is elusive, the Abert's Towhee is one of the more stable species in the Southwestern lowlands.

Supplemental Information

Birds can have many different sound patterns, even within a single species. Some sound patterns are referred to as songs, and other sounds are referred to as call notes. Various call notes communicate different needs such as sounding an alarm, extending greetings, intimidating predators, finding food, and simply calling to find one another. Abert's Towhees do not seem to have a song and have only one short call note that sounds like a single peep. Frequently, they can be heard peeping softly to one another while hiding under low, dense growth. It occurs to me that they must have tremendous distinguishing abilities to decipher the different intentions of what sounds to me to be the same note each time!

Chipping Sparrow
Spizella passerina

Description: Gray rump; thin, black line through eye; rufous
crown; white wingbars

A very tame and common sparrow, the Chipping Sparrow has distinct plumage changes from breeding season to winter. Regardless of season, however, look for the black line through the eye in conjunction with the gray rump. In breeding season, both sexes have a rufous cap and a stark white superciliary contrasting with the black eye line. The throat is whitish while the nape, ear patch, and remaining underparts are plain gray. The upperparts are mottled brown with two white wingbars. In winter the adults' crown becomes lighter, thus appearing streaked, while the face shows brown. Juveniles have brown streaking on gray underparts and lack the rufous crown. This gentle bird measures five to five and three-quarters inches.

True to its name, this familiar sparrow has a chipping song on one pitch. Its call is a high, sharp *seep*.

Habitat and Diet

In the lowlands, the Chipping Sparrow is an abundant transient and winter resident in grasslands with brushy vegetation. It is one of the most insectivorous of all sparrows, eating almost equal parts insects and vegetable matter. Most sparrows are primarily seed eaters, but the Chipping Sparrow supplements its weed seed intake with ants, wasps, caterpillars, and spiders.

Nesting and Mating Behaviors

The Chipping Sparrow moves to oak-juniper, pine-oak, and coniferous habitat for breeding. The female builds the compact nest of dried grasses and rootlets, meticulously lining it with finer grasses as well as an abundance of horsehair. The male assists by bringing materials for her use. She lays three to five light blue, slightly glossy eggs blotched with dark purple, then incubates them for eleven to fourteen days. There are usually two broods per season.

BREWER'S SPARROW
Spizella breweri

Description: Finely streaked crown; plain breast; brown ear
patch; distinct white eye ring

The Brewer's Sparrow has light brown upperparts streaked with dark
brown. The finely streaked crown lacks the buffy central stripe of the
rare Clay-colored Sparrow. Like the Chipping Sparrow, the Brewer's has
a plain, unmarked breast and belly. Note the well-defined, white eye ring,
buffy-white wingbars, and small bill with pink lower mandible. The sexes
are similar, and the juvenile has brown streaking on the breast and flanks.

Its voice consists of buzzy trills that may be heard all winter. The call is
a sweet *seep.*

Habitat and Diet

The Brewer's Sparrow is an abundant transient and winter resident in
the Southwestern lowlands, especially in the more open deserts. Look
for it among creosotes. Its diet consists mainly of grass seeds, but insects
and spiders are consumed as well.

Nesting and Mating Behaviors

By April, the deserts are void of this bubbly songster that prefers the
sage or salt brush found in cold desert regions further north. The cup-
shaped nest is hidden in a bush low to the ground and is made of dry
grasses, small twigs, and rootlets, then lined with horsehair. The three to
five blue-green eggs are marked with dark brown spots and incubated for
about eleven days.

VESPER SPARROW
Pooecetes gramineus

Description: Distinct outer white tail feathers; rufous wing patch;
white eye ring; all-over streaking

The Vesper Sparrow measures five to six and one-half inches from beak
to tail. It shows light brown above and white below, with dark streaking

on its head, back, throat, and breast. The white outer tail feathers are most conspicuous in flight, but the rufous wing patch is not always as visible. A dark ear patch outlined with black highlights the white eye ring. There are no apparent plumage differences between the sexes.

"Vesper" suggests an evening songster, but actually this species sings at any time of the day and even at night, rendering a series of notes similar to that of the Song Sparrow with high trills giving way to a fast melody. During breeding season, the male delivers an elaborate flight song from fifty to seventy feet in the air.

Habitat and Diet

A common migrant and winter resident in the Southwestern lowlands, the Vesper Sparrow chooses grasslands and weedy fields as its primary habitat. This is prime territory to find seeds and insects, both of which are consumed in large portions in proportion to its small size. Migratory and wintering birds often form loose flocks while feeding. Insects fed upon include grasshoppers and beetles, while cutworms, army worms, and caterpillars are also treasured delicacies.

Nesting and Mating Behaviors

By the end of April, most Vesper Sparrows have migrated northward to breed in mountain meadows and sagebrush habitat. The nest is a bulky, cupped-shaped affair placed in a depression in the ground and protected by undergrowth. Dried grasses and roots form the foundation, then hair is woven into the inner cradle.

The female lays three to six creamy-white eggs with brown spots and incubates them for twelve to thirteen days. There are usually two broods per season.

Black-throated Sparrow
Amphispiza bilineata

Description: Black bib; white face stripes

The Black-throated Sparrow was formerly named Desert Sparrow. As its current name indicates, a jet-black throat and chin adorn this little species, making a striking contrast with the small white face stripes. Its head and upperparts are grayish-brown, and the tail is black with whitish underparts. About four and one-half to five and one-half inches long, both sexes have the same markings. The immature lacks the black throat and is sometimes mistaken for the Sage Sparrow.

In spring, the Black-throated Sparrow may be heard at any time of the day. The song has a very clear, sweet sound, beginning with a series of short notes and ending in a fast trill on a different pitch. The call notes are used to communicate a variety of needs: Territorial calls are loud and begin as soon as a nesting site has been established; mating calls are varied and softer; and communication around the nest is subtle in order to quietly guard the privacy of the well-concealed nest.

Habitat and Diet

The Black-throated Sparrow is a common year-round resident in the desertscrub. An extreme tolerance for the hot, dry season suits this sparrow well for desert survival. Seeds are the main food choice, but it readily goes to water when available. When the dry, hot month of June rolls around, however, it seems to be able to adapt and obtain the necessary liquids from insects and plant life.

The Black-throated Sparrow lives in graceful harmony with people and is easily attracted to feeders. It is readily found in picnic areas scavenging for subtle treats left behind by humans. Its gentle disposition and optimistic sounding medley make it a delightful little bird of the lowlands.

Nesting and Mating Behaviors

The Black-throated Sparrow nests in dense, low bushes or often in the center of cholla cacti. Although the nest is sometimes only two to three feet off the ground, and even occasionally on the ground, it is very well concealed. The cup-shaped nest is very efficiently made of small twigs and grasses; then lined with hair and feathers. The female lays two to four bluish-white eggs, and has at least two broods a year. The fact that its nesting season goes into the hottest, driest months is another indication of how well this little sparrow fits into the extreme temperature variations of the desert.

SAGE SPARROW
Amphispiza belli

Description: Dark central breast spot; white eye ring and
eyebrow; dark whisker strip

Many sparrows give us identification fits in the field, but the five- to six-inch-long Sage Sparrow is an easier one. Pure white plumage underneath sports a dark, bold spot in the center of the breast; the head is brownish-gray contrasting with a white eye ring and superciliary; and a white mustache is bordered by dark whiskers. Two pale wingbars adorn the brown, streaked back. The sexes are similar, but desert-dwelling birds appear lighter than coastal birds. Juveniles are duller overall with more streaking.

Because the Sage Sparrow spends most of its time on the ground in open areas, you should be able to spot it very easily. In a wren-like fashion, this little sparrow wags a long, black tail, sometimes cocking it upward while retreating from danger. A melodious finch-like song sounding like *tsit-tsoo-tseee-tsey* fills the air during breeding season.

Habitat and Diet

The Sage Sparrow is an uncommon winter resident in desert areas supporting mesquite, creosote, sagebrush, saltbush, and grasses. This active bird feeds mainly on the ground, moving about flicking its tail while searching for seeds and insects.

Nesting and Mating Behaviors

By the end of March, most Sage Sparrows have left the lower desert areas to move to arid, higher, brushy habitat in the foothills. The nest is well hidden in sagebrush or other scrub and is made of sticks or dry twigs of the host bush. The cup-shaped structure is then lined with grasses, hair, and fur.

The female lays three to five bluish-white eggs, which are heavily marked with brown or black. Both adults take turns incubating the eggs for about thirteen days, and will leave the nest only if forced to do so. Both adults continue to participate in rearing the young.

LARK BUNTING*
Calamospiza melanocorys

Description: Breeding male–black body; white wing patch.
Female, non-breeding male–brownish body with
streaking

Beginning in April, the male Lark Bunting dressed in breeding
plumage is really quite spectacular. This six- to seven-inch bird becomes
jet black with starkly contrasting white wing patches. After the summer
molt, he appears more subdued in plumage similar to the female. She has
brown streaking above, white below, and sometimes a whitish wing
patch. The tail feathers are rounded and tipped with white. Also visible is
a white eye line. In this similar winter plumage, males can be identified
by their heavier bill and larger patches of white on the wings. Immature
birds are similar to the female.

The Lark Bunting has a stout conical bill used for cracking seeds. A
gregarious bird, this bunting is often seen in flocks. Its song is a loud
sequence of whistles and trills repeated up to eleven times. Its call is a
two-note whistle.

Habitat and Diet

The Lark Bunting is a winter resident of the grasslands, deserts, and
farmlands in the Southwest. It is mainly a seed eater, and it hops around
on the ground as it feeds. Nearly all birds, including seed-eating species,
first feed their young with insects. This is true of the Lark Bunting, which
later makes a gradual switch to a vegetable diet.

Nesting and Mating Behaviors

The nest consists of a simple depression scraped in the ground sometimes under a protective, low, leafy branch or next to weeds. This cup-
shaped home is first layered with grasses and rootlets, then lined with
finer materials such as down or hair. The depth of the nest is only about
one and one-half inches, and the inside diameter is close to three inches.

The female lays four or five pale blue eggs, which are oval-shaped and
slightly glossy. They are usually plain, but occasionally they contain red-

* Plate 36

dish-brown spots. The female incubates the eggs by herself for approximately twelve days. Often there are two broods.

Supplemental Information

I don't ever remember seeing Lark Buntings when I was a youngster, so I was excited one day when a birding friend suggested we make a little trip to some grasslands where she had seen a flock of them. It was mid-April, a perfect time to see them in various stages of their annual molt. I was so surprised, because as it turned out, she took me to the grasslands where I had been raised! Indeed, a flock of Lark Buntings posed for us, some displaying the female-type plumage, some with their spectacular black and white, and yet others with a mottled appearance, obviously still in the molting process. I couldn't believe my friend had taken me back to McNeal, my home territory!

SAVANNAH SPARROW
Passerculus sandwichensis

Description: Streaking below; light superciliary; pale crown stripe; yellow lores

There are vast variations of this species, including sixteen recognized subspecies named according to geographical location. Generally in the Southwest, the Savannah Sparrow is darkly streaked overall including the white underparts as well as the brown upperparts. Yellow lores and eyebrows adorn the head and are particularly visible in summer. A slender, short, notched tail enunciates rather large, strong wings. Its legs and feet are pale pink and its small bill is conical, typical of all sparrows. The sexes are similar in plumage and size, measuring approximately four and one-half to five and one-half inches. The form found at the Salton Sea lacks streaking on its head, and breast streaks appear very faintly.

The Savannah Sparrow often sings from the ground rather than finding a high perch. Listen for a series of notes beginning with two or three chips followed by trills and slurs. The call is a thin *seep* which is often heard in flight.

Habitat and Diet

The Savannah Sparrow is a common to abundant transient and winter resident in irrigated fields, grasslands, and weedy fields of the desert lowlands. Although its conical bill indicates a seed eater, nearly half of its food intake consists of insects. Beetles seem to be a favorite, but much to the farmer's benefit, this species also consumes large numbers of boll weevils.

Nesting and Mating Behaviors

The Savannah Sparrow chooses grasslands, weedy fields, savannas, marshes, and tundras for breeding territory. The female scratches a depression in the ground in an area protected by undergrowth. Using grasses, she molds the foundation, then lines it with finer substances such as hair and feathers. Her three to five slightly glossy, bluish-green eggs are heavily blotched with brown. Attending to all of the nesting business by herself, she incubates the eggs for twelve days. There are normally two broods per season.

SONG SPARROW
Melospiza melodia

Description: Pale rusty brown body; central breast spot; gray
superciliary

The Song Sparrow measures from five to six and one-half inches in length and varies in plumage according to its geographical form. Field markings include size, bill shape, streaking, and color of plumage, which appear quite different in the various subspecies. The desert type (*saltonis*) is very pale brown with heavy streaking on the white underparts, accompanied by a central breast spot and a dark stripe bordering the white throat. It sports a gray superciliary. The upperparts are striped, the tail is long and rounded at the end, and the legs and feet are pink. Both sexes are similar. The juvenile is lighter with finer streaking. (There are thirty-four recognized subspecies of Song Sparrow.)

From the top of a low tree, the avid songster throws its head backward and maintains this position while singing. The call is a nasal *chimp*, but the song, true to its name, is a repertoire of three or four clear, Blackbird-like piping notes, a buzzy *tow-wee*, and ends with a trill.

Habitat and Diet

The Song Sparrow is a common, permanent resident in riparian areas along major rivers, and is a common winter resident around reedy ponds, streams with extensive brush, farmlands, and other weedy habitats in the lowlands.

Weed and grass seeds comprise approximately three-fourths of its diet. The remaining one-fourth includes insects such as ants, wasps, and beetles. Caterpillars are also a favorite.

Nesting and Mating Behaviors

The female builds the nest on the ground in a tuft of grass, in a brush pile, or low in a bush. The cup-shaped affair is constructed of grasses, leaves, and bark strips, then lined with finer grasses and hair. Working alone, she may take up to ten days to complete this task. She lays three to six slightly glossy, pale green eggs, which are almost totally covered with dark brown and purple splotches. She incubates them by herself for twelve to thirteen days. There are sometimes as many as three broods a season.

Lincoln's Sparrow
Melospiza lincolnii

Description: Breast buffy with fine streaks; gray crown with cinnamon-brown border stripes

The melodious Lincoln's Sparrow measures five to six inches long, and plumage resembles the Song Sparrow. In order to distinguish between the two, notice the Lincoln's gray eyebrow, crown bordered with cinnamon stripes, buffy breast band with very fine streaking, and shorter tail. Upperparts are mottled buffy-brown and cinnamon, and a whitish eye ring is apparent. Juveniles show lighter plumage and lack the gray coloration.

This shy sparrow hides in the dense thickets, but when disturbed, quietly signals annoyance by raising its crest before hopping away through the brush. Also by joining other flocks of sparrows, the Lincoln's Sparrow often goes unnoticed. When singing, however, it appears robust and quite confident, but it rarely sings in its desert wintering grounds.

The full, loud song has been described as both wren-like yet similar to the notes of the Purple Finch. Gurgling stanzas alternate with low notes rising, then ending low. Two calls may be heard: The alarm call is a series of *tschips* while calls for other purposes sound like a buzzy *tzee*.

Habitat and Diet

In the Southwestern lowlands, the Lincoln's Sparrow is a common migrant and winter resident in riparian areas with dense undergrowth or in weedy/grassy locations. It is also common in towns.

This omnivorous sparrow eats grass and weed seeds, but also "exterminates" many insects including ants, grasshoppers, wasps, and beetles. Caterpillars are occasionally a delicacy for this slender sparrow.

Nesting and Mating Behaviors

The Lincoln's Sparrow leaves the lowlands in March for higher elevations to breed in mountain meadows. The female builds the tidy, compact nest directly on the ground, but well concealed among the grasses. She lays four to six slightly glossy, pale green eggs in the grass-woven cup and incubates them for thirteen days. The male, an avid songster, remains quiet during this time.

WHITE-CROWNED SPARROW*
Zonotrichia leucophrys

Description: White crown with black stripes; pink or yellow bill; lacks yellow on face

This aptly named sparrow is very conspicuous with a white crown bordered by black stripes. The eyebrow is also white with a black line between the eyes. Notice that the clear gray breast has no throat markings, the gray back is streaked with brown, and the bill is either pink or yellow. The sexes appear identical, and measure from six and one-half to seven and one-half inches in length. The immature displays a browner breast and a light, buff-colored crown with dark brown stripes on each side.

The White-crowned Sparrow is very widespread, and its song seems to vary according to geographical location. It basically consists of one or

* Plate 37

more clear, plaintive whistles followed by several husky trills of different pitches. Two call notes sound like *chink* and *tseep*.

Habitat and Diet

In the Southwestern deserts and grasslands, the White-crowned Sparrow is an abundant transient and winter resident arriving in flocks during the fall, then migrating to higher and cooler elevations for breeding. In California the sexes often separate, with the females migrating to winter habitats east of the Sierras and the males choosing areas west of the Sierras.

A seed eater by preference, this handsome sparrow consumes about seventy-five percent of its food intake in the form of grass and weed seeds. As a supplement, the remaining portion consists of insects including ants and wasps. Very small amounts of fruit are occasionally added to this menu.

Nesting and Mating Behaviors

Two races are found in the Southwest, but both forms breed to the north of the hot desert habitat. Choosing clearings of alpine meadows, burned areas, and even town parks, the female chooses a low bush or a depression on the ground for her nesting site. With fine twigs and grasses, she weaves the cup-shaped structure, then meticulously lines it with finer grasses, feathers, and hair. She lays four to six slightly glossy, pale blue eggs covered with chestnut blotches. Continuing to tend to the nesting chores alone, she incubates them for about twelve days.

Supplemental Information

The White-crowned Sparrow is one of the most widely studied species of birds. Not only do markings vary according to geographical location for this abundant and conspicuous sparrow, but the songs of those in the Eastern ranges are totally different from those in the Western regions. It has also been observed that in the far north during the summer solstice, the White-crowned Sparrow may sing all night during the breeding season.

RED-WINGED BLACKBIRD*
Agelaius phoeniceus

Description: Male—black body; red shoulder patches. Female—brown; pinkish throat; streaked breast

The male Red-winged Blackbird resembles no other North American bird. His bright red patches are confined to the epaulets, sometimes with a buffy, yellow border showing; otherwise, this blackbird is truly black. The red shoulder patches are most conspicuous during the breeding season. At other times, the red may be concealed while the yellow margin becomes the focus. This blackbird measures seven to nine inches long, which is slightly smaller than the American Robin.

The female is essentially brown with a pinkish throat; heavy, dark streaking below; and a sharp bill. A vertical, light-colored stripe appears above her eye. The immature male is darker than the female and has light-red shoulder patches.

The Red-winged Blackbird is extremely gregarious and may be found either in small groups or in large flocks. During winter it joins other blackbirds, as well as cowbirds and grackles, forming very large integrated flocks. The Red-winged Blackbird's voice resonates with a gurgling, liquid sound described as *konk-la-nee* or *o-ka-lee!*

Habitat and Diet

This beautiful blackbird abounds in the Southwest wherever it can find marshy areas or even irrigated farmlands. It is especially plentiful during the winter when northern residents join the local residents.

The Red-winged Blackbird feeds on seeds; thus it appears in great numbers in grain fields. It pays for its share, however, by ridding the environment of many pesky insects that would otherwise damage more of the crop than is actually consumed by the hungry blackbird. Most feeding takes place away from its nesting area.

Nesting and Mating Behaviors

The spring colors and types of plumage on breeding birds serve for more than an exhibition of beauty. Attracting mates and defending terri-

* Plate 37

tory are the practical applications of these attributes. Birds utilize their bodies to send messages to other birds by displaying wings and tails in various positions. Male Red-winged Blackbirds sing while displaying their red epaulets to attract females and to drive other males from their territory. Studies show that when the red shoulder patches are covered, Red-winged Blackbirds are less successful in both obtaining a mate and in maintaining a territory. This suggests that color is actually more impressive than song.

After mating, the female builds her nest in loose colonies among cattails, rushes, or bushes in marshes, as well as in grassy fields adjacent to water. The bulky, woven basket is lined with fine grasses, and neatly contains three to five blue-green eggs, marked with brown, purple, or black scrawls.

The female does the incubation alone, which takes ten to twelve days. Often she raises two broods per season. She breeds in her first year, while the male waits until the second season.

Supplemental Information

The springtime sights and sounds of the marshy, cattail-lined wetlands, as well as the lush grain fields, are quite spectacular when flocks of Red-winged Blackbirds abound. Splashed across the field, or perched on top of a reed or on the head of a grain stock, the males exuberantly display themselves. I love to listen to the chorus of loud songs when great numbers of them congregate in a relatively small area.

Next time you visit such a scene, notice how they use their whole bodies to flaunt the brilliant red epaulets while they sing. No wonder they need ample supplies of seeds and insects. This frequent little display appears to take a great deal of energy!

MEADOWLARK*
Eastern—*Sturnella magna*
Western—*Sturnella neglecta*

Description: Brownish upper body; yellow below; black bib.
Eastern—gray cheek; white on outer tail feathers;
darker crown stripes; Western—yellow lower cheek

Generally, male birds are much more conspicuous in coloration than the females. The meadowlark, however, is one species where both sexes are beautifully colored and identical in markings. The female is slightly paler than the male; otherwise, their plumage is the same. The bright yellow breast is adorned with an obvious black V-shaped ascot.

In Spanish this bird is called "pecho amarillo," which means "yellow breast." The upper head and body are an inconspicuous brown and buff color, which serves as camouflage in clumps of grass. Small black-and-white stripes appear on the top of the head, and white outer tail feathers become obvious in flight. Measuring nine inches from the tip of its beak to the end of its tail, this beautiful species has well-developed legs for ground mobility.

To distinguish between the Eastern and Western Meadowlark, look closely at the cheek. On the Western species, the yellow from the throat bleeds onto the lower cheek, while the Eastern bird sports a gray cheek. Additionally, the Eastern displays a white patch on the outer tail feathers. The song variations will clench an identification: The song of the Western Meadowlark has seven to ten flutelike notes with a gurgling sound, while that of the Eastern Meadowlark has two clear whistle-like notes. Both species can live in the same territory without interbreeding, and, therefore, each species remains distinct.

The meadowlark has an easily identifiable flight pattern, departing with great bursts of energy, then slowing to glide a short distance. It continues by alternating rapid wing movements with graceful sailing. When threatened, it makes a flushing sound similar to the explosive departure of quail.

* Plate 38

Habitat and Diet

Resident meadowlarks are joined by an influx of fall migrants who frequent grassy ranch country, and can be easily seen perching on fences along roads. Farmlands are another attractive habitat because of an abundance of grasses as well as insects. This species' posture always exhibits an upright position while displaying the stunning yellow breast and its stylish black vest. When it dives into clumps of grass, however, it is almost impossible to spot.

Nesting and Mating Behaviors

The meadowlark's nest is very carefully hidden in clumps of tall, dry grass from the previous season. First a small depression is scratched into the dirt, and then a very intricately designed, inverted dome-shaped nest is made in the hollow. The rather bulky affair is made strictly of grasses, and both sexes share in the task of its construction. Once the nest is completed and the female lays her typical clutch of three to five eggs, the male leaves and does not return to the nest during incubation. Although most of the males are monogamous, some of them are polygamous. The male returns when the nestlings are hatched, however, and then becomes very involved with the task of feeding the young.

The eggs are white and covered all over with many brown and lavender splotches, which are especially concentrated on one end. It takes approximately thirteen to fifteen days for incubation and hatching; then the nestlings stay in their home for about two weeks. Some birds that hatch on the ground, such as the Killdeer, can be ready to run and take care of themselves within hours after hatching. They have the ability to move away quickly from dangerous ground predators. But because the meadowlark does not mature so quickly, its survival is mainly dependent on the camouflaged coloration of the upper part of its body. Its main enemies are coyotes and snakes. Even roadrunners occasionally invade the nest to consume the eggs.

Supplemental Information

In the grassy lowlands, meadowlarks are found in large flocks when the food supply is plentiful. Since they conceal themselves so skillfully amid grasses, only approximately one in five can be seen easily. In response to danger, this striking bird freezes and is usually passed by unnoticed.

Meadowlarks not only entertain humankind with their musical eloquence, but are very beneficial in ridding the environment of harmful insects. A welcome visitor to farmlands, it consumes enough grasshoppers, cutworms, boll weevils, crickets, and other insects to make a noticeable difference in the harvest of some crops. For this valuable service the meadowlark only requires a small portion of grain to supplement its insect diet and a safe place to assure survival.

YELLOW-HEADED BLACKBIRD*
Xanthocephalus xanthocephalus

Description: Male—blackish body; yellow hood. Female—
          brownish; white, streaked breast

The Yellow-headed Blackbird is eight to eleven inches long, which is comparable to the size of the American Robin. As its name indicates, the male, which is essentially black, has a deep orange-yellow head, and this coloration extends to the lower breast. In flight, he displays conspicuous white wing patches.

The female is slightly smaller and has a brownish coloration, including the head. Her chest, throat, and face are yellow-brown, with white streaks emphasizing the lower breast.

Habitat and Diet

This gregarious blackbird is a migratory bird, and during the winter months, large flocks can be found roosting in the tules and cattails around marshy edges of lakes in the southernmost areas of the Southwest.

It is fun to sit quietly and unobtrusively in an area abounding with Yellow-headed Blackbirds and listen to the loud chorus produced by their raucous swarms. The song sounds somewhat like a rusty hinge and accelerates to a double forte when a large group simultaneously defends its territory against an intruding predator.

The Yellow-headed Blackbird seeks water for safety, and it can also be seen foraging in adjacent fields and open country. Its diet consists of crickets and other insects, along with various weed seeds.

* Plate 38

Nesting and Mating Behaviors

The Yellow-headed Blackbird is rarely seen during summer in the deserts and grasslands. In May, they move to higher and cooler elevations where they breed in a marshy habitat similar to that of their winter roosting site.

This species nests in colonies, with as many as 25 nests in an area of only 200 square feet. The nest is constructed entirely by the female, who may build several nests before actually choosing one in which she lays the eggs. The nest itself is a bulky structure made of aquatic vegetation woven to the growing reeds in a basket-like fashion. It is usually six inches to three feet above the water, and as the woven material dries, it shrinks to a tightly woven cup. The outside diameter is five to six inches, with a three-inch diameter for the eggs on the inside of the nest.

The female constructs the nest in two to four days, then lays three to five oval-shaped eggs, which are pale green with gray and brown dots displayed over the entire egg. The egg is very smooth and even glossy in appearance. The female not only builds the nest, she also does the entire incubation by herself. She never flies directly to the nest, however, but lands some distance away, then very slyly disappears into the reeds, often emerging unseen on the nest.

Supplemental Information

There are only fourteen species of North American birds said to be regularly polygamous, and the Yellow-headed Blackbird is one of them. This means that the male has a pair bond with more than one female. Like the Yellow-headed Blackbird, most of these species breed in marshes or areas where there is an abundance of food, for the female must feed the young unassisted. The keeping of a territory and thus the protection of food resources becomes the male's main role.

BREWER'S BLACKBIRD*
Euphagus carolinus

Description: Male–purplish-black, glossy body; yellow eye.
Female–grayish brown; brown eye

The Brewer's Blackbird is from eight to ten inches long and is very commonly seen in the lower elevations of the Southwest. The male appears all black, but in the breeding season a purplish-black sheen may be seen on his head, and iridescent green reflects from his body. The female is a brownish gray with dark eyes, which differ from the conspicuous yellow eyes of the male. As this blackbird walks, its wings are held slightly downward and its head moves in a jerking motion.

The male displays very interesting behaviors as he spends a great deal of time defending territory or in courtship rituals. He can often be seen spreading his wings and fluffing his feathers, or with tail spread, and bill pointing upward. This is the way he communicates his intentions to other birds.

The song is a creaking sound, and during the mating season the male may be seen with his tail spread and his head lowered while strutting around uttering this interesting sound.

Habitat and Diet

This winter resident may be seen at the lower elevations from September through April, and it is the blackbird most frequently seen around irrigated fields, corrals, ranches, feed lots, and along the roadside. In the cities it is commonly seen in parks, on golf courses, and in back yards. The Brewer's Blackbird is a very social species and can often be seen mixing with other blackbirds, such as the Red-winged Blackbird or the Brown-headed Cowbird.

Its diet consists mainly of seeds, but crickets and other insects are supplements. Most feeding occurs on the ground.

Nesting and Mating Behaviors

The Brewer's Blackbird nests at the higher Southwestern elevations and can be found in loose colonies or by itself. The nest is well construct-

* Plate 39

ed of interlaced twigs carefully lined with fine grasses and horsehair. The outside is often plastered with mud or cow dung, making it very durable. The nest is built solely by the female and can be found on the ground, in trees high above the ground, in low shrubs, and in thick weeds. The outside diameter of this sturdy structure is five to six inches, the height is three and one-quarter inches, and the inside diameter is three inches. The four to six eggs are oval shaped with a slightly glossy, smooth greenish gray, or grayish brown shell. Each egg is entirely speckled with dark brown or black spots. Incubation is done entirely by the female and takes twelve to fourteen days.

The male guards the nesting territory until the female begins incubation. Afterward, he may mate with yet another female, enticing her into the same territory. The male can be monogamous, but is usually polygamous with two mates and occasionally three or four.

Supplemental Information

Polygamy occurs as an efficient method of reproduction and one study concerning polygamy in Brewer's Blackbirds indicates that its practice seems to depend on the number of males versus the number of females in a given territory. When there were nearly equal numbers of males and females, polygamy was rare, but when there were twice as many females, polygamy was the rule. An interesting follow-up showed, however, that the following breeding season, the males had a tendency to re-mate with the primary female of the preceding season.

BRONZED COWBIRD*
Molothrus aeneus

Description: Male—black body with bronze sheen; red eye.

Female—gray body; red eye

The Bronzed Cowbird is six and one-half inches to eight and three-quarters inches long, which is larger than the Brown-headed Cowbird, but it has a noticeably longer bill. The Bronzed Cowbird has a conspicuous red eye. In the breeding season, look for the ruff on the male's nape. In most areas of the Southwest, the female is dull gray in coloration, but in Texas the sexes are similar—both are entirely black.

* Plate 39

The song consists of high-pitched squeaking sounds, which are prolonged and somewhat mechanical in nature.

Habitat and Diet

This common summer resident can be found in irrigated areas, feedlots, semi-open country, riparian woodland, and desertscrub. It roosts in large flocks and is easily seen in city parks where it socializes with other blackbirds.

The Bronzed Cowbird forages on the ground for weed seeds and insects, including large numbers of crickets. Occasionally this gregarious bird can also be seen feeding on ticks from the backs of cattle.

Nesting and Mating Behaviors

This "red-eyed cowbird" does not build its own nest nor does it even raise its own young. Rather, it uses a reproductive strategy called parasitism. The nesting season lasts from May through August and after copulation the female finds a nest where eggs have already been laid by some other species of bird. She often even removes one of the "host's" eggs and replaces it with one of her own pale, blue-green eggs. The unsuspecting host continues to incubate until all eggs are hatched, including the "planted" Bronzed Cowbird egg.

The major concern about this practice is that the nestling cowbird may often be bigger and grow faster than the other nestlings and can crowd them entirely out of the nest. The Bronzed Cowbird lays from one to four eggs, but only one egg per host nest.

The Bronzed Cowbird seems to be more choosey than some other parasitic species, and mainly chooses to parasitize the nests of Hooded Orioles. It also occasionally chooses to invade the nest of the Summer Tanager and Northern Oriole.

During mating season, the male raises the ruff on his neck as he prances around during the courtship display. He also may be seen hovering in the air a short distance off the ground, right in front of the female.

Supplemental Information

Even though I know it is not for us humans to judge nature's processes, I have wondered about the loss of songbirds due to the reproductive strategy employed by the Bronzed Cowbird. Thankfully, I have found in the research that the population of the "host" birds has not been significantly altered. Nature takes care of itself, and as with any parasite, the Bronzed Cowbird continues to be less populous than its host, which assures the survival of both species.

Brown-headed Cowbird
Molothrus ater

Description: Male—metallic blackish-green body; dark brown head; finch-like bill. Female—grayish-brown with slight streaking

The Brown-headed Cowbird is the smallest North American blackbird, measuring seven and one-half inches from beak to tail. Sporting a chocolate brown head, the male fits the description of its name. The rest of his body consists of glossy, dark green-black plumage. The iris is dark and the tail is slightly rounded.

The female has gray-brown upperparts and lighter brown underparts with faint, narrow streaking. Her chin and throat appear dullish-white. Juveniles are more heavily streaked than the female, and have a scaly appearance on the back and wings. Due to its small size, finch-like bill, and streaked plumage, the female and juveniles might be mistaken for a sparrow or female House Finch.

In winter, this gregarious species is often seen mixed with flocks of other blackbirds. The male's song is a combination of squealing and gurgling sounds that are quite musical. The female's response is a soft *tsip.* Calls include whistles and rattling sounds.

Habitat and Diet

The Brown-headed Cowbird is a transient and winter resident in the Southwestern lowlands, especially where there are herds of cattle. As livestock move along grazing, they flush insects from the grasses, which the cowbird quickly snatches. Because of parasitic behaviors, this species seems destructive among the avian world itself, but it does contribute by assisting in the control of grasshoppers, boll weevils, and caterpillars. Its diet also contains grass and weed seeds.

Nesting and Mating Behaviors

Promiscuity is the term given the mating behavior of the Brown-headed Cowbird. There is no pair bonding. Instead, it may mate with several partners during one season. The male communicates his desires to the female by bristling, swelling, and singing in the tree tops. With wings and tail spread, he bows and sputters until a female joins him.

Parasitic species exist both in the plant and animal world, and the Brown-headed Cowbird is one example of parasitism in the feathered society. When the female is ready to lay an egg, she searches for a "host" nest belonging to another species and already containing one or more eggs. She removes an existing egg and deposits one of her own. Seldom do the "foster parents" realize the intrusion, so they incubate and raise the young as their own. The cowbird egg usually hatches first and is often the larger and more aggressive nestling, thus demanding more time and food from the unsuspecting adults. Their own young often even perish in this process.

Supplemental Information

People often blame the Brown-headed Cowbird for the demise of other bird species, but we fail to acknowledge that the cowbird is a native species, originally restricted to the Eastern United States. Its numbers are now out of control because of expansion of agriculture and clearing of native forests, allowing the spread of this species and high overwinter survival rates. We only have ourselves to blame!

HOODED ORIOLE[*]
Icterus cucullatus

Description: Male—orange body; black wings, tail, back and bib; two white wingbars. Female—yellow body; gray tail, back, wings; no bib

Springtime colors enhance the ruggedness of the desert, and one feathered contributor is the Hooded Oriole. The male of this brightly decorated species has a yellow-orange head with matching underparts and deeply contrasting black wings, tail, and bib. The black coloration

* Plate 39

extends from the lores to the breast. Two white wingbars highlight the wings, and the bill is long and slightly decurved. (Arizona and California birds are more yellow than those of western Texas.) In winter, the black back appears scaly. This species measures seven to seven and three-quarters inches long.

The female Hooded Oriole is pale yellow and lacks the bib. Her tail, upper back, and wings are dark gray. Her longer and more deeply curved bill and solid yellow underparts distinguish her from the Northern Oriole. Immatures resemble the female, except the young male has a black throat by the first spring.

The Hooded Oriole has a sharp call sounding like *wheat,* and makes throaty, chattering noises resembling *chut chut chut whew whew.*

Habitat and Diet

The Hooded Oriole frequents the deserts during summer in areas sustaining mesquites and other desert scrub, and riparian areas with cottonwoods and sycamores. Adapted to cities, it is easily found in parks high in eucalyptus trees, or more often in its favorite tree, the fan palm.

Mainly insectivorous, orioles glean insects from the leaves of trees. Watch for this beauty in the tree tops moving slowly from branch to branch, meticulously searching for food. Additionally, it is fond of nectar from the ocotillo blooms, and will come to feeders with sugar-water. A few Hooded Orioles remain in the desert areas during winter especially those birds in residential areas who are habituated to feeders.

Nesting and Mating Behaviors

The nest of the Hooded Oriole, a real work of art, is a long, hanging basket affixed to the underside of a palm leaf or hung over a branch of another tree (sycamore, cottonwood, mesquite, eucalyptus), usually one growing near water. Constructed with grasses, or fibers stripped from palm fronds, the nest is wider at the bottom and sometimes lined with plant down. The opening is usually on the top, but may also be near the top on the sides.

Placed five to forty-five feet above the ground, the nest is relatively safe from ground predators. The Hooded Oriole's worst enemy, however, is one who approaches from the sky: the cowbird. This parasitic species ousts one of the oriole eggs, replacing it with one of its own. When hatched, the young, aggressive cowbird demands food intended for the young orioles, thus starving them. Helping to compensate for this loss, the Hooded Oriole nests two or three times a year. The three to five eggs of the Hooded Oriole are bluish-white with dark brown markings, while the cowbird's egg is larger and unmarked.

BULLOCK'S ORIOLE*
Icterus bullockii

Description: Male—orange with black nape and upper back; black throat, tail, and wings; white wing patch and edgings. Female—yellow body; olive-green tail and wings; small white wing patch and edgings

The Bullock's Oriole has regained its status as a distinct species from the Baltimore Oriole, and thus the name Northern Oriole is now obsolete. Because these two species interbreed in overlapping geographical areas in the Midwest, they were previously classified as one species. The thinking has changed, and we're back to Bullock's in the Southwestern lowlands where it is a common transient and summer resident.

The male Bullock's has a black nape, back, throat, and eye line. Additionally, his wings are black with a large white wing patch and white wing edgings. His tail is black except for the outer feathers which are bright orange as is the rump, face, and underparts. (The male Baltimore has a black head, throat, and bib. It lacks the white wing patch.) The female's head and breast are light yellow, her belly is white, and her tail and wings are olive-green. She has one small, white wing patch, and the wing feathers are edged with white.

This species measures seven to eight and one-half inches from beak to tail, and has a slender, pointed bill, and a dark iris. The extremely brilliant orange coloration of the male does not often appear until the third or fourth year. The lighter-orange birds are the younger ones. The song of the Western form consists of a series of whistles described as *chuk chucky wheew wheew wheew.* Its call is a harsh *skip.*

* Plate 40

Habitat and Diet

In the Southwestern lowlands, the Bullock's Oriole is a transient and summer resident. It is attracted to streamside growth, parks, farms, and areas where palms, mesquites, and cottonwoods thrive. This eyecatching species eats considerable numbers of insects, gleaning them from foliage high in the tree tops. Omnivorous, it also supplements the insect smorgasbord with available fruit.

Nesting and Mating Behaviors

The nest of the Bullock's Oriole is designed and situated so that it is easy to see, but nearly impossible to approach by most predators. Suspended in a cottonwood or mesquite tree five to forty feet high, the intricately woven, pensile structure, which is made entirely by the female, appears black due to the amount of horsehair she interlaces with grasses. The pendulous bag is often suspended over roads or streams. She builds a new nest each year, spending four to eight days on its delicate construction.

The three to six eggs are pale, bluish-white and scrawled with brown and black markings concentrated at the large end. There is only one brood, which the female incubates for twelve to fourteen days.

Scott's Oriole[*]
Icterus parisorum

Description: Male—black hood and breast; yellow underparts; white wingbars. Female—light yellow; light back streaks; two white wingbars

Contrast and intensity characterize the male's pure yellow-and-black plumage. The jet-black hood, back, breast, and tail abruptly give way to the bright yellow underparts, rump, and wing patch which is accompanied by one thin, white wingbar. The female has two white wingbars on dark olive-gray wings. Her hood, back, and tail are streaks of gray on the otherwise olive-yellow plumage. Juveniles appear similar to the female until the first spring; then the young male's head begins to appear black.

[*] Plate 40

(The female and the immature birds have more streaking than the female Hooded Oriole.)

The Scott's Oriole measures seven and one-half to eight and one-fourth inches long, and has a slender pointed bill and a dark iris. The call is a harsh *chuck,* but the song with flute-like notes is very melodious, resembling that of the Western Meadowlark.

Habitat and Diet

The Scott's Oriole breeds both in pinon-oak habitat as well as in the arid and semi-arid regions of the Southwest. Here it is most often found among palms, yuccas, sycamores, or cottonwoods. It is uncommon in the deserts during winter because the majority migrate to destinations further south. A few birds remain, usually finding protection in desert canyons.

This beautiful bird is mainly insectivorous and can be observed gleaning insects from foliage. Even though male plumage is brightly colored, it is amazing how well he blends with his natural environment. The female always remains less conspicuous.

The Scott's Oriole is also very fond of fruits and berries such as hackberries and saguaro fruit. Cultivated orchards also attract this species, especially those containing peach, apricot, or nectarine trees. Sugarwater in feeders has become another sought-after food source.

Nesting and Mating Behaviors

The nest is a masterpiece of craftsmanship (or craftsbirdship!), consisting of interwoven grasses, yucca fibers, or fine strips of palm fronds. Intricately lined with finer, softer materials such as hair or moss, the nest is a cup-shaped structure attached to the branches of the designated host tree, usually a yucca or palm, or even in the middle of a mistletoe clump. The two to four eggs are pale, bluish-white with gray, black, or brown markings mostly concentrated on the larger end. The female does all of the incubation, which takes fourteen days.

House Finch*
Carpodacus mexicanus

Description: Male—red breast, head, and rump. Female—plain
            head; streaking underneath

The House Finch is a very lively little bird, approximately five inches in length. The male typically exhibits red on the breast, head, and rump with streaked red and black leading down to the lighter-colored belly. Occasionally I have seen males who are yellowish-orange instead of red. This is especially common in California. It has been discovered that in captivity, many males turn yellow after the molting season, whereas in their natural habitat they would become brighter red. The female is streaked with brown and has a rather plain brown head.

It is a real pleasure to listen to this finch because it has such a cheerful song. It makes a long series of Canary-like notes, ultimately ending in a *zee.* It will find a high perch and sing for long periods of time.

Habitat and Diet

This abundant species is a year-round resident in the Southwest and is often seen congregated in large numbers. Although it loves the desert, it is quite common to see this familiar bird in cities, particularly in the parks where it finds bits of food.

Because it is easily attracted to bird feeders, the House Finch is a favorite bird for many people who are forced to be indoors. Shut-ins and sick people often long for a touch of nature, which can be a very healing element. Because the House Finch is so prevalent in civilization and very readily comes within close proximity, it is one bird that seems to aid in healing through its gentle strength and cheerful song.

Nesting and Mating Behaviors

The mating displays are extremely unique and almost comical. The male flies down, picking up a small twig which he lays before the chosen female. If she stays, the male has received the first sign of approval and moves into his more animate behavior. He struts and shimmies until he

* Plate 40

has exhausted his energy. The female calmly watches as if she had already made up her mind long ago.

In the desert, it is difficult to find an area that is not inhabited with House Finches. The favorite locale, however, seems to be the cholla cactus. This finch loves to nest high up in the skyward-reaching arms of this very thorny cactus. It appears to have one of the most secure homes in the desert, and its closest neighbors are the Cactus Wren and the Curve-billed Thrasher.

The nest is a shallow cup, which is finely made and very compactly constructed of grasses, twigs, and rootlets. The House Finch has a tight bond with its nesting site and spends the majority of the year in nesting territory. Often it simply rebuilds the same nest year after year commonly in cholla, but any tree cavity or available bush will suffice.

The four to five eggs are very distinct with a glossy, bluish tint. They are lavishly decorated with black spots, particularly at the larger end. The female is totally responsible for their incubation, which takes twelve to fourteen days. There are usually two broods per season, and occasionally more.

Supplemental Information

The most dangerous enemy of the House Finch is the Merlin Hawk, which feeds almost exclusively on this species. The Southwestern deserts are relatively safe for the House Finch, because the Merlin rarely frequents this area, and then only in the winter. Perhaps this is one reason the House Finch thrives here in such large numbers.

LESSER GOLDFINCH
Carduelis psaltria

Description: Bright yellow underparts; green back; black crown

Because of its intensely yellow throat, breast, and belly, the Lesser Goldfinch easily catches one's attention. As opposed to the black-backed Eastern bird, the Western variation displays a greenish back. The male sports a black crown with white markings, while the female is lighter overall and lacks the crown decoration.

This small bird measures three and one-half to four inches long and has an undulating flight that emphasizes the white wing and tail patches. The juveniles resemble the female, but have greener underparts. The call is a sweet, plaintive *tee-yee,* while the song is vibrant and canary-like with a rapid series of notes.

Habitat and Diet

The Lesser Goldfinch is an uncommon, permanent resident in riparian areas throughout the desert. Look in weedy fields, cottonwood or willow stream bottoms, and agricultural areas for this lively species. It will be found where its food source is abundant: weed seeds are the main attraction.

Nesting and Mating Behaviors

The most unusual characteristic of this dainty species concerns its extended breeding period. In various locations throughout the desert, it has been recorded nesting from January until well into November.

The female engineers the neatly constructed, cup-shaped nest, but the male offers some assistance. Within four to five days it is complete, including the delicate lining of thistle and cottonwood down, and is securely fastened to an upright branch or fork of a tree. The female incubates the four to six plain, pale blue eggs for twelve days while the male brings her food.

HOUSE SPARROW*
Passer domesticus

Description: Black bib; gray crown; chestnut nape

One bird familiar at every bird feeder is the ever-abundant House Sparrow. The male is brown above, grayish below, and has black striping on the wings, a gray crown, white cheeks, a chestnut nape, and a large black bib. The female is dull-brown above, grayish-white below, with a pale stripe over each eye and rust-colored wings. Her breast is plain, lacking the characteristic bib worn by the male. This species measures five and

* Plate 40

three-quarters to six and one-fourth inches long and has a short, thick bill. It bustles about, habitually flicking its tail while feeding on the ground. The House Sparrow's voice has several variations, including a loud *cheep*, several chirping sounds heard in repetition, and some rather grating noises.

Habitat and Diet

This abundant resident is very cosmopolitan and is easily found around residences, parks, farm buildings, and ranches. Its diet consists mainly of seeds, so it is easily attracted to bird feeders. Often, large numbers converge on one feeder, taking more than their fair share of seeds. The House Sparrow has its contributing moments, however, as it also eats insects, which helps to maintain the balance of nature.

Nesting and Mating Behaviors

During the breeding season, the male may be seen fanning his tail and dropping his wings as he hops around in front of the female. This occurs very early in the spring, and copulation may take place as early as two months before the eggs are laid.

The male selects the site for the nest, which is made of almost any available material and constructed by both sexes. It is placed in any number of locations including tree holes, awnings, forks of trees, rafters, and birdhouses. When completed, the loose structure is in the shape of a huge ball with a small opening on the side. There are three to seven smooth, oval, glossy eggs, which are light green and spotted with browns and grays. The female does the incubation, which takes twelve to thirteen days, then both sexes feed the young nestlings.

Supplemental Information

The House Sparrow was introduced to the United States in 1850 when eight pairs were released in Brooklyn. They did not survive, so in 1852 large numbers were again imported and released. This time they quickly multiplied and spread across the United States. By 1875 they had penetrated every corner of the country, including the Southwest.

Appendix 1

BIRD LISTS

The following eight areas represent habitat scattered throughout the hot deserts and grasslands of California, Arizona, and New Mexico. These elected refuges contain high concentrations of bird species and are herein organized for the ease of comparing information gathered by the U.S. Department of the Interior, Fish and Wildlife Service:

1. Buenos Aires National Wildlife Refuge
2. Imperial National Wildlife Refuge
3. Cibola National Wildlife Refuge
4. Havasu National Wildlife Refuge
5. Kofa National Wildlife Refuge
6. Salton Sea National Wildlife Refuge
7. Bitter Lake National Widlife Refuge
8. Bosque del Apache National Wildlife Refuge

Codes:

Sp—Spring, April through May
S—Summer, June through August
F—Fall, September through October
W—Winter, November through March
C—Common to abundant, easily found in suitable habitat.
U—Uncommon to fairly common, found where looked for in suitable habitat.
R—Rare to very uncommon, more often missed than seen, even when looked for in suitable habitat.

O–Occasional, normally less than five individuals per season during any given year, but to be looked for.

X–Accidental, less than ten records for the entire area, and not to be expected.

Xx–Accidental, exact time of year unavailable.

*–Regularly breeds in local areas in the Southwestern lowlands.

SELECTED BIRD LISTS

	Buenos Aires				Imperial Nat'l				Cibola				Havasu				Kofa				Salton Sea				Bitter Lake				Bos' Apache			
	Sp	S	F	W	Sp	S	F	W	Sp	S	F	W	Sp	S	F	W	Sp	S	F	W	Sp	S	F	W	Sp	S	F	W	Sp	S	F	W
LOONS																																
Red-throated Loon																					X	X	X	X	Xx	Xx						
Pacific Loon													Xx												Xx							
Arctic Loon														R	R														R	R		
Common Loon	O				O		O	O	Xx				O	X	O	O					R	X	O		R				R	R	R	
GREBES																																
* Least Grebe			U					X																								
* Pied-billed Grebe		U			C	C	C	C	C	C	C	C	C	U	C	C					U	U	U	U	C	U	C	C	C	C	C	C
Horned Grebe						R	R	R						R	R						O	X	O	R	R	R	R	O	R	R	U	R
Eared Grebe			U	U	C	O	C	C	C		C	C	C	O	C	C					C	C	C	C	C	R	C	U	U	U	U	O
* Western Grebe			R	R	R	C	C	C	C	C	C	C	C	C	C	C					U	U	U	U	O	R	R	R	O	O	O	O
Clark's Grebe																																
Red-Necked Grebe																									Xx							
ALBATROSS																																
Laysan Albatross																					X	X										
FULMARS, PETRELS AND SHEARWATERS																																
Cooks Petrel																						X										
Buller's Shearwater																						X										
Sooty Shearwater																						X										
STORM-PETRELS																																
Leach's Storm-Petrel																						X										
Black Storm-Petrel																						X										
Least Storm-Petrel																						X										
BOOBIES AND GANNETS																																
Blue-footed Booby																					X			O								
Brown Booby														Xx							X			X								
PELICANS AND CORMORANTS																																
American White Pelican					O	O	C	C	C	O	C	C	C	O	C	U					C	U	U	C	O	C	C	R	C	O	O	O
Brown Pelican					R	R	R	X	C	Xx	X	Xx	Xx					R	R		R	R	U	U	U	U	R		U	U	U	U
* Double-crested Cormorant			R		C	C	C	C	C	O	C	C	C	C	C	C					C	X	X	C	C	R	U	R	C	C	U	U
* Olivaceous Cormorant												C			C	R			R		X	X	X	X							C	R
FRIGATEBIRDS																																
Magnificent Frigatebird						X															O	R	X	Xx								
BITTERNS, HERONS AND EGRETS																																
* American Bittern			R		R	U	U	U	R	U	U	O	O	U	U	U					R	O	U	U	U	R	R	U	U	U	U	U
* Least Bittern					U	U	U	U	U	U	U	U	C	C	C	O					R	U	R	O	U	U	U	R	U	U	U	U
* Great Blue Heron		U	U	U	U	U	C	C	C	U	C	C	C	C	C	C					C	C	C	C	U	U	U	C	U	U	C	C
* Great Egret					U	U	C	C	C	C	C	C	C	C	C	C					C	C	C	C	U	U	U	U	U	U	O	O
* Snowy Egret			U		C	C	C	U	C	C	C	C	C	C	C	C					C	X	X	X	U	U	U	R	C	C	R	R
Tricolored Heron																					X	X	R	R					Xx			
Little Blue Heron			R							Xx											O	O	X	X	R		O					
Reddish Egret							X														X	X	X	X					Xx			
* Cattle Egret			R	R	C	C	C	C	C	C	C	C	C	C	C	C					C	U	U	U	O	C	C	R	U	U	O	O
Green Heron	U	R	U	R	O	O	U	O	U	U	U	U	C	C	C	C			O		C	C	C	X	R	U	R	R	U	U	O	O
* Black-crowned Night-Heron			U	U	U	U	U	U	U	U	U	U	C	C	U	C					C	C	C	C	R	U	R	R	O	O	C	O

SELECTED BIRD LISTS

		Buenos Aires				Imperial Nat'l				Cibola				Havasu				Kofa				Salton Sea				Bitter Lake				Bos' Apache			
		Sp	S	F	W	Sp	S	F	W	Sp	S	F	W	Sp	S	F	W	Sp	S	F	W	Sp	S	F	W	Sp	S	F	W	Sp	S	F	W
	Yellow-crowned Night-Heron																																	Xx
IBIS AND SPOONBILLS																																		
	White Ibis	X																									Xx				Xx		
	White-faced Ibis		C			O	U	O	O	U	U	U	R		U	U	U					U	U	U	O	U	C	U	C	U	U	U	
*	Roseate Spoonbill					X		X	Xx																		Xx							
STORKS																																		
*	Wood Stork										O	O			R	R									X						Xx		
FLAMINGOS																																		
	Lesser Flamingo																					O		O	O								
	Chilean Flamingo																					O		O	O								
WATERFOWL																																		
	Fulvous Whistling-Duck					R	R	R		Xx																							
	Black-bellied Whistling-Duck	R																				Xx		Xx									
	Tundra Swan							O	O			U	U			O	O					R	R		O			R	O				
	Greater White-fronted Goose	R	R			R	R				U	U	U	O	O	R	R					X	X	X		R		O	O	O	O	O	O
	Snow Goose	R	R			O	O			U	U	C	C	O	O	C	C	X				X	X	C	C	O	O	C	C	C	C	C	C
	Ross' Goose		R				O	U	R	U	U	C	C	R	R	C	C					R	O	C	C	U	U	C	C	U	U	C	C
	Brant			X		R							Xx									O		X	X								
*	Canada Goose	R	O			R	O	X	U	C	C	O	U		O	O	R				X	R	O	O	X	C	C	C	C	C	C	C	C
*	Wood Duck		R			R	R	U	U	U	U	R	O	R	O	O	O					X		X	O	O	O	O	U	O	O	O	C
*	Green-winged Teal	C	C			U	R	O	C	C	C	O	R	O	R	C	C					C	R	C	C	U	C	C	U	C	C	O	C
	Baikal Teal																							X									
	American Black Duck																																Xx
	Harlequin Duck																							X									
*	Mallard	U	C	U	U	C	C	C	C	C	C	C	C	U	C	C	C				X	O	U	U	U	C	C	C	C	C	C	C	C
*	Northern Pintail	C	C	U	U	U	C	O	O	C	C	O	O	U	C	U	C			O	R	R	R	C	C	C	C	C	C	C	C	U	C
*	Blue-winged Teal	U	U	U		O	R	O	O	C		O	O	C	U	C	U				R	R	O	R	O	U	C	U	C	U	U	U	C
	Garganey	X																															
*	Cinnamon Teal	C	U	C		C	U	U	C	C		C	C	O	O	O	O		R	R	R	O	U	C	R	C	U	C	U	O	O	O	
*	Northern Shoveler	C	C	C	C	C	U	U	C	C	C	C	C	O	R	C	C		R	O	O	O	X	R	C	U	R	C	C	U	U	C	C
*	Gadwall	C	C	U		U	U	C		C	C	C		U	R	C	C					R	R	U	C	U	U	U	U	U	U	C	C
	Eurasian Wigeon	X															R								X								Xx
	American Wigeon	C	C	C		C	C	U		C	C	U	C	O	U	C	C					R	O	O	O	C	C	C	C	C	C	U	U
*	Canvasback	C	U	U		U	O	U		O	O	O		R	U	R	U					O	X	U	O	C	U	U	R	O	O	U	U
*	Redhead	U	U	U		O	U	U		O	O	U		U	U	U						X	C	O	C	C	C	C	C	O	O	U	U
*	Ring-necked Duck	U	C	U		O	R	U		C	O	C		R	C	C						O	O	R	O	U	U	U	U	U	U	U	C
	Tufted Duck																R																
	Greater Scaup								O								R					O	X	R	R	X		R		Xx			R
*	Lesser Scaup	U	U			U	U	U		R	U	U		O	O	C	U			U	U	O	X	X	X	U	R	U	O	U	O	U	U
	Oldsquaw	O	X					X														O	X	X	R	O		R		X			Xx
	Black Scoter																					X		X		X			R	X			Xx
	Surf Scoter							X														X		X		R			R	X			Xx
	White-winged Scoter																					O		X		O			R	X			Xx
	Common Goldeneye	R	C					O	R	U		U		O	O							O	R	O	R	O	O		R	O			R
	Barrow's Goldeneye							O	R			R												X	Xx				R	R	R		Xx

SELECTED BIRD LISTS

	Buenos Aires				Imperial Nat'l				Cibola				Havasu				Kofa				Salton Sea				Bitter Lake				Bos' Apache			
	Sp	S	F	W	Sp	S	F	W	Sp	S	F	W	Sp	S	F	W	Sp	S	F	W	Sp	S	F	W	Sp	S	F	W	Sp	S	F	W
Bufflehead							R	C			C	C			U	C				R	U		O	O		C	R	C		U	U	C
Hooded Merganser							R	C			U	C			R	R							R	O		O	O	O		O	O	C
Common Merganser								O			U	U			O	O			O	C				O		R	U	R		O	R	R
Red-breasted Merganser												O			R	R			C	C			X	R		R	R	R		R	C	R
* Ruddy Duck		U	U	U		U	U	C			C	C	C	O	C	C	O	C	U	U	U	R	U	U	C	U	C	C		U	C	C
VULTURES																																
Black Vulture	R	R																											Xx			
* Turkey Vulture	C	C			R	C	C	C	U	U	U		O	R	R	C			R		C	R	U	U	O	C	O			C	C	
OSPREY, KITES, EAGLES AND HAWKS																																
Osprey					O	R	R	R	R	R	U	R	R	R	R	R	R	R	R		R	R	R	R	R	O	R				O	
Black-shouldered Kite					R	R	R	R	R	R	R	R	R	R							O	O	X	O	O	R						Xx
Bald Eagle	R	R	R	R	R			O			U	U				C									C		U	C			O	U
* Northern Harrier	C		C	C	C		C	C	U		U	U	C	X	U	C	C	C	C	C	U		U	U	O		U	C	O		O	C
Sharp-shinned Hawk		U	U	U	O		O	O	O		U	U	U		U	C			R	R	O		U	U	O		O	O	C		C	C
* Cooper's Hawk		U	U	U	U		U	U	O		U	U	U	R	C	C			R	R	O		U	U	O		O	O	C	O	O	O
* Harris's Hawk	R				O	O	O	O	U	U	U	U																	O	C	O	O
Red-shouldered Hawk									U	U	U	U									O		R	R					O	R		O
Gray Hawk	C	C																														
* Broad-winged Hawk																					X											
Swainson's Hawk		U	U						Xx				R	R			O				O			O	U	U	U		U	U	U	R
Zone-tailed Hawk		R															R	X							Xx							
* Red-tailed Hawk	C		C	C	U	U	U	U	C	U	U	C	C	C	C	C	C	C	C	C	X	X	U	U	C	O	C	C	C	U	C	C
Ferruginous Hawk					R		R	R								R				R			R	R	O		O	R	O		O	O
Rough-legged Hawk																								O	O			U	O		O	O
Common Black Hawk																					X											
* Golden Eagle	R	R	R						O	O	O	U	O	O	O	U	U	U	U	U								O	U	U	U	U
Northern Goshawk									Xx				Xx					X										O				R
Mississippi Kite																							O						R	R	R	R
CARACARAS AND FALCONS																																
Crested Caracara	X																															
* American Kestrel	U	U		C	O	O	O	C	C	C	C	C	C	U	C	C	C	C	C	C	C	C	C	C	U	C	U	U	C	U	C	C
Merlin							R	R							O	O			R	R			R	R		R	R	R	O		O	O
Peregrine Falcon			R	R	O		O	O					R	R	R	R	R	R	R	R	O	O	O	O		R	R	R	R	R	R	R
* Prairie Falcon			R	R	R	R	O	O					R		R	R	O	O	O	O	R	R	R	R	U	U	O	U	U	U	O	U
GALINACEOUS BIRDS																																
* Wild Turkey																													U	U	U	U
Montezuma Quail		U	U	U																												
* Masked Bobwhite Quail		U	U	U																												
* Scaled Quail	C	C	C																						U	U	U	U				
California Quail																																
Gambel's Quail	C	C	C	C	C	C	C	C	C	C	C	C	C	C	C	C	C	C	C	C	C	C	C	C					C	C	C	C
* Ring-necked Pheasant																					U	U	U	U	C	C	C	C				
* Lesser Prairie-Chicken																					R	R	R	R	R	R	R	R				
Northern Bobwhite																					U	U	U		U	U	U					
RAILS, GALLINULES AND COOTS																																

SELECTED BIRD LISTS

			Buenos Aires				Imperial Nat'l				Cibola				Havasu				Kofa				Salton Sea				Bitter Lake				Bos' Apache			
			Sp	S	F	W	Sp	S	F	W	Sp	S	F	W	Sp	S	F	W	Sp	S	F	W	Sp	S	F	W	Sp	S	F	W	Sp	S	F	W
	*	Black Rail					O	O	O				O	O										O	O	O	O								O
	*	Clapper Rail													U	U	U						R	R	R	R					C	C	C	C
	*	Virginia Rail			U	U	U	C	U	C	O	O	C	C	U	U	U	U					U	U	U	U	U	U	U	U	U	C	C	C
	*	Sora		U			U	C	U	C	C	C	C	C	U	C	C	C					C	U	U	U	U	U	U	U	U	C	C	C
	*	Common Moorhen					C	C	C	C	C	C	C	C	C	C	C	C					C	C	C	C	R		R					
	*	American Coot		U		U	C	C	C	C	C	C	C	C	C	C	C	C					C	C	C	C	C	C	C	C	C	C	C	C
		Purple Gallinule																										R	R	R	R				
		Yellow Rail																					X					R							
CRANES																																		
	*	Greater Sandhill Crane			X			O	O	U		O	O	U		O	O							U	U	U		U	C	C		C	C	C	C
		Whooping Crane																														U	U	U	U
		Common Crane																										Xx							
PLOVERS																																		
	*	Black-bellied Plover					O	O	O		Xx			O	O	O	O						O	C	C	C	O	O	O	O		R		R
	*	Lesser Golden-Plover																		R	R			O	O	X	R	R						
	*	Snowy Plover					O	O	O	O	O	O	O		R	U	C	R				R	U	U	U	R	C	C	C	C	U	C	C	U
		Wilson's Plover										Xx											X												
	*	Semipalmated Plover	X			X	O	O	O	O	O	O	O	O	O	O	O						C	O	U	R	O	O	O	O	O	O	O	O
	*	Killdeer	C	C	C	R	C	C	C	C	C	C	C	C	C	C	C	C		O	O		C	C	O	C	C	C	C	C	C	C	C	C
		Mountain Plover													Xx	U	U						O	O	O				R					
OYSTERCATCHERS																																		
		American Oystercatcher																					X												
STILTS AND AVOCETS																																	
	*	Black-necked Stilt	U	U			U	U	U		C	U	C	C	O	C	C				R		C	C	C	U	C	C	C	U	C	U	U	U
	*	American Avocet	U	U			U	U	U	O	U	C	R	U	R	U	U	R			R		C	C	O	U	C	C	C	R	O	U	U	U
SHOREBIRDS																																		
		Greater Yellowlegs	U		U		U	O	O	O	O		U	U	U	U	C	O				X	C	O	U	C	C	C	C	C	C	C	C	O
		Lesser Yellowlegs	U		U		U	O	O	O	O	O	U	U	U	U	C	O		R	R	X	U	C	U	R	C	C	C	R	U	O	U	O
		Spotted Redshank									Xx											X												
		Solitary Sandpiper		R			O	O	O		O	O	O		R	U	U					X	X	O			O		O		O	O		
		Willet	R				U	O	O	R	U	O	O	U	U	U	C	O					O	O	C	U	C	C	C	U	O	U	C	U
		Wandering Tattler																			X			X	X									
	*	Spotted Sandpiper	R			R	C	U	C	C	C	U	C	R	C	U	C	U		R			U	O	C	C	U	R	R		C	O	C	C
		Upland Sandpiper								X														X			R						R	
		Whimbrel							X								R							O	O			O	O				Xx	
		Long-billed Curlew	R		R		R	O	O	R	U		U		U	U	U	U			O		C	C	C	O	C		O		O	O	O	O
		Hudsonian Godwit						X															X												
	*	Marbled Godwit	X	X			U	U	U	O	U	U	U	O	O	C	O				R		C	U	U	X	C	R	R		C	U	C	C
	*	Ruddy Turnstone									Xx												O	O	U	O	R	R	R		U	Xx	U	O
		Black Turnstone																					O											
	*	Surfbird																					O											
	*	Red Knot																					U	X	R	O		R			U			
	*	Sanderling						O				O		O		R	R						U		O	U		R	R	R	U	U	O	U
	*	Semipalmated Sandpiper																			R			X			R	R			R	R	R	R
	*	Western Sandpiper	R				C	C	O	C	C		O	C	U	C	C	R			X		C	C	U	C	C	C	C	C	O	U	O	U

SELECTED BIRD LISTS

	Buenos Aires				Imperial Nat'l				Cibola				Havasu				Kofa				Salton Sea				Bitter Lake				Bos' Apache			
	Sp	S	F	W	Sp	S	F	W	Sp	S	F	W	Sp	S	F	W	Sp	S	F	W	Sp	S	F	W	Sp	S	F	W	Sp	S	F	W
White-rumped Sandpiper																																R
Little Stint																													R		R	
* Least Sandpiper	C		C	C	C	U	C	C	C	U	C	C	U	C	C	C					C	O	C	C	C	C	C	O	U	U	U	R
* Pectoral Sandpiper						O	X			O	R			O	O						X	O	O	X	R	R	R		O	O	U	
* Baird's Sandpiper		X								U	U			U	U						O		R		U	O	O		U	U	U	
* Stilt Sandpiper										C	C			O	O						C	X	X		U	O	O		R	R	R	
* Dunlin		X				O			O	O	O	O	O	O	R	R					C	X	C	U	C	C	C	R	R	R	O	
Curlew Sandpiper										O	O			O	R					X	X		R	O		R						
Buff-breasted Sandpiper																								X					Xx			
Ruff																							X									
* Short-billed Dowitcher			R			U				U	U	U		U	U	U					U	O	U	R	R	R	R		X		C	O
* Long-billed Dowitcher		C					C	C	U	U	C	C	C	C	C	C	X				C	U	C	C	C	C	C	R	C	O	C	O
SNIPES AND PHALAROPES																																
* Common Snipe	U		U		U	O	U	U	U	U	U	U	C	C	C	C					U		U	R	R	U	O	U	C	U	C	U
American Woodcock		C			U	U	O		O		O	O	C	C	C	C					C	C	C	X	C	C	C	U	C	C	C	
* Wilson's Phalarope	U		U		U	U	O		U		O	O	U	C	C			X			C	C	X	O	C	O	O	C	O	C	O	
* Red-necked Phalarope	U		U		R	O	O		U		O	O	U	C	C			X			X	X	X	O	O	R	O	O	O	O	O	
Red Phalarope			R			R					Xx			R	R						O											
JAEGERS																																
Pomarine Jaeger																					X	X	X									
Parasitic Jaeger						X								Xx							X	X	R						Xx			
Long-tailed Jaeger																							X									
GULLS, TERNS AND SKIMMERS																																
* Laughing Gull																					O	C	C	O	U		O					
* Franklin's Gull			X		R	R			R	Xx	O			R	R						R	O	R	R		R			R	R	R	
Little Gull							X														X	X	X	X	Xx							
Heermann's Gull	X					X	O			O	O										X	R	R	O	R							
* Bonaparte's Gull	R		R	O	R	O	O	O	O	O	O			R	R						C	R	R	O	O	O	R	O	O	O	O	R
* Mew Gull							X														O	X	O	O								
* Ring-billed Gull	R	U	R	R	R	U	O	C	C	C	C	C	R	U	C	C					C	U	C	C	C	C	R	C	C	C	C	U
* California Gull	X	O	O		O	O	R	O	C	O	O	U	C								C	U	U	U	R	R		C	Xx	Xx	Xx	
* Herring Gull							X		Xx		Xx	R	C								R	O	U	C	R	C	R	C	O	O	O	O
* Thayer's Gull																					O		X	R								
Lesser Black-backed Gull																					X	R	X	O								
* Yellow-footed Gull																					R	R	R									
* Western Gull																					O	O	O	O								
* Glaucous-winged Gull							X		O		O				R						O	O	R	O								
Glaucous Gull																					X	R	O	X								
Black-legged Kittiwake																					X		X	O								
Sabine's Gull					R	R			Xx												X	O	O	O					Xx		O	
* Gull-billed Tern	R		O	U	R	U	U	R	C	C		U	U	U	C	C					U	O	U	X	U	R		U	U	C	C	U
* Caspian Tern	X		U	U	O	U	U		C	C		C	C	C	C	C					O	X	O	U	C	C	C		C	C	C	U
Elegant Tern																					X	X										
* Common Tern		O	O			O	O		O	Xx			R			R	X				R	R	C	R	R	U	R		R	R	R	O
Artic Tern																					X	X	O	X		X						

SELECTED BIRD LISTS

	Species	BA Sp	BA S	BA F	BA W	IM Sp	IM S	IM F	IM W	CI Sp	CI S	CI F	CI W	HA Sp	HA S	HA F	HA W	KO Sp	KO S	KO F	KO W	SS Sp	SS S	SS F	SS W	BL Sp	BL S	BL F	BL W	BA' Sp	BA' S	BA' F	BA' W
SEABIRDS																																	
*	Foster's Tern					O	U	U	O	O	O	O	C	R	U	U	R					C	C	C	U	U	U	O		O	O	O	
*	Least Tern						X																X							Xx			
	Black Tern			R			U	U	U		O	O	O	O	O	U	C					U	U	C	X	C	C	C	C	U	O	U	
*	Black Skimmer							X	X							O						U	R	R	X					Xx	O	U	
	Ancient Murrelet																					X	X										
PIGEONS AND DOVES																																	
	Band-tailed Pigeon													Xx												Xx				Xx			
	Rock Dove			R					X																X	R	R	C	C	R	O	R	
	Spotted Dove																								X								
*	White-winged Dove	C	C		U	C	C	C	U	C	C		C	U	U	U	O	C	C	C		C	C	C	C	O	O	O	X	R	O	C	C
*	Mourning Dove	C	C	C	C	C	C	C	C	C	C	C	C	C	C	C	C	C	C	C	U	U	U	O	X	C	C	C	C	C	C	C	C
*	Inca Dove	R	R					R	R					C	C	U	O					C	C	R	R	R	R	R	R	Xx	Xx		
*	Common Ground Dove		U		C	U	U	U	U			O		R	R	R	R	O	O	O		R	R	R	U					Xx	Xx		
CUCKOOS AND ROADRUNNERS																																	
*	Yellow-billed Cuckoo	U		U			U			U	U			U	U			U	U			X				O	O	U		U	U	U	U
*	Greater Roadrunner	C	C	C	C	C	C	C	C	C	C	C	C	C	C	C	C	O	O	O	O	C	C	C	C	C	C	C	C	C	C	C	C
	Groove-billed Ani																							X	X	R				Xx			
OWLS																																	
*	Common Barn Owl	U	U	U	C	O	O	O	O					O	O	O	O					R	R	R	R	U	U	U	R	O	O	O	R
	Flammulated Owl																		X				X										
*	Western Screech-Owl	R	R	U	R	C	C	C	C	C	C	C	C	C	C	C	C	C	C	C	C	R	R	R	R	R	R	R	R	U	U	U	
*	Great Horned Owl	C	C	C	C	C	C	C	C	C	C	C	C	U	U	U	U	O	O	O	O	O	O	O	O	C	C	C	O	U	U	U	U
	Ferruginous Pygmy-Owl	R	R																		R												
*	Elf Owl	R				U		U		U	C			U	U			C	C														
*	Burrowing Owl	R	R	U		U	U	U	U	R	R	R	R	U	U	C	C					C	C	C	C	U	U	U	U	U	U	U	O
	Long-eared Owl	R	R	R		R	R	R	R					R	R			U	U	U				O	O	R	R	R		Xx			
	Short-eared Owl			R				R	R			Xx				Xx						O	R	U	U			R		R	R	R	R
	Northern Saw-whet Owl																					X	X							R	R	R	
	Northern Pygmy-Owl											Xx																					
NIGHTJARS																																	
*	Lesser Nighthawk	C	C			C	C	C		R	C	C	C	C	C	C	C	O	O	O	R	U	U	U	R	O	O	O	R	C	C	C	
*	Common Nighthawk	R	R																							C	C	C	C	U	U	U	
*	Common Poorwill	U	C	C		U	U	U	U	U	U	U		U	U	U		C	C	C	R			O	O			Xx		O	O	O	
	Buff-collared Nightjar		R																X					X									
	Whip-poor-will																																
SWIFTS																																	
	Black Swift																					X								X			
	Vaux's Swift																					U	C			C				U			
*	White-throated Swift	U		U		O	O	O	O	U	U	O		U	U	U	C	O	O	R	O	R	R	R	R					R	R		
	Chimney Swift																						X							Xx			
HUMMINGBIRDS																																	
	Broad-billed Hummingbird	U	U											O	O			O	O			R	R										
*	Black-chinned Hummingbird	C	C		U	C	C			C	C			C	C			O	O			R	R	O	O	R	R	R		C	C	C	C
	Anna's Hummingbird	U				C	C	C	C	C	C			C	C					U		U	U	R	R	Xx							

SELECTED BIRD LISTS

	Buenos Aires				Imperial Nat'l				Cihola				Havasu				Kofa				Salton Sea				Bitter Lake				Bos' Apache			
	Sp	S	F	W	Sp	S	F	W	Sp	S	F	W	Sp	S	F	W	Sp	S	F	W	Sp	S	F	W	Sp	S	F	W	Sp	S	F	W
* Costa's Hummingbird	R	C			C	C	C			C	C		C																			Xx
Calliope Hummingbird	R						X		Xx																				U	U	U	U
Broad-tailed Hummingbird	C	C																						O					U	U	U	U
Rufous Hummingbird					O		O		Xx				O	O							R	O	O		O	O	O		O	O	O	
Allen's Hummingbird		C				O							O	O							X	O			R	R						
KINGFISHERS																																
Belted Kingfisher	U	U			C	C	C	U	U	U	U	U	C	C	C	C	O	O	O	O	U	U	U	U	U	O	U	U	U	O	U	O
Green Kingfisher			X			U	U	U	U	U			C	C	C	C	O		R		R	U	U	X		O		U	U	O	U	O
WOODPECKERS																																
Lewis' Woodpecker		X				X			Xx					R	R	R	R	O	O		O	O	O	O	R	Xx						
Red-headed Woodpecker															R	R		X			X		O	O	O	R	R					
Acorn Woodpecker									Xx									X	R	R	R			R	R	R						O
* Gila Woodpecker	C	C	C	C	C	C	C	C	C	C	C	C	C	C	C	C	C	C	R	R	C	R	R	R	C	C						
Yellow-bellied Sapsucker	R	R			U	U			O		O	U	U	U					X	X	X		R						Xx			
Red-naped Sapsucker	U	U	U	U	U	U				R	R						R		R	R	X	X	R	O	R	O			U	U	U	U
Red-breasted Sapsucker																	O				R		O		O		O		U	U	U	U
* Ladder-backed Woodpecker	C	C	C	C	C	C	C	C	C	C	C	C	C	C	C	C	O	O	O	O	O	U	U	U	O	O	O	O	C	C	C	C
Nuttall's Woodpecker																																
Downy Woodpecker	R				R	U	C	U	U	U	C	C	U	U	C	C					O	R	O	O	O	R		O	U	U	U	U
* Gilded Flicker	C	U			U		U		U	U	C	C	C	C	C	C	C	U	U		C	O		C	R	R	R	C	C	C	C	C
* Hairy Woodpecker									Xx				C	C	C	C	O	O			O	O			R	R			C	O	O	R
Williamson's Sapsucker									Xx				Xx																			
TYRANT FLYCATCHER																																
Olive-sided Flycatcher	U	U	U		O	O		O	O	O	O	O	O	O	O	O	O	O	R	R	O	R	R									R
Northern Beardless Tyrannulet	C	C							Xx				Xx								Xx											
Greater Pewee	C	C			C	U	C		C	U	C		C	U	U	C	C												C	U	C	
* Western Wood-Pewee	C	C			U		U		R	R			O	O			C		C		U	U			U	U			O	O	C	O
Willow Flycatcher		U	U		U	U			R	R	R		C	O	O		U	U	C		O	O			O	O					X	
Least Flycatcher																			C											U		
Dusky Flycatcher	U		U		R	O	R		R	O	O	O	R	U	R	R	O	O			O	O	O		O	O						
Hammond's Flycatcher	U		U		O	O	R	R	O	O	R	R	U	R	U	D	U	D			O	D	R	O	O	O			O	U		
Gray Flycatcher					R	C	O	O	C	C	C	C	O	O	O	O	O	R	O	X	R	R	O	X	R	O						
Western Flycatcher (Cordilleran)	C	U	C		O	O	C	C	O	O	C	C	C	C	C	C	C	O	O		O	O	O		O	O			O	O	O	
* Black Phoebe	C	C	C	C	O	O	C	C	C	C	C	C	C	C	C	C	C	U	U	C	C	C	C	C	C	C	C	C	C	U	C	U
Eastern Phoebe					X									R	R	R			X	X			X	X		R	R					
* Say's Phoebe	U	U	U	U	U	U	U	U	U	U	C	C	C	C	C	C	U	U	U	U	U	U	U	U	U	D	U	R	R	C	C	U
* Vermilion Flycatcher	C	C	C	C	U	U	C	C	U	U	U	C	R	R	O	R	R	O	R	C	R	O	R	R	C	U	C	R	C	C	O	C
Dusky-capped Flycatcher	R	R			C	C	R		R	C	R	R	C	C	C	R	U	O	X		O	R	R	R	R	O			C	C	C	R
* Ash-throated Flycatcher	C	C			C	C	R		R	C	O	O	C	U	C	R	C	C	C		C	C	U	U	U	U			U	O	C	
* Brown-crested Flycatcher	U	U			C	C	O	O	O	O			C	C			R	C						X					R	R		
Tropical Kingbird	R	R				R				R			R	R			R	C			X								O	O		
Cassin's Kingbird	R	R				O	R	R	Xx	C	C	C	Xx				X			X	O	R	O	X	X							
Thick-billed Kingbird	R	R							Xx				Xx												R	R			O	R		
* Western Kingbird	C	C			C	C	C		C	O	O	C	C	C	R	C	C	C	U		C	O	O	C	C	C	C		C	C	C	C
* Coach's Kingbird					C	C	U		C	C	C	C	C	C	C	U	C	C	U	U	C	C	C	C	U	U			Xx		C	C

SELECTED BIRD LISTS

		Buenos Aires				Imperial Nat'l				Cibola				Havasu				Kofa				Salton Sea				Bitter Lake				Bos' Apache			
		Sp	S	F	W	Sp	S	F	W	Sp	S	F	W	Sp	S	F	W	Sp	S	F	W	Sp	S	F	W	Sp	S	F	W	Sp	S	F	W
Eastern Kingbird																								X	X	R	R	R	O	O		O	
Scissor-tailed Flycatcher																										O	R	O	R	R			
Rose-throated Becard		R	R																														
LARKS AND SWALLOWS																																	
Horned Lark		C	C		C							C	C			O	O			O	R			C	C	C	C	C	C	C	U	U	C
Purple Martin	*			U												R								O	O						O	O	
Tree Swallow			U		U	C	O	U	C	U		U	U			C	C			X		C	O	O	C			R	R	C	O	O	C
Violet-green Swallow			U		U	C	O	U	U	C		U	U	U	U	C	O					C	O	O	C			O	O	C	O	O	C
Northern Rough-winged Swallow		U	U			C	C	U	U	C	O	O	O	C	C	C	O	U	O	O		C	O	X	O			C	C	C	O	O	C
Bank Swallow						C	O	O		O	O	O	O	O	O	O	O					R	O	R	R			O	O	X	O	O	
Cliff Swallow	*	R	R			C	C	U	C	C	O	C	C	C	C	O		O	O	R		C	R	X	R			C	O		C	C	C
Barn Swallow	*	U	U			U	O	O	U	C	C	C	C	C	U	U			R		R	C	O	O	C	C	C	U	U	C	U	U	C
JAYS, CROWS, AND RAVENS																																	
Gray-breasted Jay		U	U	U	U																					R	R	R	R			R	R
Steller's Jay												Xx				R	R			R	R					R	R	R	R	R	R	U	U
Scrub Jay	*					X				Xx		X		R	R	O	O	R	O	O	O			O		O	O	O	R	U	U	U	U
Pinyon Jay								R	X	Xx		U	U	Xx	R		R	R		R	R			R		R	O	R	O	U	U	U	U
Clark's Nutcracker								X					O	Xx													Xx						
Black-billed Magpie																											Xx		Xx	Xx			
American Crow		C	C	C	C							C	C			R	R							O	R						C	C	C
Chihuahuan Raven	*	C	C	C	C				R		R	R	R	C	C	R	R	O	O	O		O	R	R	U	U	U	O	O	O	U	U	O
Common Raven		C	C	C	C				R	R	R	R	R	C	C	C	C	O	O	O	O	C	R	R	R	R	R	O	R	C	C	C	C
Blue Jay								R				C	C									O	R	R	R	O		O	R	Xx		O	O
CHICKADEES AND TITMICE																																	
Mountain Chickadee												Xx				Xx										Xx							
Bridled Titmouse												Xx				Xx									X	X					U		U	C
Plain Titmouse		U	U	U	U																										O	O	O	O
VERDIN																																	
Verdin	*	C	C	C	C	C	C	C	C	C	C	C	C	C	C	C	C	C	C	C	C	C	C	C	C					U	U	U	U
BUSHTITS AND NUTHATCHES																																	
Common Bushtit	*		R									Xx				R	R									Xx					O		O
White-breasted Nuthatch			R					X	X	Xx		Xx				Xx				O				X	R		R	R	R		O	U	U	U
Red-breasted Nuthatch								R	R	Xx		R				R	R			O				R	O		O	R	O		O	U	U	U
Pygmy Nuthatch			U																		O					Xx					O		O
CREEPERS																																	
Brown Creeper								R																O	R			R	R				O
WRENS																																	
Cactus Wren	*	C	C	C	C	C	C	C	C	C	U	U	U	U	U	C	C	C	C	C	C	C	C	C	C		R	R	R	O	O	O	O
Rock Wren	*	U	U	U	U	C	C	U	U	U	U	U	U	U	U	C	C	C	C	C	C	C	R	R	R	R	U	U	U	U	U	U	U
Canyon Wren	*	U	U	U	U	C	O	O	O	Xx		U	U	C	C	O	O	C	C	C	R			X	O	U	U	U	U	R	R	R	R
Berwick's Wren	*	C	C	C	C					O	O	O	O	U	U	O	O	O	O	O	U	R	R	U	U	U	U	O	O	O	O	U	U
House Wren						O	O	O	C	O	C	O	U	U	U	O	O	O	O	C	U	U	U	U	U	O	O	O	O	O	O	U	U
Winter Wren															O	Q	O							X						Xx	Xx		
Marsh Wren	*	C	C	C	C	C	C	C	C	C	U	U	U	C	C	C	C	C	C	C	C	C	C	C	C	C	U	C	C	O	O	C	C
Carolina Wren																								R			R	R	R	Xx	Xx		

SELECTED BIRD LISTS

Key to locations: Buenos Aires, Imperial Nat'l, Cibola, Havasu, Kofa, Salton Sea, Bitter Lake, Bos' Apache. Seasons: Sp = Spring, S = Summer, F = Fall, W = Winter.

Species	BA Sp	BA S	BA F	BA W	IN Sp	IN S	IN F	IN W	CI Sp	CI S	CI F	CI W	HA Sp	HA S	HA F	HA W	KO Sp	KO S	KO F	KO W	SS Sp	SS S	SS F	SS W	BL Sp	BL S	BL F	BL W	AP Sp	AP S	AP F	AP W
KINGLETS AND GNATCATCHERS																																
Sedge Wren																												O	Xx			
Golden-crowned Kinglet								X	C		C	C			R	C	C			C	C		O	C	R	R	C	C			C	O
Ruby-crowned Kinglet			C	C	C		C	C	C		C	C	C		U	U	C		U	U	C		C	C	C	O	C	O	O		U	U
Blue-gray Gnatcatcher			R	C	C		C	U	C		C	C	U		U	U	C		U	O	U		O	O	U		U	O	O		U	O
* Black-tailed Gnatcatcher	U		U	U	C	C	C	C	C	C	C	C	C	C	C	C	C	C	C	C	C	U	U	U	Xx				U	U	U	U
BLUEBIRDS AND THRUSHES																																
Eastern Bluebird																	O			O	O		X	O	R		O	R	R		O	R
Western Bluebird				R	O		O	O	O		O	O	U		U	U				P	O		X	O	R	O	R	U	C	O	U	C
Mountain Bluebird	R			O	O		O	O	O		O	O	U		U	U	O		R	O	O		O	O	O	O	O	O	U		O	O
Townsend's Solitaire	R			O				U	O		U	U	O		O	O	O		R	U	O		U	U					U		O	O
Swainson's Thrush					U				U		U		U		U		U		U		U		U	X	U		U					
Hermit Thrush				C				X	U		U	U	R		R	U	O		R	O	O		R	O	U		U	R	U		U	R
Varied Thrush				X												R				X	X				Xx							
Rufous-backed Robin				X									R		R	R	R			R												
* American Robin	U			O	O			O	U		U	U	U		U	U	U		O	R	R		U	O	U	O	O	O	U		U	U
Wood Thrush																																
Gray-cheeked Thrush																									Xx							
MIMICS AND THRASHERS																																
Gray Catbird					C	C					Xx														R	R	C	C			Xx	
* Northern Mockingbird	C	C	C	C	U	U	U	U	C	C	C	C	C	C	C	C	U	U	U	U	C	C	C	C	C	C	U	C	C	C	C	C
Sage Thrasher					O		O	O	O		O	O	U		U	U	O		O	O	O		X	X	R			R	C		O	R
Brown Thrasher							R																				R		R			R
Bendire's Thrasher	R	R	R										U	U	U		O	O	O		X	X	X		R	R			Xx			
* Curve-billed Thrasher	U	U	U	U	C	C	C	C	C	C	C	C	C	C	C	C	O	O	O	O	X	X	X	R								
* Crissal Thrasher	R	R	R	R	C	C	C	C	C	C	C	C	C	C	C	C	O	O	O	O	R	R	R	R					U	U	U	U
Le Conte's Thrasher					C	C	C	C	C	C	C	C	U	U	U	U	U	U	U	U	R	R	R	R								
PIPITS																																
American Pipit			U	C	C			C	C		C	C	U		U	U	O			R	R		R	U	U		U	U	R	U	U	C
Water Pipit																									R		R					Xx
Sprague's Pipit																																Xx
WAXWINGS																																
Cedar Waxwing			U	O	U			O	O		O	O	O	O	R	R	O			O	R	U	O		R		U	O	O		O	O
PHAINOPEPLA																																
* Phainopepla	C	C	U	C	C	C	U	C	C	C	U	C	C	C	O	U	U	C	U	C	U	U	U	U	R		U	R	R		O	O
SHRIKES																																
Northern Shrike												X																			O	
* Loggerhead Shrike	C	C	C	C	C	C	C	C	C	C	C	C	C	C	C	C	C	C	C	C	C	C	C	C	U	C	C	C	U		U	C
STARLINGS																																
* European Starling	U	U	U	U	O	O	O	O	C	C	C	C	C	C	C	C	O	O	O	O	C	C	C	C	U	C	U	U	C	C	C	C
VIREOS																																
* Bell's Vireo	C	C			C	C	O		O	O	O		U	U	U						U	U							O	O	O	
Gray Vireo					U				O				R	R			O	O														
* Solitary Vireo	R			R	O			U	U		O	U	U	R	U	R	O	O		O	R		O	O	R			R	O		O	
Hutton's Vireo	R				U			Xx			Xx				R	R	O	O	R				X									

SELECTED BIRD LISTS

	Buenos Aires				Imperial Nat'l				Cibola				Havasu				Kofa				Salton Sea				Bitter Lake				Bos' Apache			
	Sp	S	F	W	Sp	S	F	W	Sp	S	F	W	Sp	S	F	W	Sp	S	F	W	Sp	S	F	W	Sp	S	F	W	Sp	S	F	W
Warbling Vireo	R				C		C		C	C	C		C	U	U		C		C		C				R				O			
Red-eyed Vireo					X										R			X									R		O		O	
Philadelphia Vireo																		X														
Yellow-throated Vireo													Xx																			
WOOD WARBLERS																																
Tennessee Warbler																						X										
Orange-crowned Warbler		U			C		C		C		C		C	C	C	C	C		C		C	C	C		R		O			U		O
Nashville Warbler	U				U		U		C		U		U		U		C		U		C		U		O				Xx		U	
Virginia's Warbler											Xx		R	X	X						O		R						Xx		U	
* Lucy's Warbler	U	C			C	C			C	C			R	X	C		R	R			X								O	O		
Northern Parula								X	C	O			Xx	O	C						X	R			O		R	O	Xx		O	
* Yellow Warbler	C	C			C	O	C		R	O		R	C	O	C	R	C		C		C	R	U	R	C	R	U	R	C	U	U	O
Chestnut-sided Warbler																			X	X	X	X	X		U	Xx			Xx			
Magnolia Warbler																					X	X			X	Xx			Xx			
Cape May Warbler																					X	X	X		X	X						
Yellow-rumped Warbler	C	C			C		C		C		C		C		C		C		C		C	U	C	C	C	C	C	R	C	O	C	U
Black-throated Gray Warbler		R			U		U		U		U		U		U		U		U		U		O		R	R			O		O	O
Black-throated Blue Warbler																		C			X	X	O		R	R	R		Xx			
Townsend's Warbler	R		U	X	U		U	X	U		U		U		U		C		O		X	R	X	R	R	O	R		Xx			
Hermit Warbler	X		R		O		O		O		O		U		O		U		U		U	R	R		O		R		Xx			
Prairie Warbler																					X		X									
Bay-breasted Warbler																					X											
Cerulean Warbler																						X										
Grace's Warbler																						X				Xx						
Palm Warbler	C						X														X	X	X			X						
Blackpole Warbler					X								R								O	O	O		O	O			Xx			
Black-and-white Warbler	R				C		X		Xx				Xx		R	R					O	O	R		O	R	R		O		O	
Golden-winged Warbler													Xx																			
Northern Waterthrust	R		R		U		C		U		U		U		U		C		O		R	R	X	R	O	R	R		O		O	
Louisianna Waterthrust	X				O		O		O		O		O		O		U		U		U	X	R	X	O	R	R		Xx			
Prothonotary Warbler													Xx																			
Black-throated Green Warbler	R	R											Xx																Xx		Xx	
* MacGillivary's Warbler	U	U	U		C		C		C		C		C		C		U		U		R	R	U	O	O	C	C		O	C	O	
Common Yellowthroat	C	C	U	U	C		C		C		C		C	C	C	U	U		U		U	U	U	U	U	C	U	U	C	C	U	C
Wilson's Warbler	U	C	R	R	C		C		C		C		C		C		C		U		X	O	O		U	R	O		C	C	C	C
Ovenbird													R								X		X		R	R			R			
American Redstart					R		R		O		O		R	R	R	R	X				O	R	R		O	C			O		O	
Painted Redstart													R			R				R												
* Yellow-breasted Chat	C	C			C	C	C		C	C	C		C	C	U						U	U	U		O	C	U		O	C	C	U
Yellow-throated Warbler																					X	X	X			R			Xx			
Blue-winged Warbler		X											Xx																			
Worm-eating Warbler													Xx													Xx						
TANAGERS																																
Hepatic Tanager																	O				X						R		O		O	
* Summer Tanager	C	C			O	O	O		C	C	C		C	C	C						X	O	X		R	O	R		U	U	U	

SELECTED BIRD LISTS

	Buenos Aires				Imperial Nat'l				Cibola				Havasu				Kofa				Salton Sea				Bitter Lake				Bos' Apache			
	Sp	S	F	W	Sp	S	F	W	Sp	S	F	W	Sp	S	F	W	Sp	S	F	W	Sp	S	F	W	Sp	S	F	W	Sp	S	F	W
CARDINALS, GROSBEAKS AND BUNTINGS																																
* Western Tanager	U		U		U	U	U						O	O	O	O				O	C	U	U		O	U	O		C	R	R	O
Scarlet Tanager																												R	O	O		
CARDINALS, GROSBEAKS AND BUNTINGS																																
* Northern Cardinal	C	C	C	C									O	O	O	O								O	R			O				
* Pyrrhuloxia	U	U	U	U									C	C	C	R	R	O	R		X	U	R	R	O	U	O	U	U	U	U	U
Black-headed Grosbeak	U	U	U		C	U	C		C	U	C		C	C	C		U	O	U		C	U	R	C	U	U	O		U	U	C	C
* Blue Grosbeak	C	C			C	C	C		C	C	C		O	C	O		R		R		U	U	R	U	C	U	C		C	C	U	R
Blue Bunting																					X											
Lazuli Bunting	C	C		R	U		U		U	U			U	U		C	C			C	C		U	C	O	O	R	C	O	R	R	R
* Indigo Bunting		R	R		O		O		U		U		O	O		R				U	X	X	X	X	R	R		R	O	R	R	U
Varied Bunting	U	U											Xx								X	X	X		R	R						
Painted Bunting													Xx												R	R						
Rose-breasted Grosbeak			X										R	O	R	R	X			R	X	X			O	O			U	U	U	O
Dickcissel	X												Xx												R	R						
TOWHEES AND SPARROWS																																
Green-tailed Towhee			C	U			U	U	U		U	U	U		U	U	U	U	U	O	R	R	R	O	C	O	C	O	U	U	U	O
* Spotted Towhee			U	U			O	O	O		O	O	U	U	U	U	U	U	U	O	R	R	R	O	R	U	U	R	C	U	C	C
* Canyon Towhee	C	C	C	C									C	C	C	C	C	C	C	C	C	C	C	C					U	U	U	U
* Abert's Towhee	U		U	U	C	C	C	C	C	C	C	C	C	C	C	X	X				C	C	C	C								
Brown Towhee																													R			R
American Tree Sparrow																																
Botteri's Sparrow	C																															
Cassin's Sparrow	C																												O	O		
Rufous-winged Sparrow	U	U	U	U																					C	C	C					
Rufous-crowned Sparrow	C	C	C	C									C	C	U	R	C	C	C	C					O	U	U		O	O	O	O
Chipping Sparrow			X		X								O	C	U	O	C	C	C	C	R	R	R	R	O	R	C	O	C	C	C	C
Clay-colored Sparrow																																
Brewer's Sparrow			C	C	C	C	O	O	C	O	O	O	C	C	C	C	O	O	O	O	U	U	R	U	U	C	C	U	U	C	C	C
Vesper Sparrow	C		C	U	O	U	U	R	O		U	R	O	C	U	O	O	O	O	O	R	R	R	O	C	C	C	R	C	O	C	C
* Lark Sparrow	U	U	U	U	O	R	O	O	O	Xx	O	Xx	O	O	O	Xx	O	O	O	O	X	X	X	X	C	C	C	C	O	R	O	O
Black-chinned Sparrow	C	C	C									O	U	C	U	R	C	C	C	C		O			O	O	O	R	C	U	U	U
* Black-throated Sparrow			R	R	O	O	U	U	O	U			C	C	U	C	C	C	C	C	R	R	R	R	R	R	R	R	U	U	U	U
Sage Sparrow	R														U			C			O	U	O	R	O	O						
Five-striped Sparrow	X																															
Lark Bunting			C	C	R	R	R	O	C	Xx	R	O	C	R	O	O	C				C	C	C		U	U	O		O	O	O	
Savannah Sparrow	C	C	C		C	U	C	O	U	C	O	C	C	C	C	C	C	O		X	O	C	U	O	O	C	C	R	C	C	C	C
Grasshopper Sparrow	C	C	C		X		X		U	X			R	U		R	C	C			X	X			R	R	R	R	R	R	R	R
Fox Sparrow	U				R	R	R		R		O	O	R	R		R					R	R	R	O	O	O	O		U	U	O	
* Song Sparrow	U	U	U	U	C	C	C	C	C	C	C	C	C	C	C	C					C	C	C	C	U	U	U	C	C	C	C	C
Lincoln's Sparrow	C	C	U	U	C	C	C	C	C	C	U	C	C	R	U	U	C	C	C	C	O	O	O	O	R	R	D	O	O	O	O	O
Swamp Sparrow	U		U		O		O		U		C	C	C		U	U	O	C	U	U	X	X	X		R	R	R		O	O	O	O
White-throated Sparrow	X	R	X	R	R	R	R	R	R	R	R	R	R		R	R					R	R		X	R	R		X	R	R	R	
Golden-crowned Sparrow													Xx		Xx														Xx		Xx	
Harris' Sparrow			U										R	O	R	O							O	O	R				R	R	R	
White-crowned Sparrow	C		C	C	C		C	C	C		C	C	C		C	C	C	C	U	U	C	C	C	C	C	R	C	C	C	O	C	C

SELECTED BIRD LISTS

Species	Buenos Aires Sp	S	F	W	Imperial Nat'l Sp	S	F	W	Cibola Sp	S	F	W	Havasu Sp	S	F	W	Kofa Sp	S	F	W	Salton Sea Sp	S	F	W	Bitter Lake Sp	S	F	W	Bos' Apache Sp	S	F	W
Dark-eyed Junco					O				O			O	O			O					O		O	O	U		U	C			O	O
McCown's Longspur		U			O				O																				Xx			
Lapland Longspur		X																														
Chestnut-sided Longspur		X					R																									
Baird's Sparrow																									R			U	R			
Chestnut-collared Longspur							O				O															U			O	O		
Field Sparrow																									R		R		R		R	
Le Conte's Sparrow																																
BLACKBIRDS, MEADOWLARKS AND ORIOLES																																
Bobolink																					X	X			Xx							
* Red-winged Blackbird	U	U	U	U	C	C	C	C	U	C	C	C	C	C	C	C				R	C	C	C	C	C	C	C	C	C	C	C	C
Tricolored Blackbird	C	C	C	C																	R										R	
* Eastern Meadowlark																				R							C	C	R	R	C	C
* Western Meadowlark	U	U	U	U	U		U	C	U	C	C	C	C			C	O	O	O	O	U		U		C	C	C	C	C	C	C	C
* Yellow-headed Blackbird	R	R	C		C			C	C	U	C	C	C	U	U	U	O	O	O	U	C	C	U	U	C	C	O	O	C	U	C	C
Rusty Blackbird				R											R	R											R	O				O
Brewer's Blackbird	C		U	U	C	U	C	C	C		C		U		U	U			R	U	U		O	O	C	R	C		C	C	C	C
* Great-tailed Grackle	U	U			C	C	C	C	C		C	C	C	U	U	U				O	U	U	U	U	U	U	U	O	C	C	C	C
Bronzed Cowbird	U	U			C	C	O	O					R								O	R			R	R						
* Brown-headed Cowbird	C	C	U	U	C	C	C	C	C	C	C	C	C	C	C	R	U	U	U	O	C	O	R		C	C	U		C	C	O	O
Orchard Oriole	C	C																			X	X	X	X	U	O	O	U				
* Hooded Oriole	C	C			U	U	O		O	O	O		O	O	O		U	U	R		U	U			U	U			O	O		
* Northern Oriole	R	R			U	U	U		U	U	U		C	C	C		O	O	R		C	R	U	X	C	C	U		O	O	O	
Scott's Oriole													Xx				C	C	U		U	X	X		U		U		C	C	C	C
Streak-backed Oriole																				O												
Common Grackle		X																														
FINCHES																																
Cassin's Finch		R													R								O	O			R	R			O	O
Purple Finch	R														R	R							O	O			R	R			O	O
* House Finch	C	C	C	C	C	C	C	C	C	C	C	C	C	C	C	C	C	C	C	C	C	C	C	C	C	C	C	C	C	C	C	C
Red Crossbill																				O	O	O	O	O								
Pine Siskin	R	R			R	R	O	U	O	O	O	O	U	U	O	O			O	U	R	R	U	U	O	O	R	O	O	O	R	U
* Lesser Goldfinch	U	U	U		U	R	U	U	U	U	U	U	U	U	U	U	O	O	U	R	U	U	U	U	O	O	R	U	C	C	O	R
American Goldfinch				R			O	O	O	O	O	O	O	O	O	O				U	R	R	R	R	R	R	R	U	U	U	R	C
Lawrence's Goldfinch	R	R			R	R							R			R				O	R	R	R	R	R	R			U	U		U
Evening Grosbeak		X																						X			R					R
OLD WORLD SPARROWS																																
* House Sparrow	U	U	U	U	O	O	O	O	C	C	C	C	U	U	U	U	O	O	O	O	C	C	C	C	C	C	C	C	C	C	C	C

Appendix 2

DESERT BIRDING HOTSPOTS

The following areas are accessible to the public and obtain either high concentrations of bird species or specialties. Write or call for specific directions and/or bird lists.

Arizona

Buenos Aires National Wildlife Refuge
P.O. Box 109
Sasabe, AZ 85633
(520) 823-4251

Cabeza Prieta National Wildlife Refuge
1611 N. Second Avenue
Ajo, AZ 85321
(520) 387-6483

Catalina State Park
P.O. Box 36986
Tucson, AZ 85740
(520) 628-5740

Kofa National Wildlife Refuge
P.O. Box 6290
Yuma, AZ 85366-6290
(520) 783-7861

Lost Dutchman State Park
6109 N. Apache Trail
Apache Junction, AZ 85219
(602) 982-4485

Muleshoe Ranch Headquarters (Nature Conservancy)
RR l, Box 1542
Wilcox, AZ 85643

Organ Pipe Cactus National Monument
Rt. l, Box 100
Ajo, AZ 85321
(520) 387-6849

Saguaro National Park Headquarters
3693 S. Old Spanish Trail
Tucson, AZ 85730
(520) 733-5100

San Bernardino National Wildlife Refuge
1800 Estrella
Douglas, AZ 85607
(520) 364-2104

San Pedro Riparian National Conservation Area
Bureau of Land Management
RR l, Box 9853
Huachuca City, AZ 95616

Arizona/California

Cibola National Wildlife Refuge
P.O. Box AP
Blythe, CA 92226
(520) 857-3253

Havasu National Wildlife Refuge
1406 Bailey Avenue
Suite B
P.O. Box 3009
Needles, CA 92363
(520) 667-4144

Imperial National Wildlife Refuge
P.O. Box 72217
Martinez Lake, AZ 85365
(520) 783-3371

California

Anza-Borrego State Park
P.O. Box 299
Borrego Springs, CA 92004
(619) 767-5311

Joshua Tree National Park
Oasis Visitor Center
74485 National Park Dr.
Twenty-Nine Palms, CA 92277
(619) 367-7511

Salton Sea National Wildlife Refuge
P.O. Box 120
Calipatria, CA 92233
(619) 348-5278

New Mexico

Bitter Lake National Wildlife Refuge
P.O. Box 7
Roswell, NM 88220-0007
(505) 622-6755

Bosque Del Apache National Wildlife Refuge
P.O. Box 1246
Socorro, NM 87801
(505) 835-1828

Carlsbad Cavern National Park
3225 National Park Highway
Carlsbad, NM 88220
(505) 785-2232

Elephant Butte Lake State Park
P.O. Box 13
Elephant Butte, NM 87935
(505) 744-5421

White Sands National Monument
P.O. Box 1086
Holloman AFB, NM 88330-1086
(505) 479-6124

Appendix 3

SELECTED REFERENCES

Audubon Society, *Field Guide to North American Birds*, New York: Alfred A. Knopf, Inc., 1977.

Audubon Society, *Master Guide to Birding, Loons to Sandpipers*, New York: Alfred A. Knopf, Inc., 1983.

Bach, Richard, *Jonathan Livingston Seagull*, Old Tappan, NJ: McMillan Publishers, 1970, 1990.

Berger, Andrew J., *Bird Study*, New York: Dover Publications, Inc., 1961.

Brown, Davis E., and Lowe, Charles H., *Biotic Communities of the Southwest*, Salt Lake City: University of Utah Press, 1994.

Childs, Jr., Henry E., *Where Birders Go In Southern California*, Los Angeles Audubon Society, 1990.

Clark, William S., and Wheeler, Brian K., *Peterson Field Guides: Hawks*, Boston: Houghton Mifflin Company, 1987.

Craighead, John J., and Craighead, Frank C. Jr., *Hawks, Owls, and Wildlife*, New York: Dover Publications, Inc., 1969.

Harrison, Hal H., *Peterson Field Guides: Western Birds' Nests*, Boston: Houghton Mifflin Company, 1979.

Holt, Harold, *A Birder's Guide to Southern California*, Colorado Springs: American Birding Association, Inc., 1990.

Phillips, Allan, Marshall, Joe, and Monson, Gale, *The Birds of Arizona*, Tucson: The University of Arizona Press, 1964.

Kaufman, Kenn, *Peterson Field Guides: Advanced Birding*, Boston: Houghton Mifflin Company, 1990.

MacMahon, James A., *The Audubon Society Nature Guides: Deserts*, New York: Alfred A. Knopf, 1985.

National Geographic Society, *Field Guide to the Birds of North America*, second edition, Washington: National Geographic Society, 1987.

National Geographic Society, *Water, Prey, and Game Birds of North America,* Washington: National Geographic Society, 1965.

New Mexico Ornithological Society, *New Mexico Bird Finding Guide,* Albuquerque: New Mexico Ornithological Society, 1992.

Peterson, Roger Tory, *Peterson Field Guides: Western Birds,* Boston: Houghton Mifflin Company, 1990.

Taylor, Richard Cachor, *A Birder's Guide To Southeastern Arizona,* Colorado Springs: American Birding Association, Inc., 1995.

Timbergen, Nikolaas, *The Herring Gull's World,* New York: Lyons and Burford, 1989.

Tucson Audubon Society, *Davis and Russell's Finding Birds In Southeast Arizona,* Tucson Audubon Society, 1995.

Wilt, Richard A., *Birds of Organ Pipe Cactus National Monument,* Globe, Arizona: Southwest Parks and Monuments Association, 1976.

INDEX

*Asterisk indicates rare, occasional, and accidental birds included only on list starting on page 298.
Bold-faced type indicates birds included in color section.